A

DETROIT

ANTHOLOGY

Edited by
Anna Clark

A Detroit Anthology
Rust Belt Chic Press

Selection and Introduction copyright ©2014 by Anna Clark
All individual pieces copyright the author; reprint permissions on page 232
All rights reserved.
Printed in the United States of America
First Printing, 2014

Cover and interiors designed by Haley Stone
Cover photograph by Amy Sacka

Print edition: 978-0-9859441-4-8

www.beltmag.com

Grand River and Book Tower / Megan Snow

TABLE OF CONTENTS

ACT II

Aaron Waterman

Introduction

DETROIT IS A CITY OF STORIES. In this way, we are rich. We begin with abundance. But while much is written about our city these hard days, it is typically oriented to those who are not from here. Even local writers often pen stories that are meant to explain Detroit to those who live elsewhere. Much of this writing is brilliant, but our anthology, this anthology, is different: It is a collection of Detroit stories for Detroiters. These are the stories we tell each other over late nights at the pub and long afternoons on the porch. We share them in coffee shops, at church social hours, in living rooms, and while waiting for the bus. These are stories full of nodding asides and knowing laughs. These are stories addressed to the rhetorical "you"—with the ratcheted-up language that comes with it. Many of these pieces took real legwork to investigate. We may be lifelong residents, newcomers, or former Detroiters; we may be activists, workers, teachers, artists, healers, or students. But a common undercurrent alights the work that is collected here: These stories are for us.

This is a city made of many voices, and so, too, is this book. Here, you will find reportage and confessionals, comic anecdotes and sweeping analyses. Again and again, Detroit writers turn to the heated lyricism of poetry; some stories of this place can be translated no other way. Readers will hear the language of a living city in the multiplicity of style and tone—though it is true that this might create some sharp edges and woozy gaps between the pieces. And in substance, some writers patently disagree with other writers. Nothing is in unison. But it is music all the same, an ensemble of parts that contribute to a whole.

Also audible: the absences. This book is not intended to be a comprehensive anthology of the city. For all the breaking news coming out of bankrupt Detroit, for all the attention the city attracts from artists, ruin explorers, and urbanophiles, our untold stories are legion, and this book only fills a small bit of the void. It shouldn't be used as an excuse to cease listening for more.

I don't expect you to read this book straight through, any more than I expect you to explore the city by walking straight up Woodward, notching each essay and poem as if it were a mile marker. But if you do move page by page through this book, you will see a collective narrative emerge. This is a story of leaving, and of being left. It is a story of not having enough money, and of having much more than your neighbors. It is a story of fires. Of inventing music. Of trying to get from one part of town to another—by bike, car, bus, foot, or sheer force of will. A story of sports, play, and the heart-thrust of fandom. Of shame and wonder. Of laughter and self-deprecation. Of remembering and misremembering history. Of fear. Of skyscrapers and gardens. Of suburbs—little towns in their own right. It is a story of having more power than we know.

This anthology is loosely arranged like a stage play (overture, two acts, and an intermission) not because there is anything false or costumed about the writing here, but because theater is a uniquely collaborative art form; so, too, are cities. Theater stitches together prose and poetry, music and oratory; so do cities. Comedy and tragedy are the two archetypal forms of theater; likewise, I'll venture to say that no place stages comedy and tragedy better than Detroit. And while it's hard to shake the feeling sometimes that the spectacle of this city is defined more by the distant "audience"—watching us from their safe seats in the dark as we improvise our way through an epic drama—in the end, it is thrilling to realize that we are all players here, each with the power to impact our shared story. On this stage, each choice we make matters.

However you navigate this book, you will find the dissonant chorus of people so often tasked with justifying themselves because of where they live, no matter which side of 8 Mile they are on. A watchfulness comes forth that I have rarely seen in other places I have lived or visited. Detroiters notice the details. As a result, you will not find "positive" stories about Detroit in this collection, or "negative" ones. But you will find true stories.

My hope is that the pieces in this Detroit anthology will ignite recognition: not (just) for our similarities, but for our differences. Our experiences are not the same, after all. Sometimes our search for connection leads to the washing away of our distinctive shapes, as if difference equals conflict and futility. But it needn't be so. Friction creates energy, and it is our choice how we use it.

We are a city moving through the fire of transformation. We are afire. There is no place I would rather be.

Anna Clark
Detroit, Michigan

Aaron Waterman

Aaron Waterman

We Love Detroit, Even If You Don't

Aaron Foley

Detroit is bankrupt. Does it hurt to write those words? Honestly, it doesn't. It hurts as much as ripping a Band-Aid off. Detroit is bankrupt. Detroit is bankrupt. Detroit is bankrupt. I can say it a million times, but the emotional effects are minimal. Call it being jaded, or maybe just putting my head in the sand. But after we've withstood so much, can it really get any worse?

Detroit is broke. Detroit has been broke. Detroit has been broke all of my twenty-nine, years. I am not a lifelong resident. I have spent the majority of my life here. My parents' parents' parents—one side from North Carolina, the other from Alabama—have been here longer than I have. And during all that time, Detroit has been broke.

It is a reality we have come to accept and, for many of us, a reality we were born into. It doesn't mean that the love is lost.

Detroit is a lot of things. It is not the small town you grew up in, where you went to a crappy high school in the country and dreamed daily of flying the coop to New York City or Hollywood. It is, by and large, still a city where people migrate, or maintain.

Detroit didn't need a bankruptcy filing to tell us we were broke because we already knew. It's an enigmatic tangled web in the darkest abyss that takes more than a *Slate* piece here or a CNN panel there to explain. Still, I'll attempt a TL;DR: A crowded city full of a rising middle class that reached its peak when freeways provided access to spacious land beyond city limits. A crowded city that also faced rising tensions between black residents and white residents. Redlining. Access. Police brutality. Draining economic resources. Unequal pay. Riots. Rising costs. Dwindling tax base. Legacy costs incurred by pensions, unions, city services. Inflation. Industry collapse. Taxes. Corruption. Crime. Schools. Jobs, and the lack of them. All against the backdrop of a shitty American economy in general.

A twisted Rube Goldberg machine running on a never-ending cycle is what Detroit is. And we know this. But here's the thing: We've been trying and trying and trying to stop the cycle.

But did you think that it would happen overnight?

Did you think that your tax dollars going to Chrysler and General Motors—private corporations, one of which is not even headquartered in the city limits, that have somehow been conflated with city government in the last few years—would just fix everything? That Chrysler and GM were the only two employers in Detroit, and that solving their problems would solve our decades-long issues with racism, finances, corruption, and the rest?

Did you really think that Detroit was the new Silicon Valley, the new Brooklyn, or the new Pittsburgh? Or that startup-savvy college grads with pie-in-the-sky ideas would keep the fires from burning every Halloween, or kids from walking past abandoned homes on their way to school each morning?

Yeah, we need Chrysler and GM. Ford, too. And every hipstapreneur that's willing to register to vote here as well. But they're not the only ones here.

I live in Detroit. It's hot as hell right now, and we're having biblical rainstorms. Grass is growing like crazy. But you know, I see people cutting the grass on lots that aren't theirs. Everyday when I pass through my neighborhood on my way to work.

I see little old ladies tending to their annuals, kids—black and white—playing football in the street (even though they can be annoying because they block the street sometimes). I see a bunch of regular-ass people doing regular-ass shit because Detroit is a regular-ass city with regular-ass problems just like everyone else.

Which is why I wholeheartedly believe that Detroit will be just fine.

"Bankruptcy" is a scary term, exacerbated by *Wheel of Fortune* losses, that has more bark than bite. Society discourages individuals from talking about finances; we don't talk about salaries outside of job interviews, we withhold the cost of the new house we just bought, we don't mention the raise we just got. So to find out someone declared—*gasp!*—bankruptcy provokes gossip, feigned concern, funny stares, distrust, and, most notably, shame.

Detroit is already the butt of jokes and the target of pity, so the nonstop flow of jokes and *tsk-tsking* was just as inevitable as the bankruptcy filing. I was dreading the former long after having accepted the latter.

Please tell me another Les Gold joke. Please post your OCP logos. Can you remind me again what Romney said in that *NYT* opinion that one time, I forgot just that quick. And my goodness, *please* spout another "It's So Cold in the D" lyric. But whatever you do, don't feel sorry for Detroit.

A headline like "Detroit Is Bankrupt" underneath a photo, *another fucking photo*, of a rundown house in the shadow of the city skyline tells half the story. The devil in the details is this: Detroit's biggest issue is dealing with pensions for retirees. It's a $3.5 billion open wound and no one knows how the city will deal with it. (You know who else has that problem? Chicago.) We don't know exactly what will happen in the course of bankruptcy, but we're fully aware that we'll all have to share in some painful cuts.

It does not mean we're selling our art, or turning off all the lights, or selling our land to Canada or China, or fencing off the city from the rest of America. It simply means we fucked up (we know, we know!) and we have no money to pay our bills.

That's it. Emergency Manager Kevyn Orr also has promised—and we're all holding him to this—to steer as many funds as possible to restoring city services and improving emergency response, a process in place before the papers were filed.

(It doesn't mean we're the next Stockton, California, or the next Vallejo, California, or the next San Bernadino, California, either. Really, guys? Stop comparing us to these random places in California. I have nothing but love for the West Coast, and it is undeniable there are issues in those cities. But none of these coffee shop artists are waking up and saying, "Hmm, where can I live cheap and network with a bunch of young minds to make a real difference in the world? Oh, I know—STOCKTON!" OK, they've gone through municipal bankruptcies, but the cultures of those towns are far different than Detroit's, and the way these stories unfold will take varied paths.)

I could go on and on about how the car you're driving was possibly designed here and how we're the home of Motown and stuff like that, but fuck it. You know that already. At least you should.

I don't want to say "Detroit will rise again." We built a whole mantra around the idea of rebirth in the '70s with the Renaissance Center, Renaissance High School, Renaissance everything pretty much. Fact is, Detroit is still on the uphill climb it has been on for more than forty years. We didn't rise then, and saying *Speramus Meliora, Resurget Cineribus* a bunch of times isn't going to make it happen any sooner.

I'm just going to say that for as much shit as you talk about Detroit, where you live is probably just as fucked up somehow.

Are you black? Good luck in Florida, or pretty much all of America at this point. Are you gay? You must have a peachy time getting your state to legally recognize your marriage. Are you a woman? Don't be knocked up in the wrong state at the wrong time. Are you a recent college graduate? How do you even afford to live anywhere?

Sounds petty? Then hell yeah, I'm being petty. Just as petty as your tired *RoboCop* jokes. But guess what? We all live somewhere that's fucked up to some degree, and even if you move somewhere else, your life still won't be Instagram perfection.

Despite all of its fucked-uppedness, I still love Detroit. And there are a lot of people here who love this city and want to reduce that fucked-uppedness to a minimum. You love your fucked-up city, too.

A bid last summer to bring the X Games here to Detroit got a lot of national press, and we were appropriately disheartened when ESPN chose Austin over us. It's fine, because the masterminds behind that bid have put the wheels in motion to come up with an alternative. It sounds cheesy as all hell to say this, but Detroit never says die.

On the other end of the spectrum, hundreds of volunteers are planning a mass cleanup of the city's North End neighborhood, an event that won't get nearly as much attention as the X Games bid. I'm not complaining about the coverage at all, don't get me wrong. But the point here is, people mobilize for causes here—be it skateboarding in abandoned lots or boarding up abandoned homes.

Those are just two examples, I know. And that won't convince you, I know. I can't yell about the "good parts" of Detroit or complain about the national media coverage anymore, so just go ahead and click through that slideshow of black-and-white photos of Motown stars and assembly-line workers, and tell us again how Obama and the Democrats killed Detroit or whatever. At this point, sticks and fucking stones.

I love Detroit, I know a ton of people who love Detroit. It's a twisted love that runs the gamut of emotions: joy, disappointment, hurt, anger, fear, elation, delight, apprehension, courage, resentment, cynicism, stubbornness, optimism, and confusion. Then again, maybe that's something we all have in common. Have you ever loved? You mean to tell me that everything you've loved was just cut and clear? There was never any condition or obstacle?

When it's love, you know it's real. And love conquers all, even the stigma of Chapter 9 bankruptcy and the national headshaking that's come with it. So yeah, Detroit will be just fine. Even if you don't think so.

Notown

Thomas J. Sugrue

Editor's note: *What follows is Thomas J. Sugrue's response to the book* Detroit City Is the Place to Be: The Afterlife of an American Metropolis *by Mark Binelli. It first appeared, in slightly different form, in the journal* Democracy.

"NO ONE LIVES THERE ANYMORE." I have heard those five words uttered again and again over the four decades since my parents joined the Great Boer Trek from city to suburb. Detroit has lost a lot of people—about 1.3 million—since its population peak of nearly two million in the early 1950s. Between 2000 and 2010 alone, Detroit lost a remarkable 25 percent of its population, as massive long-term disinvestment, the collapse of the public infrastructure, and the near-death of the American auto industry devastated the city. Today, more than 40 of the city's 139 square miles are empty, at least 90,000 houses stand abandoned, and neighborhood shopping districts are scarce. Once-grand factories are gutted and crumbling. A few years ago, *The Onion* ran a headline "Detroit Sold for Scrap." Funny because it's true: One of the city's few growth industries is scrapping. Inept scavengers pulled down a substantial part of a pedestrian bridge at the defunct Packard Plant (a mile-long complex that stopped making cars in 1957) in an effort to retrieve its steel support beams. When I visited shortly afterward, an electrical crew was replacing copper wire that had been stripped out of nearby live power lines. Drivers learn to veer around sewer openings in the streets because every time iron prices rise, sewer lids disappear, leaving car-eating holes in their place.

For most of the colorful characters in Mark Binelli's gripping, tragicomic account of Detroit, the city's emptiness is its future. Newcomers to Detroit describe the city as "the Wild West" and themselves as "pioneers" staking claim to new land. For them, the Motor City is a tabula rasa, a place to undo, remake, rebuild, reinvent. Among them is wealthy investor John Hantz, who won approval for his plan to convert part of Detroit's East Side urban prairie into a commercial tree farm—a striking turnabout for a neighborhood that was once the city's densest. A short distance from Hantz Farms, artist Tyree Guyton has turned a few mostly abandoned blocks into a post-apocalyptic art installation, using abandoned houses as canvases, urban detritus as statuary, and half-dead trees, covered doll heads, and old shoes as totems. Detroit's most famous radical, Grace Lee Boggs, now 98, who is still on a journey that began with Trotskyite factionalism, moved through Black Power, and shifted to neighborhood and anti-violence organizing, leads a devoted band of utopians who envision Detroit as a collective of communal farms, the world's largest wholly self-sustaining city. That vision is more than a little far-fetched, but with at least 875 urban farms and community gardens in Detroit today, it's no more unreal than long-dashed dreams of somehow restoring the city's mid-century industrial might.

Detroit represents, in extremis, the realities of urban America today. American cities have long embodied the paradoxes of poverty amidst progress. They attract migrants in search of opportunity or outcasts in search of liberty, but they also repel those discomfited by insecurity, anonymity, and anomie. Detroit offers one version of this story: The Motor City was the nation's Arsenal of Democracy and the engine of its massive postwar consumer economy, then the epitome of deindustrialization, racial conflict, and decay.

Binelli offers a brief overview of the city's sometimes glorious and often troubled history, but primarily turns his attention to the future: How does a city reinvent itself? Is it possible for a place left for dead to come back to life? Can we save the city? Who is that elusive "we"? On each of these questions, Binelli is a pessimist of the intellect but an optimist of the will. He offers an unflinching analysis of the city's problems but an intimate portrayal of those longtime Detroiters and newcomers alike who are trapped in the city's present while reimagining its possible (and impossible) futures.

A contributing editor at *Rolling Stone* and *Men's Journal,* Binelli is a former suburban Detroiter turned New Yorker. He moved back to Detroit to write his book and quickly found himself in the company of various expatriates, from New York to the Netherlands. He spends much of his time with the city's burgeoning cadre of hipsters—mostly white, mostly young—whose migration set the local news atwitter when the 2008 and 2009 American Community Surveys showed that Detroit's white population had grown for the first time since the mid-twentieth century. The small upticks in those years, however, scarcely affected overall trends: In 2000, Detroit had almost 100,000 white residents; ten years later the number had fallen to 55,604, or only 7.8 percent of the city's population.

However small in number, Detroit's white newcomers are both optimistic and messianic. They see Detroit as the Brooklyn of the prairies or, even more ambitiously, the next Berlin, a magnet for what urban planner Richard Florida calls the "creative class." For struggling artists, Detroit's bargain-basement prices are a lure, with single-family homes averaging just $21,000 and vast studios for a tiny fraction of New York rents. The city has become a mecca for Germans who revere the city's innovative techno music scene. It is now home to several trendy art galleries, including a cutting-edge modern-art museum (MOCAD—the Museum of Contemporary Art Detroit). And the hip now have watering holes, many of them retrofitted dives that serve microbrews and local food amid their iconic and now ironic knotty pine paneling, stainless steel bars, and flickering vintage neon signs that have never left the premises. Detroit's Midtown district, perhaps the city's hippest enclave (even if all of its residents could fit into a few blocks in Brooklyn), has even attracted the Holy Grail of a dying Midwestern city: a Whole Foods.

But as Binelli shows, it's not just cheap property that lures the hip to Detroit: It's a sense of missionary zeal that they will save the city. The young white denizens of what Binelli cheekily and brilliantly calls the "DIY city" see Detroit as a blank slate—a city with the people (at least the "wrong" kind of people) mostly left out. That vision of Detroit is most evident in what wags have come to call "ruin porn," the often stunningly beautiful photographs of empty factories, vacant classrooms, and haunted churches that look like they have been hit by a neutron bomb. Many of downtown Detroit's glorious Beaux-Arts and Art Deco skyscrapers stand so empty that visionary photographer Camilo José Vergara once proposed that they be turned into an American acropolis, stabilized and preserved as monuments to a lost civilization, looming over the decaying city like the Parthenon over Athens. It is now fashionable for European tourists and local urban explorers to spelunk through long-empty factories. Scrappy urban DIYers have turned the flooded basement of a long-defunct manufactory into a subterranean hockey rink; pop-up entrepreneurs refashion the crumbling shells of old motor plants into surreptitious night clubs. The steampunk artist and the witty journalist alike look upon Detroit as did Shelley the ruins of Rome's Baths of Caracalla or Wordsworth the bare-ruined choirs of Tintern Abbey. "I came to see the end of the world!" proclaims a German college student to Binelli, outside the rotting hulk of the grand, abandoned Michigan Central Station.

Though he finds their optimism irresistible, Binelli is justifiably skeptical of Detroit's would-be saviors and their dreams. "Aside from burned-out buildings and overgrown lots, what's missing from the Tomorrowland renderings of Detroit 2030, with its monorails and Christmas tree farms and office parks and Apple Stores? Oh, right: poor people." Detroit might be depopulated, but it is not a blank slate. Over 700,000 people, more than four-fifths of them black, call the city home. For them, Detroit's ruins are not romantic: They are a taunting reminder of how the city has lost capital and jobs, and how many lives have been ruined in the process.

Binelli's skepticism is justified. For the last forty years, American urban policy has been motivated by what I call trickle-down urbanism. Big-city mayors have long placed their bets on glitzy downtown redevelopment, providing subsidies to lure corporate headquarters back from the suburbs. They point to pockets of gentrification with their busy bistros, coffee shops whose patrons' faces glow with the light from their laptops, and pricey lofts carved out of old factories as evidence that cities are coming back. The more desperate, underfunded city governments, including Detroit, have placed their chips on casino gambling, with hopes that they will somehow become the next Las Vegas. Even in Detroit, the impact of such redevelopment is undeniable: It's possible to enjoy a pinot noir at a sidewalk café on downtown's main strip, Woodward Avenue, once left for dead. Suburbanites who dared not enter the city a few decades ago now fill Detroit's well-guarded casino parking lots. But apart from some unionized casino jobs and some extra tax revenue in the city's depleted coffers, few city residents have seen any direct benefits from much-touted urban redevelopment schemes. For those with a little disposable income, like me, Detroit is a far livelier place than it has been in decades. For everyone else, not so much.

The grim reality is that Detroit is home to one of the poorest, most segregated urban populations in the country. Detroiters are disproportionately unemployed, impoverished, and in poor health. The city—infamous for its murder rate—still ranks among the most violent places in the United States. Detroit averaged 90,000 fires in 2008, twice the number of New York City, even though the latter is eleven times more populous. The nearly complete disappearance of industry and commerce and the collapse of the housing market have devastated the city's tax base, making it almost impossible to provide even rudimentary police and fire protection. Binelli notes that the average police response time for a life-threatening crime in the city is a scarcely believable twenty-four minutes. In the enclave of Highland Park, local firefighters must buy their own equipment and work for ten dollars per hour, with little training and no capacity to investigate arson.

The fundamental question facing Detroit is how to deal with the mountain of social and economic problems the city faces. And that is the tragic part of Binelli's story. He chronicles the efforts of Detroiters, from mayors to union leaders to teachers, to grapple with the city's troubles. All of them have the will, but none have the capacity to make more than a difference on the margins. Some of Binelli's stories are moving, like that of charismatic Asenath Andrews, the principal of the Catherine Ferguson Academy, a high school for pregnant teenagers and mothers with a 90 percent graduation rate. He follows John Zimmick, president of UAW Local 174 (once led by labor giant Walter Reuther), who helplessly laments that "the middle class really is going away and I don't have the answers for it." And he attends the pathetic trial of Kevin Howell, a hapless crack dealer who goes to jail for murder after his mother testifies against him. These single moms, struggling unionists, and the perpetrators and victims of crime are the other side of the DIY city, all stranded with little help in a city of failing schools, collapsing wages, and endemic violence.

Ultimately, the causes of Detroit's problems—and their solutions—are far bigger than the city itself. For the last forty years, cities have fallen mostly to the bottom of the list of national policy priorities. After a burst of spending on community development and social services in the 1960s and early 1970s, federal urban spending has steadily spiraled downward. President Ford told cities to drop dead, President Carter sacrificed an urban policy to his anti-inflation agenda, and President Reagan cut urban spending from 12 percent to 3 percent of the federal budget. The first Bush Administration's Enterprise Zone programs—repackaged as Empowerment Zones under Clinton—did little to create new jobs or reinvigorate impoverished neighborhoods. Even the Obama administration, which ceremoniously created an Office of Urban Affairs, put cities on the back burner (even if, for a time, city governments and school districts did benefit from the infusion of stimulus money).

Detroit has also fallen prey to suburban indifference or outright hostility to cities, their residents, and their problems. Advocates of regional cooperation like Bruce Katz, Myron Orfield, and David Rusk have made a persuasive case that the fates of cities and suburbs are intertwined and that metropolitan economic growth depends on improving central-city economies and schools. The balkanization of the big metros creates separate and unequally funded school districts, duplicative services, and bureaucratic inefficiencies. But the obstacles to regionalism are huge, especially in places like Detroit where generations of racial hostility have poisoned city-suburb relations. As Binelli pointedly argues, for decades suburban Detroiters "saw themselves as displaced persons, refugees of a race and culture war forced to build dissident strongholds, where the true way forward would be demonstrated." Not surprisingly,

Detroit's black majority looked outward with distrust, fearful that regionalism would simply be another mechanism for suburban control.

In this climate of hostility, Detroiters were largely left to fend for themselves—and the story is not a happy one. Binelli takes a long look at the pervasive corruption in Detroit's city government, but he swiftly and persuasively debunks the time-honored myth that Detroit's woes are primarily the consequence of black misrule. Many journalists, policy-makers, and white suburbanites still point their finger at supposed race-baiters like Mayor Coleman Young, who held the office from 1974 to 1993. Binelli is too smart to fall into that common journalistic trap. "Even today," he writes, "there's an unsettling fervency to the hatred of Young among certain white ex-Detroiters who will tell you *Coleman Young ruined this city* with such venom it's impossible not to see Young as a proxy for every black Detroiter who walks the halls of their old high schools or sleeps in the bedrooms of their childhood homes." After all, Young built close working relations with corporate leaders, set aside city positions for whites, and oversaw the (controversial) construction of two major auto plants and a downtown corporate complex. But there simply wasn't a lot that a mayor could do when he took over a city that had already been on the skids for a quarter century, a city whose economy depended on the auto industry during the oil shocks and was forced to endure the massive restructuring and Chrysler bankruptcy of the 1970s. Young had the misfortune to rule when legislators in both Washington and Lansing alike shunted cities to the margins.

Binelli does justifiably skewer some of the city's urban policy follies, like the "People Mover" monorail that loops through the downtown in a ghostly parody of an urban transit system and a vestige of the suburban opposition to a regional transportation policy. He has scarcely a good word—and correctly so—for former Mayor Kwame Kilpatrick, the charismatic "hip-hop mayor," who was (at first) heralded by the Democratic Leadership Council as one of a new generation of fiscally conservative, culturally relevant big-city leaders, but was caught having an affair with his chief of staff, using city police to cover up the mess, and lying about it until hundreds of tawdry text messages surfaced in the investigation.

But Binelli's most devastating criticism falls on the inept rather than the corrupt. He offers a detailed and unsparing discussion of the half-baked efforts by Detroit's recently retired mayor, former basketball star Dave Bing, to "right-size" the city. Bing, who fashioned himself (like so many big-city mayors these days) after New York's Michael Bloomberg, stumbled partly because of incompetent staff and poor political skills, but primarily by falling back on the tired shibboleth that somehow, if the city were run like a business, it could rebound. At "listening" meetings held throughout the city to consider what Detroit would look like in the future, Bing showed up late and offered little more than vague plans for improvement: Provide better city services to a "demonstration area," and leave behind others in an "Urban Homestead Sector," where "in return for giving up services such as street lights, the homeowner would get lower taxes (in exchange for experimenting with alternative energy and, where possible, using well water.)"

In the meantime, the state government has stepped in, first assigning Detroit schools an emergency financial manager charged with closing the city's undersubscribed schools, and reducing administrative staff, wages, and benefits. This story too was one of irony—at the same time that the first school manager, Robert Bobb, painted the school district as ill fated and corrupt, he had to recruit parents to enroll their children because state and federal funding is contingent upon head counts. In 2012, just as Binelli was finishing his book, Republican Governor Rick Snyder threatened to take control of city government, on the premise that it would take an outsider to dismantle city employment, reorganize government, and privatize some of the city's few relatively well-paying jobs: those in the public sector. But the feedback loop—fewer city services, fewer middle-class workers in the city, and ongoing depopulation and disinvestment—doesn't bode well for the city's future.

Binelli offers no policy prescriptions—and for good reason. There are no obvious solutions to the city's problems, at least in the short to medium run. It may be that, over time, as old central cities regain population, they will regain some of their lost political clout on Capitol Hill. It may be that as suburbs grow increasingly diverse and struggle with what were once seen as distinctly urban problems, such as rising poverty, aging schools and infrastructure, and declining tax revenues, they will form coalitions to push for greater public spending. For now, though, Binelli has it right. In the absence of an approach to urban and metropolitan problems that goes beyond state receivership and austerity, Detroit's fate, for better and worse, has been left in the hands of its hardscrabble residents, its leftist utopians, its underpaid firefighters and teachers, and its inept would-be reformers. It's hard to imagine a story grimmer than the one Binelli tells, yet in the end he captures something about Detroit and its people that flies in the face of the city's squalor. Detroiters—and Binelli himself—are hard-edged optimists, fighting against the odds for the city that, for all its troubles, haunts their imaginations. That optimism might, in the end, be the only thing Detroit has left going for it.

I'm From Detroit

Shannon Shelton Miller

"WHERE ARE YOU FROM?"
"Detroit."
An easy answer to an easy question, I once believed. During those initial getting-to-know-you exchanges I'd have when meeting new people, especially if they were from Southeast Michigan, I figured my answer spoke for itself.

"Detroit" was rarely good enough, inevitably triggering a follow-up question.

"What part?"

"Northwest side."

"Um, what suburb is that? Like, Royal Oak, Farmington Hills…"

"No, on West Outer Drive, between Six and Seven Mile Road. Near the Lodge Freeway."

Their faces went blank.

"Oh, you mean in the actual *city* of Detroit."

"Yes, that's what I said from the beginning. Detroit."

As I got to know these people better, I overheard them tell others they were from Detroit, despite hailing from one of Detroit's suburbs. To them, Detroit was Warren, Rochester Hills, Livonia, Novi, or even Wixom, an exurb up to thirty miles from the city center.

"How would someone from San Francisco know where Livonia is?" they'd explain. "It's just easier to say you're from Detroit."

I understood that. I do the same thing now that I live in a suburb of Dayton, Ohio. Only those with some connection to the Dayton area know where Centerville is, so it makes more sense to consider Dayton my hometown. Still, I wonder if these faux Detroiters recognized the irony of claiming a city they never visited aside from the occasional trip downtown to watch a sporting event or to party in Greektown.

Before claiming Detroit as their home, perhaps they should spend a little more time in Detroit.

§

The first time this exchange happened, I didn't think much of it. By the time it became a regular occurrence, I started noticing a few commonalities among those who expressed confusion and even surprise that I grew up in the city.

"I've never met anyone actually from Detroit."

I knew the implication of that statement, but, depending on the person, I decided to be a little cheeky.

"It's a city of almost one million people, and you've never met one?" I'd ask.

"No, can't say I have."

You've never met any black people then, I thought.

The question-askers were always white. The Detroit natives—those of us born and raised in the city—were almost always black. Black friends from other Rust Belt cities like Chicago and Cleveland told me they shared the same experience— when we all started in college and left the confines of our all-black neighborhoods to interact with significant numbers of whites for the first time, we began encountering these self-proclaimed Detroiters, Chicagoans, and Clevelanders, only to learn upon further questioning they were from Troy, Schaumburg, and North Olmsted.

And they, the suburban white students, seemed shocked that we were from the city—after all, we were neither poor nor downtrodden, and we were occupying the same collegiate space as them. Yes, a student expressed that to me once.

As I became better versed in Detroit's history, I recognized this was the consequence of three decades of white flight that rendered Caucasians and African Americans sometimes hostile strangers although we occupied the same metropolitan area. The parents of my white peers might have been born in the city, but moved in their youth to what's now considered the inner-ring suburbs of Oakland and Macomb counties. By the 1990s, when their children were finishing high school, they had few memories of their old neighborhoods and rarely, if ever, took their children to see their old homes. This, perhaps, was understandable—a good number of those areas are a shell of their 1950s selves, falling victim to the forces of redlining that often converted solid neighborhoods of owner-occupied homes to unstable areas of rental dwellings with a revolving door of occupants.

As property values decreased, white flight increased. By the middle of the 1970s, many neighborhoods hit their nadir, and they still haven't recovered. When I reached adulthood in the 1990s, Detroit was 83 percent black, a percentage that remains steady today.

My white peers in Generation X and Y had no memories of Detroit. If they visited the city, they went downtown and made a beeline for I-75, I-96, or I-94 to quickly head home.

Life still progressed in Detroit. A burgeoning black middle class, often first-generation college graduates, took advantage of the lowered housing costs in the neighborhoods whites left behind, scooping up well-constructed brick three- and four-bedroom colonials for $30,000 or less in the 1970s. They planted flowers and gardens in front yards and backyards, had barbecues and cookouts for the neighborhood, and chatted with neighbors across picket fences.

They raised their children in these neighborhoods. We took dance lessons and martial arts classes; we joined baseball teams, football leagues, and scouting troops. Our parents ferried us from place to place, wanting to ensure we had a wealth of extracurricular experiences to balance what we learned in school—which often happened to be a school of the Detroit public variety. Granted, these were typically magnet high schools such as Renaissance or Cass Tech, which churn out future college graduates with the same regularity as many suburban schools, but they still fell under the erratic and oft-mismanaged umbrella of Detroit Public Schools. Somehow, we turned out fine.

Our childhoods were pretty similar to those of our suburban white colleagues who shared a middle-class upbringing—except ours took place south of 8 Mile, where the teachers, coaches, and scout leaders were all black, as were we.

My parents were first-generation college graduates. After taking teaching jobs in the late '60s and early '70s, they began shopping for a single-family residence to house their growing family. In 1978, they found their dream home on West Outer Drive in the heart of what was once Detroit's thriving Jewish community. A block away from the JCC, now the Northwest Activities Center, the house was a steal.

My mother said she never imagined living on Outer Drive growing up poor near 12th Street on Detroit's near west side. Eleven years earlier, she'd witnessed National Guard members clad in riot gear marching down the street outside the home she shared with her mother and sister.

In the 1980s, the world and our suburban neighbors saw images of Devil's Night and blight on the nightly news, reminding them of the danger that supposedly lurked miles south of their homes. In the supposed epicenter of it all, I remained blissfully unaware of it. Even as I grew older, I was shocked to learn of the poverty that existed in parts of Detroit. I never saw it around my part of the city.

By living there, though, I was able to understand that Detroit, like any major city, had its good and bad parts. Crushing pockets of poverty certainly existed, but so did comfortable middle-class neighborhoods. Palmer Woods and Indian Village were enclaves of wealth with fabulous homes rivaling those seen in magazines—their zip codes just rendered them undesirable to many.

And unlike our white suburban counterparts, we were able to see where they lived when we ventured to the suburbs to shop or visit a relative who began leading the wave of black flight out of Detroit by moving north of 8 Mile in the 1980s.

We knew about the suburbs, but they didn't know much about us besides what they saw on TV.

§

Our segregated worlds began to cross in high school, when we attended summer enrichment programs with suburban kids at the University of Michigan, Michigan State, and other universities. We entertained questions and comments that made us roll our eyes. No, we didn't have any homeless kids in our school that we knew of, and no, all of us didn't have good basketball teams at our schools.

Some programs offered excursions that took the group through city neighborhoods, including mine. This was in the early 1990s, some two decades after Detroit living had supposedly become untenable.

"There are nice houses here," a student from West Bloomfield said.

"Of course," I responded. "Why wouldn't there be?"

By college, I had become used to this, although certain statements couldn't be left unchecked. Mere unfamiliarity with Detroit was one thing; none of us had a say in where our parents chose to raise us.

Snarky, uninformed commentary, however, had to be addressed.

"So, what part of Detroit is the bad part?" a guy from New York asked a woman from Rochester Hills during a study abroad program.

"Pretty much anything south of Eight Mile is ghetto," she said.

I was within earshot, and I wasn't going to let this one go.

"Oh, you mean the part where I grew up and where my family still lives? By Seven Mile? That's the ghetto part?"

She turned multiple shades of red. I wondered how exactly she could make such a determination considering that she probably hadn't ventured very far south of Maple Road, let alone visited the city itself outside downtown.

Even after college, when I met suburbanites in their late twenties and early thirties, the lack of familiarity with Detroit remained surprising. A guy I dated grew up in Bloomfield Hills and lived in Troy; he didn't have any idea how to get to my parents' home, and thought we needed to traverse I-75. I told him the main street near his apartment could simply be driven six miles south, directly into Detroit. The name changed from Coolidge to Schaefer once you hit 8 Mile, but it was the same street.

We'd grown up just six miles away from each other, yet it seemed worlds apart.

§

I left Michigan in 2010 after marrying a Daytonian (who lived in Dayton!) and moving there. I read stories on my Facebook feed from friends of all races who are working, living, playing, and partying in Detroit. Mostly downtown, but they're venturing into the neighborhoods as well, buying homes in Brightmoor, East English Village, and other areas that few outside the city knew in the past.

Maybe they're also tired of the division between city and suburb, and want to know what they missed during their childhood when they learned that Detroit was a place to be feared. Even if they still live in the suburbs, their willingness to explore Detroit beyond obligatory stops at Comerica Park, Joe Louis Arena, and Pizza Papalis is refreshing. I completely understand the draw of suburban life, especially when one has children, but I'll make sure my children living outside the city limits won't claim it without having much knowledge of life inside.

I still make a point to say I'm a native Detroiter, raised on West Outer Drive and 7 Mile. My parents still live there, and I visit often with my husband and our son.

My husband, a native of western Pennsylvania, has no ties to Detroit other than marrying me. For years, he didn't understand my insistence on asserting I was *really* from Detroit.

While playing golf at a Dayton country club one day, he spotted a man wearing a baseball cap with the distinctive old English D.

"Are you from Detroit?" my husband asked.

"Yes," the man answered with excitement, glad to find someone who recognized the symbol.

My husband was also excited. "My wife is from Detroit," he said.

"Oh really? What part?"

"Northwest side, West Outer Drive, kind of close to Seven Mile."

The man looked confused. "Is that near Lake Orion? That's where I lived when I was in Michigan."

Lake Orion…thirty-five miles from my Detroit home.

My husband smiled. When he shared the story with me, he joked that he's probably spent more time in Detroit than most self-proclaimed Detroiters. He gets it.

Two Women at Cass and Temple / David Clements

The Portrait / Gabriela Santiago-Romero

Turner Ronald Carter the Third

Kat Harrison

WE WERE THE THIRD COLORED FAMILY to move onto the 5100 block of Linsdale Avenue in Detroit. The Horton clan next door and Howard and Mattie Brogdon, across the street with their four children, had taken gold and silver honors a few months earlier. My parents gladly accepted the bronze, and we settled into the six-room lower unit of our brick two-family flat at 5080-82 Linsdale.

It was late in the year in 1952. I was three years old, living in a toddler's paradise. I wasted no time musing over the social significance of moving to this tree-lined street from the tiny attic apartment in my aunt and uncle's A-frame bungalow in River Rouge. Instead, I busied myself with more urgent matters: Finding hiding places, playing peek-a-boo in the hall mirror, making noises (all sorts) in the big, echoey rooms. What could I have known or cared about prejudice and discrimination at that age?

Whether I understood it or not was immaterial. The reality was this: We—along with the Hortons, the Brogdons, and others dotted across our neighborhood—were in the *avant garde* of a cresting *pas de deux* that was shifting blocks in a few west-side neighborhoods like ours from all-white to all-black, often in the time it took the sun to set and rise.

Giving credit where it is due, our move would have been impossible without the U. S. Supreme Court's 1948 ruling in *Shelley versus Kraemer* and *McGhee versus Sipes*. This decision settled several lawsuits that arose, in part, out of the purchase of a house at 4626 Seebaldt Street in Detroit by Minnie and Orsel McGhee Sr., which is located only eight blocks from ours on Linsdale.

The facts of the case are simple and familiar. (Think *Raisin in the Sun* played out in real-time in Detroit in 1945.) When white neighbors discovered the McGhees, a very light-skinned colored couple, had purchased the Seebaldt house, they tried to get the McGhees to abandon their home. Mr. and Mrs. McGhee, who were my friends Reggie and Kathleen's grandparents, neither bent nor broke.

They rejected offers to buy them out, endured blazing crosses on their lawn, and fought escalating lawsuits through local, state, and federal courts. Supported by the NAACP, a young lawyer named Thurgood Marshall led the legal team that took their case, which had been joined with the St. Louis-based *Shelley* case due to the factual similarities, to the Supreme Court.

To call the Court's verdict in the *Shelley* and *McGhee* cases "landmark decisions" buffers the cushions of understatement. Despite post-World War II frigidity on issues of racial equality, a pre-Civil Rights-era Supreme Court ruled that restrictive covenants in deeds intended to prohibit the sale of residential property to non-whites were unenforceable. Say what?

It wasn't that the Supreme Court sided with the McGhees and the Shelleys on their right to live wherever they pleased. The pivotal issue dealt with the ability of state courts to enforce the covenants in light of the equal protection clause of the Fourteenth Amendment to the US Constitution. Said differently, a state court cannot overrule the US Constitution—ever.

With that ruling, colored homebuyers' field of residential dreams widened considerably, not only in Detroit, but across the country. Nevertheless, purchasing a home in a white neighborhood was not an adventure for the timid. Colored home seekers were often quoted substantially higher prices than their white counterparts. For instance, my parents bought our house for twice the amount the seller—a single white man named James McNaughton—had paid for it a few years earlier.

Then, there was the problem of long-term financing for the purchase. Conventional mortgages were not available to colored homebuyers—even those, like my parents, with a $3,000 down payment and solid jobs at US Rubber and the US Post Office as references. Like others of their race, they settled for a land contract through Bank of the Commonwealth to purchase the house at 5080-82 Linsdale. It was, at the time and for many years, the only bank in town that would handle real estate transactions involving colored people.

The Supreme Court decision didn't fling wide the doors of housing equity, either. It took one weapon out of the well-stocked arsenal of bigots who, driven by fear and prejudice, worked hard to maintain racial segregation in their own back- (and front-) yards. Some even enlisted their children in the battle, as I was to find out one not-so-normal summer day.

Ours was a quiet street in a quiet neighborhood, even during the transition from white to colored. I was four or five years old, and my mother allowed me to play outside by myself, as long as I didn't venture any farther than the walkway that led to the sidewalk. I'm sure she was no more than a whimper away, but I felt like a big girl being left on my own like that.

Mindful of the weight of the trust she'd placed on my tiny shoulders, I usually stuck to the porch, which was partially shielded from the street by several tallish pine trees that grew between the house and a well-trimmed row of reddish prickly bayberry bushes. As an only child, I was used to finding my own amusements. Being outside and alone was not a problem for me.

One day my solitary playtime was interrupted when a little blond boy joined me. I don't think at this time in my life I knew the difference between white and black. My mother was light-skinned, "high yellow" some would have said, and my father was dark, dark brown, "black as the ace of spades" as I was once told by a man at his workplace. With both ends of the spectrum on display at my dinner table, color was irrelevant to me. I was not surprised when a white boy appeared, simply because I didn't know what a "white boy" was.

My visitor seemed older than me but not by much. When I think of how he looked, I am reminded of Tommy Rettig, the original child actor on the *Lassie* series, or Macaulay Culkin of *Home Alone* fame.

"I'm Turner Ronald Carter the Third," he announced.

Always in hostess mode, even as a youngster, I welcomed him, introduced myself, and offered to share whatever toys were handy. He must have turned out to be a decent playmate, and we enjoyed whatever we did until it was time for him to go. The signal for his departure, I believe, was a whistle that cut through the curtain of white noise that surrounded that unremarkable summer day. Turner Ronald Carter the Third perked up at the sound, like a dog that heard his master's call. We said goodbye, and he left, walking exactly five houses down the street to the four-family flat in which he lived.

The houses on our block were mostly two-family flats. Owners, like my family, usually lived on the first floor, and renters occupied the upper flats. The four-family flats were rental properties. Their owners—absentee landlords—lived elsewhere. They were transient lodgings, some more well-tended than others, through which most tenants, who were on their way to someplace else, better or worse, sojourned for only a little while.

Turner Ronald Carter the Third, child of the rented four-family flat down the street, came and played with me, daughter of homeowners, a couple of times after that. I was glad for his visits. As an only child, living in an all-adult world, it was nice to spend time with someone who saw things closer to my eye level. He must have been appropriately behaved and played fair, although I did suspect him of stealing my teddy bear, but maybe that's because of what came next.

The last time I saw Turner, he marched down the street toward my house like a boy with something serious on his mind. I was standing on the walkway as he passed me. I don't think he uttered a word of greeting. I started to follow, thinking he was heading to the porch, but reconsidered, stopped, and watched. What was he up to? Something was different because he halted midway up the steps. Then he hopped onto the lower of two concrete slabs that capped the brick balusters flanking each side of the stairs.

Turner turned toward his four-family flat, facing the space between the house and the lawn where the pine trees rose behind the bayberry bushes. He stood there for a second or two. Then, he undid his pants. And as I watched, Turner Ronald Carter the Third shot a stream of urine into our shrubbery.

I didn't need an anatomy lesson to know that he had pulled out his you-know-what and did number one on my shrubs. I also didn't need to consult Emily Post to know that his conduct breached every rule of etiquette and polite behavior for a visitor on someone else's property.

Well, I never! Had I been wearing pearls, I would most certainly have clutched them. "Ewwwww," or a sound to that effect, is what I said.

Turner closed his pants and jumped from the stairs, his expression a blend of pride and embarrassment. No need for the summoning whistle. He ran, as if chased by a posse or my outraged parents. Maybe he ran because he needed to reach the safety of his own home before he could be caught. Maybe he ran because he knew what he had done was just plain wrong. Maybe he ran because we had been playmates and he was ashamed to look me in the face. Or maybe he ran because that is what he had been told to do. Who knows? Of course, we never played together again. I suspect his family moved shortly after this incident

When I reported his gross, indecent behavior to my mother, my story focused on his naughtiness. She probably understood the motive and the message it was intended to send, having grown up in segregated coal towns in West Virginia. Rather than tarnish my young soul with a discourse on the many, varied, and sordid ways racial prejudice could be expressed, she took a higher road.

Mama agreed. Turner Ronald Carter the Third was indeed a very bad boy who lacked home training of the most basic sort. But, as a little pitcher with very big ears, I might have overheard the phrase "poor white trash" whispered when the incident was discussed with my father and other adults.

For many years, I dismissed Turner and his violation of our shrubbery simply for the *gauche*, low-class act it was. After all, he lived in rented space, while I lived in a home that was owned by my parents. Maybe that's the way his sort behaved, I thought. Marx was right, although he was making a completely different point. Class was the essence of life's struggles. Turner Ronald Carter the Third and Kathryn Ann Bryant belonged to different classes, mine being more refined and elevated than his, and that was that.

In later years, my musings about Turner's defiant and deviant act led me to think that he was the weapon his parents used to register their displeasure with the arrival of unwanted colored neighbors. He became a one-boy *un*welcome wagon, a symbol to be manipulated, like a flaming cross or a rock tossed through a window.

Now a sixty-something adult, I can't imagine how such a young child in the 1950s could have devised such a plan by himself. Nor can I believe that the call of nature had been so sudden and urgent that he could not have been more discreet in answering it. How sad and cowardly it was to use a child to insult another child, neither of whom could have possibly understood the motivations and bigger issues at play.

I googled Turner Ronald Carter the Third as I was finishing this essay. The search was fueled by curiosity and the ease of finding people on the Internet. I didn't have a plan if I found him. What might I do? Confront him? Make him 'fess up? Go for coffee at Starbucks?

I found someone who might have been an older version of the boy about whom I wrote. The images I found startled me. They were in a lovingly assembled pictorial memorial to a man who lived in Taylor, and served and died in the Vietnam War. About the right age, his name was Turner Ronald Carter, *Junior*.

Could Linsdale Turner be Taylor/Vietnam Turner? Could he have announced his name as "Junior" rather than "the Third"? Possibly. It was a long time ago and, while the story is true, my recollection of his familial suffix could be faulty. Now, I'll never be sure if he was second or third in the line of Turner Ronald Carters.

When I read of his death, I felt sad, and I hoped the young man captured in the smiling blond images was not "my" Turner. Inexplicably, I felt linked to him, somehow, maybe because we were both Baby Boomers, whose shared experiences—from Milky the Clown to the *Mickey Mouse Club*, from Edgewater Park to the Bob-Lo

Boat, and from Soupy Sales to the Selective Service—were greater than someone else's perceived differences between us on a summer day on Linsdale Avenue in the 1950s.

Postscript: *I believe the boy in my story is the same person whose pictures I found as a young man on the Internet. I gave him a fictitious name because I was truly saddened to learn of his death and didn't want to disturb his family's memories of him, should this essay reach them somehow. —KH*

Gas Station on Second Street, Detroit

Matthew Olzmann

Dusk. A quick stop you think, five bucks of gas
then onward into the rest of your life.
But as you stand by the pump and look for your card,
a stranger grabs your shoulder. His other hand hides
in his jacket. What's in the jacket? He's got a knife
to cut you like a piece of rib eye. No,
he's got a nine-millimeter with holes drilled
in the barrel to muffle the shot. No, his name
is Kevin and he only wants to give
you a flyer for The Blood Now Church of Christ.
Kevin emerges from twilight, silent as twilight.
Kevin almost gives you a heart attack as he leans
in to say, *Hi. My name is Kevin!*
You don't have time for this.
You think about your studio apartment,
your girlfriend's breezy little sundress.
You want so badly to return to that world
but that's another planet now. This here is Planet Kevin
and Planet Kevin's only resident knows Hell is very real.
If you won't listen, he yells, *you'll suffer for eternity.*

It works like this, fear. You, afraid of Kevin, Kevin afraid
of forever. He steps closer. You inch away.
And a hundred feet above, a horned owl flies south.
To the owl, your circling looks like the beginning
of a fight, or two small figures about to dance
the way people have always danced
when the world grows dark and they think they understand.

Desire Lines

Michael Eugene Burdick
and Francis Grunow

Take me to water and the vast inland sea. Ottawa. Huron. Pottawatomi. Slice across corners, curve through the block. Get me to the store. Find me a rock. Lead me and connect me, to spite building and grid. As we always have, as we ever did. The path I follow another has made. Started by one for barter and trade. Some became Gratiot and Grand River, these lines of desire. Pat down from footfall, then wagon wheel, and tire. Expanded with lanes, wood, brick, and stone. Came so far, and so fast, and so wide, and emptied us out from the inside.

Things I Lost in the Fire

dream hampton

IN 1976, MY MOTHER AND STEPFATHER moved from our two-family flat on Eastlawn and Kercheval, an increasingly dangerous intersection, to a painted gray brick, three-bedroom house on Newport, one block over and a mile north, and what felt like worlds apart. My mother divorced my father when I was two. He stayed in my life, but I also don't remember a time before my stepfather. The apartment on Eastlawn was a rental. I remember a landlord yelling at my parents about the waterbed in the living room. I spent most of my time beneath a faux velvet black quilt on that water-bed because my block and the ones around it felt unsafe to me, whatever that means to a five-year-old black girl, and I chose my developing reading habit over the outside.

My stepfather had owned a home before, with his before-us family, but even as a child I understood how important homeownership was to my waitress mom and mechanic dad. We bought the house on Newport the summer before I began first grade, from a white family in flight.

They'd built an above-ground pool in the backyard and had decorated the bedroom walls with the fake wood paneling that was then somewhat chic. Somehow, my mother became friendly enough with the outgoing family to be invited to their new home in Adrian. They had a daughter my age who told me in her new bedroom that she'd miss the cherry tree in the backyard across the alley from the home we'd just bought from her family. When I asked her why her mom was leaving a house with a pool and access to a cherry tree, she whispered, conspiratorially, "…the blacks."

By the following summer, the few white families still left on our block when we moved there also fled, leaving my mother to be, I believed at the time, the last white person still in Detroit.

During the ice storm of 1978, when we lost power for days, we lost our pool, too, when a giant branch from the ancient oak in our backyard crushed one of its walls beyond repair. The pool was leverage for my brother and me, providing instant neighborhood friends, some who bullied my brother, taking over our backyard a half dozen at a time. Even then, the block was divided by the adults into good kids and bad. Bad kids were yelled off manicured lawns; good ones were paid a dollar to mow.

During the ice storm of 1978, when we lost power for days, we lost our pool, too, when a giant branch from the ancient oak in our backyard crushed one of its walls beyond repair. The pool was leverage for my brother and me, providing instant neighborhood friends, some who bullied my brother, taking over our backyard a half dozen at a time. Even then, the block was divided by the adults into good kids and bad. Bad kids were yelled off manicured lawns; good ones were paid a dollar to mow.

By the mid-eighties, my brother moved from the mowing crowd to the trespassing crew. Crack seemed to make its nationwide debut on the east side of Detroit, and unlike the boys his age who sold it, my brother, who'd taken to hanging with older boys, became a user.

Our gray brick home with the fallen pool and fake wood paneling was burglarized no fewer than a dozen times during my brother's addiction. Our neighbors began buying iron bars for their windows and doors and complicated locks for their steering wheels, but our family knew our intruder had keys.

By the late eighties, the black families on our block who could always afford new model cars disappeared to exotic places like Southfield and Oak Park. Chandler Park, where I'd had several birthday parties and spent most weekends, became off-limits because of shootouts. Still, we stayed.

Inside, our house began to fall apart, the ceiling above the breakfast nook began to leak and open a moldy hole in the wall in the kitchen. My parents didn't have the money or interest in home repairs.

My dad went to work every day, then came home and sat in his favorite spot in the crook of the staircase watching sports or science fiction on TV. He barbecued steaks on his Weber on the weekends. But he and the men his age withdrew from the outside, conceding our neighborhood to the boys my age who turned Detroit into a murder capital my entire high school career. My mother checked out by drinking. I'd walk from Cass Tech to the library, or sit in the Rivera Court till it closed, avoiding my house, our block. When I graduated, I left for New York and didn't come home three Christmas breaks in a row. My mom got sober, went to nursing school, and she and my dad raised my niece in our home. Flush with cash one spring, I paid a friend to repaint our exterior gray. I paid another friend to repair the kitchen.

Those improvements put us back on the side of the people on the block who still invested in upkeep, rather than the ones whose homes had crossed over into total disrepair. By the mid-nineties, burned-houses-turned-vacant lots were as common in my neighborhood as they were across the city.

Our neighbor, Mr. Louis, a veteran, died, leaving his home to his four sons, only one of whom was the grass-mowing kind. The house became our block's burden, with twice-monthly police visits, usually breaking up parties that began Thursday night and lasted until Monday afternoon.

Then, Mr. Herman, our next-door neighbor whose beautiful flowering plants seemed to nudge my mother to plant salvia each summer, died in his sleep. Ms. Erma and her husband remained, as did a single ex-police officer who took great pride in her house across the street, another painted gray brick. But most of our neighbors were new, people who cared very little for the falling-apart homes they were renting for a few hundred dollars a month.

One summer night five years ago, after my niece's birthday dinner, my dad had a heart attack in our home. My mother did what she was trained to do as a nurse, but it was no mitigation against an ambulance that took twenty-eight minutes to arrive.

Two days after my dad's funeral, a man in his thirties, annoyed by our dog's barking, stopped in front of our house and yelled, "I'll shoot that damn dog! Now that Bill's dead, I'll shoot this whole house up."

I told my brother, who drove over and dropped off a handgun.

I canceled my flight home to New York and spent six weeks finding my mother the Grosse Pointe condo she moved to a few months later.

My mother knew how vulnerable an unoccupied house on Detroit's east side could be, even one as worn as ours.

So she rented. First to a woman escaping an abusive marriage, who decorated our windows with silly pink sheer curtains. Then to a young man whose neighbors now tell me would open his trunk where he kept an enormous speaker and blast music till four in the morning, drinking with his friends on our lawn.

Mr. Herman's grandson inherited the house next door and is doing an excellent job keeping it up, so he considered it his right to confront the renter with the loud trunk speakers and the four a.m. parties.

Because Mr. Herman's grandson is a big and self-possessed man, our renters complied, for a time. My mother served her tenant an eviction notice after months of missed rent and bad behavior. One morning around two a.m., Mr. Herman's grandson felt heat from our home, which was on fire.

Firefighters saved his home from severe damage and ours from collapse, but our roof, which we'd replaced a decade ago at great expense, melted. Neighbors tell me our house smelled like gas for days.

The fire department confirmed the renters pulled the stove from the wall to better saturate my childhood home, then torched it after midnight.

I've no sweeping, poetic sentiment or condemnation about my city's particular appetite for arson, just a shell of a home that now contributes to the blight on my block. I'd long ago moved on from that neighborhood, but I did move back to Detroit a few years ago. I want to be a part of the rebuilding of my beloved city. But first, I must tear down the scorched brick house that was my home for most of my life.

Letter From Detroit

Ingrid Norton

I WAS SITTING IN THE TELWAY DINER around the edge of midnight. The Telway is a story in itself: a chrome island built during the 1940s, floating on a blighted stretch of Michigan Avenue. Telway is staffed by the Appalachian whites that long ago moved to Detroit for work and, more recently, to the suburbs to live. It's open twenty-four hours and nothing costs more than $2.25. I ordered a fish sandwich and had the place to myself, except for the short-order cook, the waitress, and the cashier. A pair of bulky night workers stood in the vestibule and asked for hamburgers, heads framed by the take-away window. Then an ambulance pulled off Michigan Avenue and parked on the sidewalk outside. A stocky, balding EMS worker with reddened skin and tired eyes came in.

"How much time you got?" he asked the powder-faced redheaded woman working the counter.

"How much time you need?"

"I just watched the cops beat the shit out of somebody," the EMT said to all of us. "He was being stupid."

He ordered a large coffee with double cream and proceeded to tell us the convoluted story. He spoke with a flat affect and blank eyes. It was a robbery/assault at some house "by the train station." He'd waited outside with the woman who had called 911. She kept telling him to go inside and help the man who'd been assaulted. "'He's spitting up, you gotta get in there.' And I told her again," he said, "'I can't go into a violent situation before the police get here, so we'll have to wait for the police.'"

It took the police over half an hour to get there, and so they waited on the sidewalk while the woman grew steadily more agitated, railing about it being the EMT's duty to save lives. She said, "I'm going in to get him! If he dies while we're waiting and you aren't helping him, I'm gonna sue the city." The EMT replied, "Well, that's a great idea, ma'am. Because in case you haven't heard, the city's broke. They don't have the money to pay my pension. They're taking away retirement benefits. *I'm* suing the city. So you can just get in line."

"That's Detroit," said the lanky blue-eyed counterman, with a laugh. He had white hair and was probably of the first generation of Appalachian migrants to come to the city.

The young, pale fry cook, who seemed a bit slow-minded, started saying something about a stabbing that had happened around the corner earlier that night.

"When?" asked the EMT.

"About 9:30."

"Wonder where we were . . . The other day we went out to Harper and Cadieux," he said, naming an intersection clear on the other side of town. Detroit takes in a sprawling 140 square miles, just under 30 percent of which is vacant (the emptied properties alone occupy an area nearly the size of San Francisco); emergency services here have the worst response time in the nation because there aren't enough staff to cover the ground. "A guy'd been shot with an AK-47," the EMT continued. "Lying in the middle of the street. They waited half an hour—*half an hour*—to call an ambulance."

Fry cook: "That guy isn't alive anymore."

EMT: "Well, I had better get going . . .,"

He took his cup of coffee, paid absently, thanked the waitress, and left without explaining how the first story had devolved into the police beating the man in the house.

As he drove the ambulance back off the curb, the woman said, "I seen him on TV."

"He's the union rep," the older, gap-toothed man explained. "That's why."

"I see him on TV all the time . . . Need anything, honey?" she asked, turning to me.

What can I tell you about Detroit that isn't contained in that story? There's Telway and a score of hamburger stands and diners like it, vestiges of the gritty, working-class mid-twentieth century city that would have been pushed out anywhere else but that hang on here. The EMT is just one of the beleaguered, unionized blue-collar workers who bear the brunt of the violence and disorder that stalk the urban poor. It is common for city first responders to live in the suburbs themselves: Over half the Detroit police force live outside the city, and the number is estimated to be higher for firefighters and EMTs. The city used to require its employees to live inside Detroit, but the law was controversially repealed in 1999, which led to massive suburban flight among emergency responders and other city employees. The mayor when I lived there, Dave Bing, had an initiative called "Project 14" to lure police to live in the city again with massive subsidies ("14" is police code for "return to normal operations"). Bing argued that having police live inside city neighborhoods bulwarks safety. Detroit police who live in the suburbs counter that the city—with its high insurance rates, limited services, and poor school options—is a very difficult place to raise a family.

The "train station" the EMT referred to is Michigan Central, the most renowned symbol of Detroit's ruination. It stands eighteen stories tall, once magnificent and now in distress: all pocked window-frames and crumbling arches. You can see the sky clear through it. When people here give directions it's simply "the train station," from which no trains have departed since Ronald Reagan was president. That's the ghost city that runs parallel to present-day Detroit.

Over the last sixty years, the city has lost 1.3 million residents from its 1950 peak of two million. The continual bleed of people moving to suburbs and other regions of the country means that Detroit's current population is as low as it has been since 1910. The massive abandonment has invidious, far-reaching effects for the Detroiters who remain. Over the last year, there have been an average of 35 major fires a day in the city. A lack of maintenance funds and property abandonment mean it is not uncommon for power lines to hang low over the empty houses and cracked sidewalks. In September 2010, a combination of dry weather, high winds, and downed power lines caused eighty-five fires to break out in one 24-hour period. Five suburban fire departments were called in to help Detroit's department combat the blazes. Whole blocks were incinerated. Louvenia Wallace, a hair stylist and mother of three whose east side duplex burned, told a reporter from *The Detroit Free Press*: "It was like blankets of smoke were everywhere, and the next thing I knew everybody's house was on fire . . . My kids couldn't sleep because it smells like smoke ... My daughter is asthmatic, so she can't be around here, no way . . . I don't have the money to just move."

An editorial in the following day's paper concluded that though the fifty-eight Detroit fire companies available worked "doggedly and admirably" they were "overmatched to an unsettling degree." The tragedy was no aberration. Plummeting home values mean few people can recover anywhere near what they paid for their houses, whereas insurance pays back the replacement value, creating a perverse incentive for home owners to burn property they cannot sell. Others simply walk away from houses they can't pay the back taxes on, leaving empty properties vulnerable to vandals, squatters, and drug dealers. The fire department has such a foreboding backlog of arson cases that a consortium of insurance companies recently partnered with the attorney general to conduct independent investigations.

Detroit is also home to "Devil's Night," a weekend of arson and vandalism beginning on Halloween eve, which peaked in the 1980s with eight hundred fires in a single night. Thanks to community patrols ("Angel's Night") and a citywide curfew on unaccompanied adolescents and children under eighteen, "Devil's Night" has slowly declined since then, with 169 fires in 2010 and 94 in 2011.

One Halloween my friend Claire Nowak-Boyd and I participated in a community patrol, driving slowly through blighted neighborhoods in northwest Detroit with our flashers on. Passing a fire in progress in Brightmoor—sometimes known as "Blightmoor"—we saw a firefighter on a ladder silhouetted by smoke over a small single-family house. We drove down dozens of other streets in that neighborhood, where houses stand exposed and ruined, their walls marked with Xs, signaling utility shutoffs, and yards full of discarded mattresses and furniture. (The city doesn't collect trash from vacant lots.)

In a December 2010 *Free Press* article about the neighborhood, African-American residents recalled the area's vibrancy in the eighties and its slow decline. The reporter spoke to Eddie Holmes, a 55-year-old woman living in a house on Rochelle Street. Most of her neighbors left a couple years ago after a drive-by shooting at the drug house next door. Another drug addict moved into the house next door. She recalled having recently chased burglars from her porch. "Almost everyone is gone out here," she said. "We feel abandoned and forgotten."

Camping on Michigan's Upper Peninsula in the summer, I met a white retiree who grew up in the area. He could remember that in the 1930s when his father built their house at Schoolcraft and Greenfield—a neighborhood near Brightmoor—people thought he was crazy; it was so far on the city's edge. Back then, the man said, the area was full of vacant lots being sold by builders. As a child he watched them fill with houses. That seventy years later the area should be full of vacant lots again is one of the unbearable ironies that characterize life in Detroit.

The mid-twentieth century explosion of industry that made Detroit a leader in home-ownership also made it a leader in redlining and lending discrimination. Recent immigrants and internal migrants—whether southern whites, Arabs, or Eastern Europeans—adopted racial hierarchies by which their status could be elevated at the expense of African Americans. As inner-city neighborhoods integrated in the middle of the century, suburbs and townships that had carefully protected racial, ethnic, and religious profiles (often by restrictive deeds) grew around the city like an ever-replicating tumor, killing its host.

As of the 2010 census, only 18 percent of the metro region's overall population lives in the city of Detroit. Only 2.8 percent of the region's white population does. Every year since the 1950s, Detroit has lost citizens while the suburbs have grown. Over the last decade, the city lost over a quarter of its residents—the equivalent of a busload of Detroiters leaving every day—while Livingston, Macomb, and Oakland, three suburban counties, held steady or gained population. Detroit is currently more than 84 percent black, a figure that represents approximately 61 percent of the metro area's total African American population. The rest live in suburbs: large-scale African American flight from the inner city began in the 1990s and has accelerated with the recent real estate crisis, which opened up housing options for black families in suburbs that discriminated against them in more prosperous times. One disturbing trend of the past decade has been for white parents in the integrating inner-ring suburbs to send their children to whiter, more affluent school districts farther from Detroit. Typically, the farther from the inner city, the richer the suburbs: West Bloomfield, 27.5 miles from downtown Detroit, is one of the ten wealthiest towns in the United States.

For every abandoned business, store, school, or church in the city, a new one has been built in the suburbs. Only 38 percent of employed Detroiters work in the city. Many suburban business names refer to streets in Detroit, though their original locations closed years ago. Telway has a second and larger location in Auburn Hills, a prosperous east-side suburb to which Chrysler relocated its main plant decades ago. Huge shopping and strip malls, office parks, and satellite downtowns mean that many suburbanites, the children of early white flight, brag about having never been into the city, while others visit it once a year to see one of the museums or attend a sporting event or a festival.

Detroit holds only 14 percent of the region's jobs. On any given day after a heavy snow, young African American men go door to door, seeing if anyone will pay them to shovel walks. The unemployed third of the city's population roughly corresponds to the third that doesn't own a car. An estimated 36 percent of the city's residents and over half of its children live below the poverty line. The Detroit school system continues to lose teachers and close schools, while grade-fixing and social promotion—where failing students are passed to the next grade regardless of performance—is rampant. Parents are expected to buy toilet paper and hand sanitizer for their children's classrooms, many of which contain between forty and fifty students.

You've doubtless read stories about Detroit's burgeoning art scene: the legions of young and generally white hipsters and artists renting cheap studios and lofts in former factories and downtown buildings. The presence of artists, entrepreneurs, and students *is* palpable in some of the neighborhoods near downtown and Wayne State University. A couple of blocks from the defunct train station, just west of downtown, sits a trendy barbecue restaurant called Slow's where there's often an hourlong wait to get a table. It's run by an international-model-turned-Detroit-impresario named Phillip Cooley. That neighborhood is called Corktown, a sliver of a neighborhood, really, once Irish, and made up of rehabbed Victorian workman's cottages. One recent autumn, I wandered through the arsoned hulk of a house, across from the train station, which had been turned into an installation called *Salvaged Landscape*. Artist and University of Michigan professor Catie Newell used burnt lumber from the back of the house to build a sculpture. Rooms that partly withstood the blaze were filled with murals. The house still smelled of charred wood and urine. For the opening, the artists placed a beer keg out back as well as a table laden with pasta and thin crust pizza. Musicians played on an impromptu stage. "This used to be a drug house, filled with squatters," explained Marianne Burrows, an acquaintance of mine who painted the murals. "So the exhibit is a way of providing neighborhood stabilization as well."

A recent *New York Times* article lauded Detroit as a "Midwestern Tribeca" of socially aware folk; but off of its bustling main drag, Corktown is surrounded by Detroit's burned-out industrial structures and houses, weedy lots, and subsidized housing. For every white entrepreneur in an inner-city neighborhood, a score of young, college-educated kids live in dense, hip suburbs like Royal Oak and Ferndale. The Detroit perceived by artists like Catie and Marianne, who are often from privileged, suburban backgrounds, is radically different from the city visible to EMS workers. I have doubts about the city's oft-vaunted creative scene, which I was part of in 2010 and 2011: to what extent were we dancing to electro-pop while Detroit burned?

On a summer night, I drove around a particularly desolate stretch of the east side. Charred foundations outnumbered houses. Grasses grew waist-high around them. On Belvidere Street, a brightly colored convenience store came into view. It had recently been refurbished: freshly painted graffiti-like letters, colorful and stylized, proclaimed it the "NEW BORN PARTY STORE," while the other wall boasted of "A MAN with a VISION . . ." The words reminded me of a speech then-Mayor Bing gave in September 2010. Bing's arrival came on the heels of the felonious ex-mayor Kwame Kilpatrick, and many looked to him for new direction; a city official introducing Bing quoted a passage from Isaiah about the restoration of Jerusalem: "[A]nd they shall build houses and inhabit them; and they shall plant vineyards, and eat the fruit of them." Restoring Detroit, however, is a formidable task. Bing announced the first stages of Detroit's strategic plan to shrink services in neighborhoods that are too far gone to recover mid-century population levels; but those neighborhoods are not entirely empty. I wondered about the optimist who had opened the New Born Party Store. It seemed like a symbol of the stubborn, creative resilience that somehow manages to thrive in Detroit's harshest, most decimated corners.

One of the great open secrets of Detroit is its spoken-word scene, which is among the most vibrant in the nation. In the spring of 2011, I went to the open mic at Nandi's Knowledge Café in Highland Park. Highland Park is a microcosm of Detroit—a small island of a city surrounded by Detroit on every side—which resisted incorporation because of its massive wealth 100 years ago when its tax base included

Henry Ford's Model T factory. Then, it was full of beautiful wide-porched houses and known as the "city of trees"; verdant elms lined its avenues. In the 1940s, the Highland Park grade school included students of more than thirty-eight nationalities. But in the 1950s, the Ford factory closed. Chrysler, which had also built a major plant there, moved operations to Auburn Hills in the early 1990s. White flight and disinvestment decimated the city, and in the meantime, Dutch elm disease wiped out Highland Park's prided trees. Today its population is almost 96 percent African-American, 40 percent of whom live below the poverty line.

Nandi's Knowledge Café is a local hub. On a Tuesday night, five dollars will admit you to the basement where soul food is served in a low-lit, mirror-paneled room and some of Detroit's most talented poets take the mic. As with many cultural spots in Detroit, when I attended one night, not only was I the only white person there, but I got the feeling that I was the only white person who had been there in a long time (the MC joked that if I was from the police or the DEA, I'd better 'fess up). The themes of the poems ranged from thwarted love ("I'm trying to be a King/But I'm still looking for my Coretta Scott") to black media stereotypes and Obama. The most impressive performance was by a petite woman named Alfie, who looked about twenty-five. Her hair was in tight pigtails, and she wore a pink T-shirt and acid-washed jeans. "I wrote this at work today, actually," she announced, taking the mic. Alfie unfolded a crumpled piece of lined paper and launched into her poem:

> I work at a Chrysler plan-
> -tation . . .

She explained how her mother told her to get a career, not a job. But college was costing too much money. So at twenty-two she took the full-time plant gig in the suburbs where her high school diploma and 3.3 grade-point average "might as well be a GED." She knows she's wasting her mind: her fifty-cent raise means she "made more than last year." Running around the office in high-heeled boots, she said, doing what the white managers tell her, she feels it's not so different from decades ago when she would have been "cooking their chicken" and making her own chitterlings. The refrain of the piece was that she should still be grateful when many friends and family don't have jobs at all. In her prayers, she tries to hold fast to gratitude instead of dwelling on all the missed opportunities:

> But I know it could be worse
> I don't mean to complain
> So every night I thank Him
> And He says, "You're welcome . . ."

As I left the open mic, I drove the long way around the residential block that surrounds Nandi's. I made a left onto Cortland Street, full of once-lovely mid-century brick houses, the stoops of which now crumble into the weeds. My headlights illuminated the pale fur of a stray dog. Right in the middle of that block, a fire was engulfing one of the two-story houses. Flames flickered between yellow and orange in the night. I slowed my car down for a moment and watched the glow reflect on my windshield and hands. I contemplated dialing 911. But the house was pretty far gone, and the buildings on either side were both vacant. Highland Park's emergency services are so overstretched that the state of Michigan seized control from the local government. So I sat there and watched it burn. Whether the continued presence of creativity, hope, and resilience amid such devastation seems a triumph or a tragedy varies second by second, block by block.

1960 What? The Motor City Was Burning. / Kofi Handon

Infernal

Tyehimba Jess

There is a riot I fit into,
a place I fled called the Motor City.
It owns a story old and forsaken
as the furnaces of Packard Plant,
as creased as the palm of my hand
in a summer I was too young to remember–
1967. My father ran into the streets
to claim a small part of my people's anger
in his Kodak, a portrait of the flame
that became our flag long enough
to tell us there was no turning back,
that we'd burned ourselves clean
of all doubt. That's the proof I've witnessed.
I've seen it up close and in headlines, a felony
sentence spelling out the reasons
my mother's house is now worth less
than my sister's Honda, how my father's worthy
rage is worth nothing at all.   In the scheme
of it all, though, my kin came out lucky.
We survived, mostly by fleeing
the flames while sealing their heat
in our minds the way a bank holds
a mortgage—the way a father holds his son's hand
while his city burns around him . . .   I almost forgot
to mention: the canary in Detroit's proverbial coal
mine who sang for my parents when they fled
the inferno of the South, its song
sweaty sweet with promise. I'm singing
myself, right now. I'm singing the best way
I know about the way I've run
from one fire to another. I've got a head full
of song, boiling away. I carry a portrait
of my father.

Greektown 1983

John Counts

S TELLA WAITED FOR ME IN GREEKTOWN. She scurried down Monroe Street in her army coat covered in patches, a dozen bright-colored barrettes in her matted grey hair, crooked face leading the way. She carried dozens of shopping bags filled with what any schizophrenic needs for life on the streets.

I couldn't imagine what they were. Cans of sardines? A thousand more hair barrettes still in their packages? Plastic bags filled with more plastic bags?

I wasn't allowed to know. I was a little boy, and I was her prey. Stella would single me out and scream obscenities until I wanted to cry whenever we encountered her on the sidewalk passing the restaurants and bars on Monroe, one of the last bustling streets in Detroit. I was being raised in the much smaller town of Bay City a few hours north, so just being in the big city was scary enough.

Detroit had been a premier destination for my immigrant forbearers in the 1910s and this street with wafting smell of lamb and baklava, the old country guys with thick mustaches sipping their tiny cups of coffee, reading the Greek newspapers was the center of it all. Jobs and opportunities were in abundance. It was the city where my great-grandpa churned chili-dog sauce at the Lafayette Coney Island until opening a haberdashery. It was the city where his wife, my great-grandma, brought a live lamb home on the streetcar to slaughter for Easter dinner. My grandma was sent to school on her first day with a sign around her neck saying she didn't know English, which the public education system eventually taught her.

By 1983, it had become a city of sharp edges, the antithesis of the overstuffed throw pillows of suburbs that ended up surrounding it, where all the Greeks would move and where I would later grow up. It became the immigrant American Dream stripped and pecked to its bones. The deepest racial conflict and the darkest side of capitalism, when manufacturing had its way and moved on to someplace cheaper. It became theory come to life. A what-if city. Armageddon city. Murder City. It had transformed into symbol.

I felt it all even as a little boy through the stories of my family. Stella, who seemed to represent this scary new city, sensed my fear.

"Motherfuckercocksucker!" she'd scream at me.

I would take a step back in shock before my parents hustled me away.

"She doesn't know what she's doing. She's got something called Tourette Syndrome," Mom would say. "The poor woman."

It didn't make my run-ins with Stella any less terrifying, but I pitied her with that extreme sadness particular to sensitive little boys.

I am only half Greek. Mom is full blooded, but Dad is "white," according to the Greeks. I was baptized at the Annunciation Orthodox church down the street where we would often go for the long Easter ceremonies. The main service didn't start until midnight Sunday when Christ's resurrection was complete and we'd all be saved, even screaming street women like Stella.

It was the one night of the year a six-year-old boy was allowed to stay up very late. Mom spit-groomed my brown hair and dressed my 11-year-old brother and me in slacks, blazers, and neckties, likely from one of Hudson's suburban mall locations. We made the trek downtown from my grandparents' house in Livonia to stand in the overflowing church holding candles until the lights cut out and hundreds of us broke into the spooky, climatic singing of "Christos Anesti," a song which I mumbled along to in Greek. Even though I didn't understand the words, the experience of chanting the syllables along with hundreds of strangers in a room lit only with candles was felt at my deepest core, filling me with all the bigness and mystery of the world.

When the service ended around two a.m., we went out to eat, which was especially a treat for those who had been fasting. Now that Christ had risen, a rack of lamb could be consumed. We went to the Laikon Café with Mom's older brother, my Uncle Tom, and his blond, Grosse Pointe-bred wife, my Aunt Betsy. Mom and Uncle Tom had grown up in a very Greek household only to pair off with whites.

The six of us were briskly seated by a waiter at the table in the front window, overlooking the street. The waiter was the same burly, bespectacled, curly-haired guy who always waited on us at the Laikon. He was pushy and direct, spoke broken English, and could carry four glasses with one hand by plunging his hairy knuckles into the liquid to grip them.

Our neighboring table, also crammed in to face the window, immediately captured my attention. The four people—two men, two women—were not Greek, and therefore not celebrating Easter, which for whites happened a few weeks earlier due to an historical complication. But they were definitely having a celebration. They had been there for some time and were noticeably drunk. Empty wine bottles littered the table, as did several large plates with scraps of the expensive stuff we didn't order—the end of a Homeric banquet feast indeed.

They were in their twenties or thirties. The women had the wispy look of hippies even though it was now the 1980s. The two guys looked more disco, wearing long-collared button-ups with no undershirts, the top buttons undone to reveal bare chests. Their table was less than a foot from ours and two of them were sitting on the same bench wrapping the semi-circle of the front window. I sat in a chair opposite the bench facing the window at the edge of the table, which I kept gripping with my young hand.

Soon after we put in our orders of roast lamb and rice pilaf, the curly-haired waiter brought our neighboring table the bill. He bumped their table with his thigh, causing the empty plates, silverware, and glasses to clink together. The bump seemed to be ignored. Instead, there was the bill that unfurled like a long scroll. After the waiter left, the group passed it around and haggled in hushed tones about who would pay. They became louder until one of the women abruptly stormed past us and out the door, which was directly to the right of our table. Then one of the guys stomped out, soon followed by the second man. Now it was just one young blond woman presiding over their spent feast, nervously looking at the bill.

When the curly-haired waiter came back to check on their table, the woman loudly informed him she wasn't going to pay.

"You've been bumping our table all night long!" she said. "Why would I pay for such terrible service?"

He demanded she pay so loud everyone in the entire two-story restaurant heard him.

"You pay bill, now!" the waiter said in a thick accent.

They stared tensely at each other. The woman still had the bill in her hand. The waiter was so close to me I could look up and see his black and abundant curly chest hairs through his sheer white polo shirt.

"You pay bill now, you fecking beetch!" he screamed.

"No!"

In a sudden act of defiance, she grabbed her table and slid it violently towards ours. My hand was on the edge in such a way that my fingers were in the crossfire. Uncle Tom was next to me and quickly grabbed my arm away before the table crashed into ours. The entire restaurant was quiet and watching the spectacle.

"You get the feck out of here, you fecking beetch," the bespectacled curly-haired waiter screamed. "You fecking beetch!"

The waiter grabbed the woman roughly by the arm and hair and pulled her to the door.

"Get the feck out!"

The woman was fighting back, which only made the Greek waiter angrier. He dragged her to the door, which was made of thick wood with a circle of stained glass at eye level. She flailed in his grip. No one in the restaurant knew what to do. The waiter took the woman and slammed her against the door. The impact of her body shattered the glass window and the woman screamed with fear and pain. The waiter yelled, "You fecking beetch! You fecking beetch!"

I was happy to see a Detroit police officer arrive on his horse, dismount, and quickly get the situation under control. More officers soon showed up and began interviewing the parties involved.

We ate our food, marveling at what just happened. The police were still there when we left. One officer had our still-raging Greek waiter inside the restaurant. The woman was outside on the sidewalk in a neon-lit doorway nervously stroking her injured head, smoking a cigarette and talking to another police officer. Another officer had located the rest of her party and was interviewing them separately down the street.

I was whisked away by my parents. Then Stella came lurching towards us down the sidewalk with her bags and crooked face. She rushed to meet us, never taking her eyes off me.

"Sonofabitchmotherfuckercocksucker. Sonofabitchmotherfuckercocksucker."

Mom stooped down and whispered to me, "She doesn't mean it, honey."

Mom clutched me even closer for the terrifying moment we passed within a few feet of Stella on the sidewalk. I felt those curses deep in the pit of my soul, in the same place that had been so stirred in church early that night.

"Sonofabitchmotherfuckercocksucker. Sonofabitchmotherfuckercocksucker."

"She doesn't mean it," Mom said. "She can't help herself."

We kept moving. We keep moving.

Coming Soon

Nichole Christian

THE HORROR OF THE CITY just rolled up in my Auntie Bettie's front yard, taking root like a wild weed. Brown boy curled on the grass, red-velvet blood coating the edges of the tulip bed. A son near lifeless, dumped, on Mother's Day. His wounds, battered face, blood-soaked skull, speak the words he cannot. Fathers and mothers take to the street, armed with cell phones and anguish. They fire cries of "nine-one-one, call nine-one-one." I am with them, a witness, wounded by what I've seen, scarred by the knowledge that my daughter's sheltered suburban eyes have seen this too. I want to hear sirens. I want to believe hope lives on in the city my heart calls home. Blind me with flashing lights and shiny badges, the signs we teach our children to believe when we tell them *all wrongs will be made right*. Maybe tonight. If we wait, justice will come rushing, swift and sudden, like the blood spilling from the boy. Just. Wait. Just. Us. Just wait. Just us. It's coming for this son on Mother's Day, for the city, for us, soon.

what you'd find
buried in the dirt under
charles f. kettering sr.
high school
(detroit, michigan)

francine j. harris

blood:
soaked and caked on white socks, on blue mesh net t-shirts.
the band leader's blue baton and drum sticks.
matchbook sulfur spilled over newport cigarette butts.
condoms in a few dull shades. tenth-grade chemistry books
modeling atomic fatty acids.
half-sucked orange dum-dums tucked under detention slips.
pictures from black hair cut out for pre-beautician consensus.
broken black glitter belts with pink buckles shaped like lips.
candle wax from last year's vigil when
de'andre "chucky" brown collapsed in the arms of his
teammate. the teammate's shoe prints rocking back and forth
where the vigil was held, biting his lip.
broken cellphones. pieces of the black rubber mat
below the entrance way, which we crossed every morning,
teeth clenched. notes of consent that girls wrote, but didn't mean
and wish they hadn't passed back.
broken teeth. lost retainers. crumpled letters written to counselors
and discarded for illegible handwriting. phone lists of
abortion clinics. deflated valentine's day balloons with
trampled white ribbon. sales ads on bassinette sets.
my first boyfriend's piano scarf. a phyllis hymen
album cover. the path from the

exit door behind the school through which certain boys
would not see certain girls leave.
torn up progress reports.
brass knuckles. two
afro picks on opposite sides of the school. germs on a hall pass
from a boy holding his crotch.
rusty rebar dust. pigeon bones. stolen phone numbers.
d.o.t. bus passes from 1960, the year of the groundbreaking.
suspended driver's licenses. broken glasses from ice
packed into snowballs. unread pamphlets on
charles f. kettering, a farmer with bad eyesight,
who invented the electric starter
and an incubator for preemies.
possum tails. original scores. balled up journal entries
written and torched, detailing abuses. genital fluids.
dna. envelopes from letters of acceptance
to states far away. math teachers' stolen answer keys
torn and burned by cigarette lighters.
cigarette lighters. hundreds of mcdonald's
fries containers because they flatten easily. weed.
imitation diamonds from homecoming tiaras
encrusted in shit-colored mud. research papers on kettering
detailing his treatments for
venereal disease
which involved heating up patients in thermal cabinets
until their body temperatures fevered at 130 degrees.
teachers' red pen marks on essay papers detailing abuses.
empty sprint cards.
a splint a football captain
was supposed to be wearing but decided made him look gay.
a fat boys tape. pieces of torn blue and white starter jackets
from the way boys wrestled each other
to the ground in spring.
my first poetry journal. pages of its poems
embossed with patterns of early name-brand gym shoes.
crumpled suicide notes written in pencil and scorched with ashes.
lost house keys. pictures of first crushes. bullets.
unpublished articles by frustrated teachers
who briefly looked into research findings,
using the charles f. kettering instrument of school
climate assessment detailing the psychological impact
on students from external stressors normally associated
with adulthood domestic patterns of abuse. fat shoelaces.
bullet casings. a jim beam whiskey flask that the old principal ditched
thinking someone was coming.
my last boyfriend's lesson plan elaborately structured

on the back
of a comic book. imprints of my mother's modest heel
from crossing the barren frontal square at my graduation.
free press articles on unnamed minors whose bodies were found
in dumpsters near kettering. the crystallized block formed
from the tissue my father handed me at graduation
for tears i couldn't explain.

Aaron Waterman

Gratiot Street Park / David Clements

Fort Gratiot

Steven Pomerantz

FROM 1948 TO 1979, my father and uncle, the sons of immigrant Russian Jews, owned a hardware store on the east side of Detroit. Similar to many new Americans, their parents had been chased from their homeland and began chasing new opportunities (and the burgeoning auto industry), first in Fort Wayne, Indiana, and then in Detroit. But life in the industrial Midwest was only slightly less harsh for the brothers, and as the city decayed the hardware store stood as a fortified outpost on the hostile prairie surrounding it.

§

The store was located on Gratiot Avenue, a major radial avenue running northeast out of downtown that had originated as an Indian trading route. It was later used as a supply road to Fort Gratiot, near Port Huron, during the War of 1812. The store occupied a WWI-era, two-story brown brick building which was half a city block long and itself reminded me of a fort, with shield-like medallions ornamenting the top and arched groupings of second-story windows that had long since been boarded up. It was in a crumbling neighborhood of empty lots and dilapidated buildings. Across the side street adjoining it was a seedy apartment building and a church, and abutting the alley behind the store was a rundown playground, which had become a thriving drug marketplace. On the other side of the building was a small, garbage-strewn lot ringed with barbed wire, next to which was a safe company whose owner, my father said, was an anti-Semite.

It was what we now term an "old-fashioned hardware store," complete with bins of nails, wire rug beaters, washboards, nuts and bolts that could be purchased by the piece, and wallpaper steamers to rent. Paint thinner was pumped from giant barrels into gallon jugs that customers brought into the store with them, and nails were weighed on an ancient set of scales. Outside, along the storefront, samples of merchandise offered inside were displayed (wheelbarrows, linoleum rugs, rolls of wiring, etc.), all chained together and secured with a padlock in case they decided to "wander off," as my father was fond of saying. There was even a giant "Mac-O-Lac" brand paint can affixed to the roof of the building so that drivers coming into the city knew what kind of business went on inside, much like businesses that had barber poles and giant eyeglasses in earlier times. Cigar-chomping Jewish sales representatives from our wholesale suppliers, with names like Irv, Seymour, and Harold, constantly seemed to be roaming the aisles, stopping only to take note of items to be re-ordered or kibitz with my father. My father gave easy credit to good customers and rarely got burned for it. Personalized service and the question "Can I help you?" meant something more than being pointed to aisle thirty-two by a slack-jawed greeter. In a pre-Home Depot world, it was a dependable and essential part of the community.

§

When the store opened for business in the '40s, it was surrounded by an Italian middle-class neighborhood that was transitioning to a black, lower-class neighborhood. By the '60s, nearly all of the customers were black, though the businesses that remained on Gratiot Avenue were still largely owned by Italians and Jews. In an amusing irony, during the early '70s, after parts of Detroit were seized by black gang violence, the store became part of "Coney-Oney" gang territory, Coney-Oney being a mangling of the Italian Corleone mob-family name from *The Godfather* movie, which had opened in 1972.

The store had regular customers whose real names you couldn't make up, such as Sugar Pie Cline, Merry Christmas and Mother Waddles, who ran a faith-based mission that still exists. If other characters at the store lacked sufficiently colorful names, they were given nicknames by my father and his brother. Among them were "Mushmouth," an employee who couldn't be understood. "Skin" was a plumbing handyman of indeterminate age with leathery skin who wore a uniform of sunglasses, a crisp white short-sleeved shirt, and a hat, and was always hanging around, as much a fixture in the store as the front counter. He was there most often to try to get work from customers, other times to get sober from too much "Sweet Lucy" the night before, all the while holding court on bags of fertilizer or rock salt (depending on the season), telling tales of his visits to New Orleans. "Bigfoots" was a tall handyman with huge mutton-chops who took every job that came through the door, a proud family man and a tireless, dependable worker. "Feets" was another handyman, who used his feet to measure projects instead of a tape measure. The default nickname given to anyone who quoted the ways of the scripture and the virtues of their church was "Reverend."

The employees reflected the many ethnicities of the city. Carl, who was black and probably the longest tenured employee of the store, was the de facto floor manager of the business and somebody my father and his brother trusted to act as their liaison with the more radicalized and empowered members of the black community. A small, wiry man with a receding hairline, mustache, and tinted glasses, he dealt effectively with those who were identified as troublemakers or as having an attitude by my father, even brokering a peace with the Coney-Oneys. He was "hip" and greeted customers by saying "What can I do you for?" or "What it is!"

Roger, the resident Pole, was a tall man with slicked-back greased hair who could fix anything and would let you know about it. Ricky, a Latino man with long hair, glazed eyes, and a wispy moustache, gave me sales tips on how to promote grass fertilizers we sold in the store as being perfectly adequate for growing weed, a thriving second career for some of our customers. And he knew more about the genius of Jimi Hendrix than anyone I ever met.

Norman, a self-styled ladies man; Ralph, a one-eyed alcoholic who had perfected the two syllable pronunciation of "shee-it"; and Chris, our Greek connection to bookies and tickets to Lions games, rounded out the colorful cast.

But when it came to the clientele, my father and uncle were always obsessed with "the Schvartz." The Schvartz (Yiddish for a black person) meant lazy, drunks, unreliable, thieves, stupid, or *chayas* (animals, in Yiddish). To the Schvartz, Dad and my uncle were Jews–greedy, exploitative, cheap, rip-off artists, devils. This much everybody understood, and it formed the basis for an uneasy alliance—they needed each other too much to let their mutual dislike get in the way. But as always in these types of things, it was more complicated than that. The neighborhood black community was made up of my father's friends and enemies. They were the source of his livelihood and the bane of his existence.

I was taught that the Schvartz were to be approached with suspicion and dehumanized as cartoon characters you could share a good laugh about. And I was told to remember that "as much as the Schvartz hate you, they hate each other more," as if that excused our attitudes about them.

§

On a July day in 1967, a race riot broke out in Detroit. The city had been simmering with racial tension for decades, and the riot was said to have been ignited by a police raid on a blind pig in the early morning. A blind pig was a private club where liquor was served illegally after hours. Looting was spreading throughout the city, and several city blocks were on fire, including some near the store.

During the following days, the city was locked down in a state of emergency; however, the police and National Guard allowed business owners to enter the city, assess their damages, and make necessary repairs. The store was found untouched, though surrounding businesses did not fare as well. My father attributed this to his good relations with the black community, but it could have been just dumb luck.

The combination of a race riot and a sprawling freeway system accelerated the white flight to the suburbs that had begun post-World War II. Three of those freeways were known as the Chrysler, the Ford, and the Fischer—the great auto barons giving their names to the enablers of the migration out of the city, in cars they had built. It was no longer an acceptable place to live or work for a lot of people. Following the civil unrest, the social and economic breakdown in this area of the city was swift, and violence became an everyday occurrence. Fear, which had always been a quiet presence, now demanded attention and gripped my father's existence from that point on. However, moving the store was never discussed and, much like the generations of mice, rats, and spiders that inhabited the store, my father and his brother were too comfortable to leave. It was easier selling what they always sold, to those they always sold it to, in a building they already owned. At least they knew fear and how to deal with it, but hope was a scarier proposition.

After the riot (Detroiters always mark time as pre- or post-riot), the store stayed in much the same condition as it had existed from the 1940s. It was either a time capsule or a tomb, depending on your perspective, and had an atmosphere of cold cement floors, inexplicably pink walls (my father read somewhere that pink made people want to buy), harsh fluorescent lighting, and dry air infused with concrete dust. Even the expansion into the carpet store space next door (it was known as the "Carpet Barn") was no occasion to change its barn-like motif, nor clean the blood-soaked carpeted area where a disgruntled ex-employee had taken an axe to its owner.

Thus, what change did occur at the store was done in the interest of protecting it against the siege of outside forces. A large fluorescent orange sign with big black letters, reading 'NOTICE! THIS STORE IS PROTECTED BY AN ARMED GUARD,' was prominently placed at the checkout counter (my father was the "armed guard"). In addition to an alarm system, most windows were boarded up, and the few storefront windows that remained were converted to plate glass. This worked out fine until the plate glass became riddled with holes from BB guns, the BBs proudly sold at our hardware store. The solution to this, in addition to halting the sale of BBs, was to replace the plate glass with a thick plastic glass that had the otherworldly name of Lexan. When even that eventually seemed vulnerable, a metal grate system was installed across the storefront, thus further suffocating what little natural light was permitted to enter. But the final step in the entombing of the store was the decision to install steel plated doors on all of the rear entrances and to secure each of those doors during closing hours with three heavy padlocks on the inside. For convenience, the keys to the padlocks were hung on chains next to the door.

The store was now impenetrable, until late one night when my father got a call from the alarm company notifying him that one of the rear doors had been breached. When we arrived early the next morning, it was clear what had happened: my father had been so focused on preventing a break-in that he overlooked the potential for a "break-out." It seemed that a couple of enterprising criminals figured out that the large, deep area under the stairs to the second floor, where we kept empty boxes and other packing material until garbage day, would be an ideal place to hide until the store was closed. So it was not hard to imagine that sometime after the store closed, the criminals emerged from their hiding place, selected the strongest sledgehammer and pick-axe that were on display, and took their time busting open the large safe in the store's office. Then, after also cleaning out the cash register, they calmly unlocked one of the rear doors with the conveniently placed keys and walked out into the night. Using another word my father cynically favored, they had "liberated" the cash.

§

Inside the store, the customers, employees, and owners now preyed upon each other like animals in a jungle. Employees exchanged knowing glances, indicating when it was safe to take cash from the register or merchandise out to their car. Customers would go to empty aisles and pocket items, sometimes confronted by my father with the phrase "Either you put that back, or I take this out." He would say it with a smile on his face while patting his front pocket where he kept a gun, akin to a sheriff in the westerns he so loved. Correspondingly, if a customer wanted a type of paint we didn't have in stock, my father would have me furiously re-label cans of paint behind the scenes so we could make the sale. "Interior white, exterior white, it's all the same shit and they'll never know the difference," he would say. And I'll never know whether the incredibly high prices our customers complained about were because the store had a near monopoly on hardware items in the area, or because, as my father told me, our costs to insure the store against fire and theft were astronomical. I want to believe that all the cheating and stealing evened itself out over the years.

But the irony is that the demise of the store didn't come because of theft, fire, violence, or any other threat my father spent years trying to insulate himself from. It didn't even happen because business was bad. In 1978, he realized that his brother had been embezzling money from the store for several years, something my uncle would confess to when later confronted, according to my parents. For a business built on offering solutions, there were none for this particular problem, and the store was soon sold to another unfortunate soul for a fraction of its value.

§

Years later, shortly before my father died, I went back to visit the store with him. The surrounding area now looked even more grim and barren, part of the transition of Detroit into its frontier status of today. I wondered if it had always looked this way and we just couldn't see it. But even before we entered the store there was the palpable sense that he couldn't wait to leave, that he was somehow tempting fate by going back, and the odds would catch up with him this time. He wore an uneasy smile, like he had cheated death. We left quickly, the weight of thirty years of fending off all the enemies too much to bear. Before we did, I glanced back and saw the familiar look of resignation, fear, and desperation on the new owner's face. He looked like my father.

Sketches of Eastern Market

Nina Misuraca Ignaczak

From 1947 to 1989, my grandfather and his brother owned a grocery store and butcher shop called the Vogue Market on the corner of Cadieux and Lanark Street in Detroit's far northeast side. The brothers were sons of grocers, having grown up in a flat above their parents' corner grocery on the corner of Canfield and Lenox, several miles closer into the city.

If you trace the sequence of homes, Catholic churches, businesses, and cemetery plots owned and occupied by my family during the twentieth century, they plot a path that migrates ever northeastward, out of the city and into the east-side suburbs.

For my first year of life, we lived in a duplex not far from the Vogue, where my father helped out on weekends while he attended law school.

By the time I came around, the store was its last decade. My grandfather—a colorful and frequently politically incorrect 1950s Archie Bunker–type character who drank Miller High Life and liked to guess peoples' ethnicities—would bestow cold hot dogs upon my sister and me from behind the white metal butcher case, snug in natural casings and skewered on a kabob sticks. We would munch the meaty treats, cold and salty, while one of my aunts rang up the order—*ching, ching*—on a mechanical cash register.

Later, I remember riding alongside my dad on humid early Saturday summer morning delivery runs in the front seat of the white Econoline delivery van with THE VOGUE MARKET emblazoned in script on the side, driving into the loading dock of Tiger Stadium on Michigan and Trumbull to deliver house-made Italian wine and cheese sausage for the press box.

I realize now that I witnessed the tail end of an era—one of neighborhood groceries and local food distribution in Detroit, a time when a small local grocer ran home deliveries in the neighborhood and supplied the city's major league baseball stadium.

My grandfather ran the Vogue Market alone for almost twenty years after his brother died; he sold it in 1989. He died in 2000, living long enough to see the rise of Meijer as a major grocer, but not long enough to see urban agriculture and the local food movements gain a foothold. During the Vogue's heyday, the neighborhood was solidly middle class and white. By the time the Vogue was sold, it was mostly poor and black.

Today, the Vogue Market is a corner liquor store. The name remains the same.

Nearly every Saturday of my childhood was spent at Eastern Market. My father would make the rounds, greeting cousins and former suppliers at the wholesale markets ringing the sheds, haggling over prices, and reminiscing over times past and people long dead. It was on these trips that I felt closest to my father and my past, gaining the tiniest glimpse into the century that had passed before I was born, when my grandparents and great-grandparents and aunts and uncles made their way in a new country as fruit peddlers and wholesalers and grocers.

Many Detroiters feel a deep sense of loss over what's happened in the city. I never knew another Detroit besides than the one in ruins. But my memories of my grandfather's store and trips to Eastern Market are enshrined in my mind, bound up with a sense of loss and wonder—and hope.

Saturday at Eastern Market today is a far cry from the one I remember growing up. Over the last five years, the market has been transformed as the result of a concerted development effort. My parents scoff a little at the high-end artisanal products on offer. There seems to be less haggling. But it attracts more people from a wider geography than ever before, and that's a good thing.

Eastern Market, 1982

It is early Saturday morning. I am seven years old, riding in the spacious backseat of my father's Cutlass, my younger sister beside me. We are cruising west on 8 Mile Road towards Gratiot Avenue with the windows rolled down. Michigan summer morning air, wet and heavy, rushes into the car. A light fog clinging to the tops of buildings is burning off rapidly. It will be hot today. My legs are already sticking to the red vinyl seats.

As we approach the market, the fog lifts, the sky is a brilliant blue, and the vacant and dilapidated buildings lining Gratiot glitter and shimmer in heat and decay. We find a parking spot in the haphazard open lots surrounding the sheds. As we climb out of the backseat, I am overwhelmed by the odor of rotting cucumbers and the sounds of farmers shouting above the crowd, "Peck of peaches, five dollars!" and "Get your watermelon!"

Nearly retching, I follow my father as we pick our way through cartons of abandoned produce left to rot in the sun.

My sister and I climb into the red metal wagon, and my father pulls us through the market. From our vantage point, we see his strong, hairy legs pushing a wide berth through the crowds. We make a sweep of the market, never making any purchases until he has perused the entire selection. There are three large sheds, and this takes about forty-five minutes.

My father negotiates with farmers, talking them down at every chance. We are allowed to get out of the wagon briefly to look at the small livestock for sale: rabbits, chickens, and ducks on display in straw-lined cages. Although we beg, we are not allowed a new pet, but are mollified by chunks of honeycomb on sticks, our fingers and lips becoming encased in the sticky, sweet waxy goodness.

As we circle back, my father fills the wagon with boxes of tomatoes, corn, cucumbers, peaches, and pears. The bottom halves of our bodies are trapped beneath the weight of produce. When we return to the car, my father frees our legs as he lifts the bags into the trunk. The car is stifling.

We roll down the windows and cruise back down Jefferson toward the east-side suburbs, the dank freshness of the Detroit River rising to fill our nostrils, the hot wind whipping through our long hair.

There are those who say urban farming and local food systems won't save Detroit. But here are some facts: Detroit is one of the few major cities with intact open food distribution hubs; in other cities, many of those nodes were lost to gentrification. Using bio-intensive farming methods, analysts predict that Detroit could produce much of its produce needs on a fraction of its vacant land. It doesn't have to be an either-or decision between food production and development. Detroit's access to freshwater as an irrigation source and for transport is virtually unlimited and unparalleled. Eastern Market is the crowning jewel, the city's strongest asset toward rebuilding a local food system.

Today, through a mix of circumstances and necessity, I find myself living in the far northern suburbs. I want my kids to know about Eastern Market, and their great-grandfather's grocery store, and the century of food mongering that makes up their heritage. So much of it is gone. I do what I can to offer my children the experience, knowing any appreciation they have will be a fraction of the truth.

Eastern Market, 2012

It is late Saturday morning. I am thirty-seven years old, riding in the passenger seat of my Honda minivan. My two children are strapped into their car seats behind me. My husband is driving. We arrive by freeway from the northern suburbs, driving past long miles of subdivisions and strip malls, giving way to the city that never seems to fully dissolve despite years of unrelenting decay. It is hot, and the windows are rolled up, the air conditioner blasting.

The market is packed with Detroiters and suburbanites, as it has always been, but there are far more of them and it takes ten minutes to find a parking place. The perimeter is still rough and unmarked, but clean. A smoky-rib aroma emanates from the barbecue-karaoke joint. We pack the kids, a boy and a girl, into a red plastic replica of the Radio Flyer.

We enter the first shed, lined with purveyors of artisanal spices, cheeses, and salad greens. Prices are as marked. The hog's head on display in the second shed is familiar, comforts me. There are no rabbits. We purchase honeycomb chunks on sticks from the same beekeeper that has been here for forty years, and the kids' fingers and faces are immediately covered in stickiness. At the end of the shed, we wait for made-to-order crepes filled with Nutella. I pick up my son as we watch a thin layer of batter swirl out and solidify on a hot plate.

Much of what is on offer I can procure at the upscale supermarkets near my home. Instead, I home in on the Detroit-grown items: Brother Nature salad mix with its spicy mizuna, Grown in Detroit–label kohlrabi, and Asian greens whose name I can't pronounce.

We return to the van, our purchases crushing the kids. The van is stifling. We roll down the windows until the air runs cold, and then roll them back up as we drive back onto the freeway, headed north.

Today, Detroiters are looking for ways to reinvent the city, with an eye toward self-sufficiency. Upstart distributors like Peaches & Greens deliver produce to corner liquor stores for SNAP recipients, many likely former neighborhood groceries like the Vogue Market. Weekday produce markets are popping up across the city, and local food businesses are being cultivated by organizations like FoodLab Detroit.

I've lived most of my life outside the city boundaries, the end result of the outward migration of my Sicilian immigrant forbears that moved a little farther with each generation. But I find myself always looking back toward the city, and for some reason, my thoughts are centered on Eastern Market.

I see the re-creation of a local food infrastructure in the city as a kind of moving full circle, taking pieces of the past—community gardens, neighborhood grocers—and meshing them with the possibilities of the future.

If anything has the potential to heal the divide between city and suburb, past and future, it will be what we put on our plates.

When the Trees Stop Giving Fruit

Shaka Senghor

I RECALL CLIMBING HIGH in the pear tree next door to retrieve the delicious fruit it offered. There was nothing I loved more than sinking my teeth into the sweet, juicy flesh of a yellowing pear. It's one of the fondest memories from my childhood. No matter what was going on in my small world, I looked forward to the fruit of one of the many fruit trees on my street. Whether it was the plum tree in our backyard, my neighbor's peach tree, or their pear tree, I could always count on these succulent fruits to erase the pain of the moment. Then, one day, the trees no longer gave fruit. It was then that I realized my neighborhood had died, leaving in its wake an iniquitous skeleton that no longer resembled the healthy, vibrant place I once called home.

The neighborhood I grew up in embodied the American Dream. Our tree-lined street on Detroit's east-side was rich with diverse culture, laughter, dancing, and the aroma of exotic foods. Summer days were spent playing freeze tag, leaping in the water that sprayed from the fire hydrant on a hot day, and eating juicy pears plucked from our neighbor Miss Moore's tree. Miss Moore was a sweet woman with a pleasant smile and frosty white hair. Out of my mother's six children, I was her favorite. Whenever she made her homemade pear preserves, she made sure to send me a mason jar full. In turn, I cut her grass and ran small errands whenever she called upon me.

A festive Italian family occupied the house on the other side of our house. We shared a grapevine that draped across our backyard fence. When the grapes were purple and plump, our families would go out back and pick them. We laughed and joked, and shared food and music. We gave them collard greens, macaroni and cheese, and Marvin Gaye, and they gave us linguini, lasagna, and opera. They had a peach tree in their backyard, and we had a plum tree. Whenever we picked fruit, we shared it with our neighbors, and they in turn shared their harvest with us.

I loved to eat, and my neighbors delighted in filling my fat belly with fruit and cookies. On any given day, you could find me in the backyard with juice from a peach or pear dripping down my chubby cheeks, until the day I got stung by a bee. After that, I enjoyed the sweet juice of these beloved fruits from the safety of our closed-in patio.

Sharing food and merriment was an everyday experience; it was the way life was meant to be. Back then, we slept with our doors open and took care of each other. Our neighbors were like family, and they made us feel welcome even though we were the first Black family on the street. Back then, I didn't know that racism existed because we never experienced it. Underneath it all, we were the same. My parents wanted for us what I imagined my childhood friends' parents wanted for them—a good education, a good job, and ultimately, a family of our own.

Sadly, the cultural and moral fibers of our neighborhood began slowly eroding, and my parents' American Dream unraveled like a ball of cheap yarn. The changes rolled out inch by inch. First, the Dodge and Chrysler factories relocated, taking with them a large part of their workforce, and transient renters who thought nothing of destroying the property of others were now replacing homeowners who took pride in caring for their homes.

Liquor stores that sold alcohol to children, turning their brains into mush, replaced the mom-and-pop corner stores. Fast food joints that served stroke–inducing burgers and cardiac arrest–producing fries replaced the comforting diners that once provided us with food prepared with love. The once manicured, lush, green lawns were now yellowing and unkempt, and the once friendly police who would stop on the street and allow children to play with their sirens were replaced by an occupying force that brutalized and shot unarmed men and boys in the back.

Out-of-work alcoholics, welfare recipients, and drug addicts replaced the teachers, firemen, dentists, and factory workers who once nurtured and cultivated our neighborhood. But the final nail in the coffin was the arrival of crack cocaine.

Crack hit our neighborhood with the force of a runaway train, causing it to implode and leaving behind the wreckage we now call the 'hood. The "neighbor" element, which is an integral part of any community's success, was destroyed. Leaving our doors open at night was like inviting death into our homes. The sound of laughter and children playing in the street was replaced with the rapid-fire bursts of AK-47 assault rifles and .40-caliber Glocks. The trees that once fed our young bellies were now camouflage for bandits looking to prey on the innocent. The white men and women who now roamed our 'hood were unlike the neighbors I had grown up with. Instead of loving and caring, they were afraid and standoffish. Or worse, they ventured into the 'hood to buy their illicit drugs or make perverted transactions before slinking back to the safety of their homes on the other side of 8 Mile.

The childhood friends that I grew up with were now enemies warring over drug turf, and by the time I turned 21, half of my friends were in prison and the other half were dead. Instead of parents gathering to celebrate a child going off to college, they now gathered to mourn a child shot down in the streets.

Today, in this 'hood that was at one time pregnant with hope, nothing remains but pain and suffering. The children dream no more, and the parents have surrendered their destiny. Teenage mothers are the norm, and young men don't expect to live past eighteen. Abandoned houses mar the land like infected scabs. Babies roam the streets at two in the morning hungry and afraid, not knowing if their parents will return from their three-day crack binge. The schools, which at one time demanded academic excellence, are now prisons with barbed wire on the windows and armed guards patrolling the campus. The inoperable bathrooms and antiquated books with missing pages only help to lower the students' self-esteem and their standardized test scores. Grocery stores, which once provided the neighborhood with healthy food, have given way to corner stores that sell us all the worst things at all the best prices—sugary concoctions offering us a sweet dose of diabetes.

Yes, the fruit of a once pristine neighborhood has all but rotted away, and the trees that once gave fruit, give no more.

Hungry Days in Detroit

Tracie McMillan

Every time I come to Detroit, no matter how long I'm staying, no matter if I'm on a friend's couch or in a hotel, I go grocery shopping. This rarely makes sense. There is no need to lug bread and cheese and jam back to Brooklyn, where I can buy all these things. But that is what love will do to you: I cannot help myself. I have to see my loves, and in Detroit that means the places that have fed me.

I lived in Detroit in 2010 for ten months, writing a book. I was so poor that I was on food stamps. Every Saturday, I went to Eastern Market, the city's biggest farmer's market. I would walk through the cavernous halls of concrete and steel, writing down prices, so that I might get three pounds of sweet potatoes for $2 instead of $2.50, and checking whether the bulk rice at Rocky's was cheaper than at E&L Supermercado (it wasn't). Many of the customers, like me, were white; many of them were not. Everyone was as likely to be in boots and Carhartts—for utilitarian, not aesthetic, reasons—as anything considered stylish.

I fell in love with the city in those hungry days. Part of it was straight-up gratitude, because it was the place that fed me well for cheap. But part of it was more complicated; it was about the deep shame I felt at being poor. It was about the frustration that welled up in my chest when I went to a suburban grocery store and realized I was eyeing the meat in other patrons' carts with envy. I was embarrassed by my longing, and of how I could not afford the food I wanted—lean ground beef, chicken thighs, fresh oranges—on the budget I had. I wondered if other shoppers might notice I didn't belong. At Eastern Market, I never wondered, because every kind of person was there.

Before I lived in Detroit, I'd heard city officials talk about the grocery gap: how millions of dollars in grocery money were spent at stores outside the city limits. I didn't doubt it, but I also wondered whether those Detroiters had bothered to stop at Honeybee Market, run by a multigenerational supermarket family with a background in produce. There, I bought El Milagro tortillas, layered rounds of corn so tasty that now I ferry thirty-packs of them back to Brooklyn. Had Detroiters somehow missed E&L, where I found the cheapest rice and oats, sold in bulk bags under a canopy of piñatas? Were they afraid to cross the pedestrian bridge at Eastern Market to visit Gratiot Central, where I buy meat and chicken when I'm downtown, or were they intimidated by the Polish signage at Bozek's in Hamtramck, where I go if I'm on the northside?

The story from city officials didn't often include my new loves. My time living and eating in Detroit taught me something, in a visceral way, about how the notions of the powerful don't always line up with reality for the rest of us. And it taught me something about how love, once it appears, has a way of pushing aside everything in its path.

In the time since I lived in Detroit, Meijer and Whole Foods opened in the city, changing its foodscape forever. Six months after they both opened, I found myself reporting in the city, running late for a meeting, and in need of breakfast. Whole Foods was on my way, so I dropped in and found myself faced with a breakfast burrito for $3.99.

I looked around. There were young professionals in line with their organic coffees, talking about their commutes to the suburbs, and there was a man in his security uniform browsing at the bakery counter. And there was me and the $4 burrito.

In Brooklyn, I wouldn't have blinked at the price. But I knew that ten minutes away sat Honeybee's hot food counter, where I could get two (very good) burritos for $2.50—the kind of price that made my life in Detroit livable, the kind of price that ushered in my love of the place.

The sensible thing would have been to buy the Whole Foods burrito and make my meeting on time. But my heart, I have found, isn't sensible. I walked out.

At Honeybee I sat in my car, dousing my burritos in salsa verde, before getting back on my way. I was fifteen minutes late for my meeting, and it was worth every second.

Catherine Ferguson Academy Farm, 2011 / Patricia Lay-Dorsey

Fishing on Belle Isle / Patricia Lay-Dorsey

There Are Birds Here

Jamaal May

for Detroit

There are birds here,
so many birds here
is what I was trying to say
when they said those birds were metaphors
for what is trapped
between buildings
and buildings. No.
The birds are here
to root around for bread
the girl's hands tear
and toss like confetti. No,
I don't mean the bread is torn like cotton,
I said confetti, and no
not the confetti
a tank can make of a building.
I mean the confetti
a boy can't stop smiling about
and no his smile isn't much
like a skeleton at all. And no
his neighborhood is not like a warzone.
I am trying to say
his neighborhood
is as tattered and feathered
as anything else,
as shadow pierced by sun
and light parted
by shadow-dance as anything else,
but they won't stop saying
how lovely the ruins,
how ruined the lovely
children must be in that birdless city.

Per Fumum *(Through Smoke)*

Jamaal May

My mother became an ornithologist
when the grackle tumbled through barbecue smoke
and fell at her feet. Soon she learned
why singers cage birds; it can take weeks
to memorize a melody—
the first days lost as they mope
and warble a friendless note,
the same tone every animal memorizes
hours into breathing. It's a note
a cologne would emit if the bottle was struck
while something mystical was aligned
with something even more mystical
but farther away. My father was an astronomer
for forty minutes in a row
the first time a bus took us so far
from streetlights he could point out constellations
that may or may not have been Draco,
Orion, Aquila, or Crux.
When they faded I resented the sun's excess,
a combination of fires I couldn't smell.
The first chemist was a perfumer
whose combinations, brushed
against pulse points, were unlocked
by quickening blood. From stolen perfumes
I concocted my personal toxin.
It was no more deadly than as much water
to any creature the size of a roach. I grew suspicious
of my plate and lighter Bunsen burner,
the tiny vials accumulating in my closet.
I was a chemist for months
before I learned the difference
between poisoned and drowned.
When my bed caught fire
it smelled like a garden.

Desolation Angel

John Carlisle

THEY STAGGER IN ONE BY ONE—each with a story, each with a life of problems. First comes the prostitute. Then comes a drinker. Every swing of the door brings another desperate person from the street outside.

People with addictions, with diseases, people living on the street. And people who suffer from none of those things but who are just drawn to this strange place.

Some talk to each other; one or two are talking to themselves, or the air, or whatever demons they hear in their heads.

It's Sunday morning. It's time for church.

At Peacemakers International on Chene Street, a little storefront ministry not far south of I-94, the congregation doesn't just help people who are addicts or poor or homeless. Those people are the congregation.

They come here because this place has taken in dozens of people fighting years of addiction and, somehow, they say, it has helped them get off drugs. People like Tony Cusmano, who gradually stole a quarter-million dollars from his family business to feed a cocaine habit before ending up behind bars. Like Shirley Robinson, who gave up a career and a house for a coke habit, which became a crack habit that left her selling herself on this street for a few years. Like Coy Welch, a longtime drinker who was found living under a bridge a couple months ago and was invited to come here.

And from this ragged crowd, the preacher emerges.

At first it's hard to distinguish him from his flock. Steve Upshur is sixty-two, and he wears jeans and cowboy boots and a leather Harley jacket. His hair is long. So is his scraggly mustache. He's a biker and looks like a biker.

He used to be an addict, so desperate he once puked up his methadone at a clinic and then got down on the ground to lap up the drug-soaked vomit. He's been a dealer. He's been jailed. He even got caught up in a bank robbery once.

His flock relates to him because he's been where they are, because he's done as much wrong in his life as they have in theirs, but more importantly because he's someone who found a way out of that hell. He's walked the walk. And because of that, he's earned their trust, earned his post as father of the wayward.

"When you get into crack and prostitution, anything goes," Upshur says. "A lot of these people will stuff people in trunks, kill people. I've had people confess murders in here. I've heard it all."

More people arrive. A homeless man. A woman one misstep away from being there. An old lady with a scowling face, muttering to herself.

The services begin right on time. But there's no prayer to start things off. No reading of the Bible. No sermon.

Instead, a high-tempo, old-time gospel song—"I Believe" by John P. Kee—blares from the stereo. And as the beat kicks in, everyone in the pews who had been sitting quietly suddenly gets up and starts clapping along. A few even dance.

Then the pastor says a few short words, but right away another song bursts out of the stereo, and the congregation is behaving like it's some kind of dance party. People who were living on the street or still are, people selling themselves there, people crippled by drug and drinking problems, are all dancing together, looking like they haven't had this kind of fun in years. It's an astonishing sight.

And just when it seems this can't possibly be the actual service, it turns out that's this is indeed how it goes at Peacemakers. Down here on Chene, going to Sunday service is almost like going to a party where, for a couple hours, the weight of everyone's troubled past falls away.

"It's just upbeat, you know?" Upshur says. "This isn't a dead place where everybody's sitting there. That ain't the way a church is supposed to be."

§

Chene Street is a disaster. The rows of burned-out storefronts between the empty blocks are reminders of how bustling it once was. But after the riot, after the freeway and an auto plant split the neighborhood in half, after everyone packed up and moved away, almost everything just died off.

Pouring into the void left behind were outcasts and cast-asides—junkies and drunks, hookers and drug dealers, the mentally ill and the physically disabled. Like a few other areas of the city, it became a refuge of the underclass, a home for everyone with nowhere else to go, where they can wander freely without being chased away by storeowners or told to move along by the cops.

"It's like the devil's playground," says John Simon, a minister here. "I mean, you got sexual acts in the middle of the day, shooting dope, smoking dope. Everything you can imagine is going on down here."

This is the world in which Peacemakers established itself in 1994. In many ways it's a typical inner-city, grassroots church. The services are nondenominational and loose. And like any Christian ministry, the place seeks to create believers and followers in Jesus, though they give food and clothing to anyone who comes here, whether they profess a belief in God or not.

But something's happening here that draws the people who work or live on the streets outside. Just about every member swears that sometime after they came here, there was a moment when everything changed for them, when their addictions simply vanished. Whether what took place for them was spiritual or psychological, whether the catalyst was from inside or out, the simple program offered here, they say, helped alter their lives. It's not a twelve-step program, more a strict combination of work, prayer, and study that uses religious belief to shield against the temptation for an addict to return to their old life.

Maybe Peacemakers gives a template to people who've never had a code of behavior to guide them. Maybe some people just need a strict system of rules to follow. Either way, its members insist that this place works.

A whole system has evolved to support them, a virtual safety net in a neighborhood that never really had one. The church operates halfway houses for ex-cons and ex-prostitutes, sets up gardens for flowers and vegetables, and keeps a chicken coop for eggs. It all goes to the neighborhood. And every day they give out food and clothes.

This place is often the last resort for neighborhood people whose choices or circumstances left them living on the lowest rungs. The program offered here is powerful and appealing because it's so simple.

"The main thing is a sincere desire to find God and get your life together, and a willingness to stick to the rules," says Jeremiah Upshur, the pastor's thirty-two-year-old son.

Those rules require members to be sober, to pray together and to participate in helping the poor by feeding and clothing them, and working to get them off the streets. But a stated belief in Jesus is not enough to stay here. Members have to demonstrate those convictions with the people of Chene Street.

"It's a hard ministry. The hardest thing that I've ever done in my entire life is to be a Christian," Simon says of the work involved. "But it's the most fulfilling."

After Peacemakers opened, the street people out front saw their old friends suddenly sober, talking about this crazy church that's feeding and clothing them and helping them get clean, even if sometimes it doesn't last, and they began showing up out of curiosity. Soon, its reputation took on a life of its own, and strange things started happening.

"We would have fires in this giant fire pit back there, and people would be coming in, throwing their syringes in, throwing their crack pipes in, just giving it all up," Simon says. "It was mind-blowing."

§

The pastor got here the long, hard way. He was a juvenile delinquent who became a teenage heroin addict. Petty crimes grew into bigger ones until he found himself nodding off at the wheel of a bank robbery getaway car one afternoon in the early '70s in Detroit's suburbs, just as the cops swarmed in. He barely escaped lengthy prison time for it.

He fled Detroit but kept his lifestyle. While in an Oklahoma jail in the early '70s for some minor offense, an inmate told him these born-again Christians had a place nearby, and they could be easily suckered into giving you food and shelter. "So I'm thinking, 'Well, go get me a sandwich; I'll go hustle them for a sandwich,'" Upshur says.

But he was drawn in by their approach. "These people are talking to Jesus like he's their buddy, and I grew up you'd have to probably be a priest or a nun to be talking firsthand to the main man," says Upshur, who was raised Catholic. "I'm thinking this is deep. All of a sudden—boom!—this spiritual world opens up. I'm like, 'You gotta be kidding me.'"

He was so inspired, he came back to Detroit at twenty-five years old, determined to stay clean, and started holding informal prayer meetings at a house next to his parents' home to talk about spirituality or God or whatever anyone wanted. At the first gathering, his audience was a bunch of teenagers who came less to hear another born-again and more to see the crazy bank robber. A week later, he had thirty-five kids there. Soon after, adults started showing up too.

The group kept growing and moved from a house to an old, unused church in Detroit, and eventually to a church in St. Clair Shores with three pastors and a large middle-class congregation. Upshur preached out there for sixteen years.

But he felt the pull of skid row. "That's always where my heart was, 'cause I come out of that," he says. "I grew up in the inner city, I've been homeless many of the years of my life, been in and out of jail all my life, a very rough life. Those were my main people that I grew up with. So when I got, quote, 'saved,' I knew I'd be back working with people that come out of my environment."

A woman in the suburban church offered him a small, old building on Chene that she owned, and he began his ministry in one of the city's most miserable, drug-addled neighborhoods. "We take people who everybody else has given up on," Bob Kaczmarek says. He's a board member of the church, sixty-four, a Catholic, a well-dressed attorney. He attends services elsewhere, but was so impressed by Peacemakers and its ragged flock that he became involved.

"This is it," he says. "For some of the people who are in the in-house programs, this is their last chance. And if they don't make it here, then you find out they're found dead somewhere."

§

There have to be at least one hundred stuffed animals inside the bedrooms at the Mercy House.

Several women stay here right now, at the Peacemakers' halfway house for those trying to escape a life of prostitution and drugs, or battered women trying to escape a violent man. Blocks away, there's a halfway house for men out of prison, off the streets, just off drugs.

What's striking about the women's house are the delicate, feminine, almost childlike touches. Though the women here have led hard lives, there's pink and softness everywhere—on the stuffed animals, in the decorations on the walls, on the clothes inside the closets. It's as if the women here are trying to reclaim an innocence they lost years ago. Denise Benn walks into her bedroom, bounces onto her bed, and grabs a blue stuffed dog. "I got this puppy I took care of right before I came in here, and it made me feel young again, 'cause I could take care of something," the forty-three-year-old says, hugging it.

Benn's history is written on her face. Her story is like one many of the women here tell. Her life collapsed at twelve, she says, when she was gang raped by six men on the way to school. Soon after, she started doing drugs to bury the trauma, hanging out with the dropouts and the druggies because they were nicer to her than anyone else.

"I liked getting high," she says. "People accepted me. I wasn't part of my family because I didn't get along with my family. But now I was part of something."

By sixteen, she was pole dancing in Detroit strip clubs, strung out on heroin, and within a couple years she went from turning tricks in VIP rooms to doing so in cars.

Her life as a street prostitute was one harrowing night after another.

"Every day something horrific was happening to me," she says. "I was either getting thrown out of moving cars or waking up with people's hands on my throat, and I had a heroin addiction and I couldn't stop. I mean, you should see the scars on my body. I'm not lying to you. I've had some horrific stuff happen to me."

The women here—five right now—watch out for each other, keep each other's spirits up when things look bleak and the street outside begins to appear appealing again. They travel in twos when they walk the neighborhood, eat group dinners, and help out at the church together.

"I got a new way of life," Benn says. "I'm productive here and I'm of use here. I've got a place here."

But there are relapses here too.

The previous spring, she violated the rules against dating someone at a nearby halfway house for men and, forced to leave, wound up back on the streets, living in an abandoned building.

"The first night I went there, I just cried, because I knew what was going to happen," Benn says. She fell right back into drugs and prostitution. "I didn't have nowhere to go. I didn't have no resources. I didn't have a dime in my pocket."

Jeremiah Upshur, the pastor's son, came looking for her and asked her to come back. Now she works for the church and tries to figure out how to build a new life. She has no money, can't even get past a minimum-wage job interview because of the long gap in her work history, and has few skills other than the ones she picked up on the streets. It makes it tough to stay hopeful, challenging to remain on the path she's trying to follow.

"It's hard," Benn says, dragging on a cigarette. "It's really hard."

§

It all comes down to a single moment, they say. A line between their old life and their new one. And they all say it like they still half can't believe it actually happened.

It happened to Simon too. He tells his story as he wanders the aisles at Joseph's Storehouse, the church's resale shop in Warren that he runs. This is where the church gets what little money it has—selling cheap things one or two at a time.

Simon's one of Peacemakers' biggest proponents because he's one of its biggest successes.

He'd already spent half a life on heroin, a habit he began at fifteen, when he first came here.

"I must've did four hundred, five hundred dollars worth of heroin every day, 'cause that was my daily do," he says. "My lottery habit was a hundred and something a day, the cocaine I used to give out for free was hundreds a day. I literally had tons of weed. I was hooked up with these Cubans and Colombians in Florida. And I was the dope man, so I had some of the finest women God put breath in. I was out of my mind. It was just a big party continuously."

He got conned into coming to Peacemakers by a concerned sister who'd heard this place seemed to work when everything else failed.

Simon walked in, thinking he'd bail after a minute, but he found a remarkable scene that had him transfixed.

"First time I went down there, I just felt something," he says. "Jeremiah, the pastor's son, was standing in the middle of the kitchen with all these dope fiends and prostitutes just standing in a circle around him. And I knew these people 'cause I used to be down on Chene."

Simon started attending services, but kept showing up wasted. He had to take one hundred dollars worth of heroin just to get into the door without being sick. He was listening to the spiritual messages but not the sobriety ones.

"I always heard you get saved and the ground's gonna shake and lightning bolts, and I didn't feel nothing. I shook his hand, went out in the car and got high," he says, laughing.

One day, much to Simon's discomfort, Upshur called him to the floor in the middle of the service. Simon had three bottles of methadone in his pocket. He was able to get them even while he was on heroin because the lady who ran the clinic would, for five dollars, give addicts a cup of her teenage daughter's urine so they could pass the drug test and get their fix. That was her hustle on the side. She kept them addicted for five dollars here and there.

The pastor asked Simon if he wanted to finally be free of drugs. Simon nervously said yes, pulled out the bottles, and set them on the pulpit in an act of re-nouncement. The addicts in the audience started drooling over them.

"You know the crowd on Chene," he says. "I heard, 'Don't do it, John! I'll buy it!' People were serious. These are drug addicts in the crowd. Each bottle could be fifty dollars or more on the street. There's people literally hollering like it's an auction. They want my drugs."

Like so many others here, from the pastor on down, he insists the spirit entered into him that day and his addiction vanished right then and there. No with-drawals, no cravings. That was twelve years ago.

"I went to meetings, NA, AA, methadone clinics, whatever they have. Nothing worked for me," he says. Now he's a minister here trying to do the same for others who come in. "God set me free that day. Everything stopped that day."

§

Jada Fields sits alone in a pew on a Sunday morning, staring forward without an ex-pression. And tears are streaming down her face.

She was a crack-smoking prostitute working Chene down the street from the church, waiting for johns to pick her up one day, and Upshur called her over. She told him flat-out what she was doing. He offered her money to instead come inside. "I've been here ever since," Fields says. She has nine children, seven grandchildren. She's thirty-nine.

That was eight years ago, eight years of relapses, of going back to the streets and then being welcomed back to Peacemakers. This time she's lasted a year here.

Behind her, a man stands there alone, and he too is crying to himself. Across the room, moments later, a man has his face buried in his hands, in tears or in shame.

This happens early in their newfound sobriety, some here will say, when the remorse of a wasted life sinks in. There's joy in starting over, but there's deep sadness too over all the time that's been lost forever. Sometimes the realization is overwhelming

But now a song interrupts their sorrow as the service begins. Once again the song is gospel, so raw it has no music backing it at all, only a quick beat driven by foot stomps and a tambourine, and carried by the raspy voice of its impassioned singer.

Everyone rises and starts clapping along. Some dance or jump up and down in place. An elderly man shadowboxes the air for lack of another way to express his emotions. A few people come to the front and start dancing in tandem, like they're doing the Hustle. The party's on.

As each song fades away, Upshur says a few things into a microphone. They're not so much religious exhortations, more like a pep talk. "Now we know we all come out of different backgrounds, all kinds of craziness, we all got a story to tell," he tells them. They shout in agreement. His manner is gentle, his tone is soothing. No yelling, no fiery eyes. "But we're gonna help one another cross that finish line, whatever it takes. We're draggin' one another through them pearly gates!"

Though the Gospels will be read aloud toward the end, though there's no doubt this is a religious gathering, the services here are more like a celebration of everyone's escape from their own hell, whether they've done it yet or are still trying. It's a sing-and-dance-along that, more than anything, is meant to cheer up people who've had little to smile about.

"Let's have a knock-down, drag-out for Jesus!" Upshur shouts excitedly as everyone starts dancing to another song. "Let it all hang out!"

Every week, the service stops midway through for a hug break, of all things. But it's actually more striking than corny. Few who come here have families, most have few real friends. So prostitutes turn to hug alcoholics with tremors, and the mentally ill embrace the homeless. Five minutes of everyone melting into each other's arms.

Kaczmarek thinks back to something he saw recently at one of the services. "One fellow got up and said he was thankful because, for the first time in his memory, he feels that he has a family, that he is loved, that he is able to love others who will receive it. From my perspective, that was the best moment of the evening to hear something like that."

These troubled people, holding onto each other in this little room in the ghetto, have created their own, safe protected world here, where they can have friends who won't pull drugs out of their pocket or have liquor on their breath. They're convinced something miraculous can happen to them here, even if it takes a bank-robbing preacher and a flock of addicts and hookers to help them do it.

"It all works somehow," Kaczmarek says, smiling. "Isn't that amazing?"

Detroit:
A City of Superheroes

Ingrid LaFleur

Without an image of tomorrow, one is trapped by blind history, economics, and politics beyond our control. One is tied up in a web, in a net, with no way to struggle free. Only by having clear and vital images of the many alternatives, good and bad, of where one can go, will we have any control over the way we may actually get there in a reality tomorrow will bring all too quickly.

—Samuel R. Delany

I'VE COME TO UNDERSTAND how the future is completely influenced by our current circumstance and past experiences. It's like there is a box we pull from to construct how the future looks, feels, smells . . . all shaped by things we have seen, read, been told. In hopes of inspiring people to think far outside their comfort zone, I made education a component of my curatorial project AFROTOPIA. I want to make sure that the magical world of Afrofuturism—science fiction, ancient mythologies, non-western cosmologies—are somewhere in that box.

I created my first class, the Young Futurist Academy, for youth at the Carr Center. For two weeks and seven hours a day, we dove into Afrofuturism. Having never taught before, I was initially scared to be in a classroom filled with teenagers. My Virgo tendencies kicked in, and I prepared the most thorough curriculum, filled with text by Prof. Derrick Bell, Octavia Butler, and Samuel R. Delany; interviews with Sun Ra; and the music videos of Janelle Monae, all with the goal of inspiring radical imagination.

On the first day of class, I quickly learned that teaching is not all about giving information; it's about learning and co-creating. One must be attentive and perceptive and open to the fluid exchange between student and teacher. It is within those moments that I also learned children already have a radical imagination—it just must be given space to flourish.

Their first assignment was to choose superhero names. For some reason, I thought this would be the easy part. I just knew everyone had a superhero name; in fact, I have three. Apparently, that puts me squarely in a nerd category. Some students knew about superheroes inside and out, but never thought of themselves as one. I promptly fixed that. They were a bit uncomfortable with the requirement to only call each other by our superhero names (which I continue to do even though class is over), but they got used to it, especially when they had to decide what their super power was. This was critical thinking on ten! They could not be like any other superhero—it had to be original—which is quite difficult, since Marvel and DC comics have been producing superheroes since the 1930s. It became a debate for about an hour. I enjoyed the seriousness with which they took the assignment. That's when I knew we were gonna have lots of fun.

There were seven students in the class: Cole-Mind, age sixteen, psychic abilities; Wink, age eleven, teleportation and the ability to walk through walls; Trinity, age twelve, multiplies herself thirteen times and super strength; Zeno, age eleven, super speed and control of nanites (tiny robots); Magic Dude, age eleven, uses dark magic for good; Sphynx, age sixteen, telekinesis; and Blaze, age twelve, manipulates fire. I am Dr. X and my villain is Monsanto. It was great way to slide in food politics. Although I was saving folks from Monsanto, my true focus as Dr. X was to help these seven superheroes harness and grow their powers.

The second assignment was imagining Detroit in 3210. I assumed my students would imagine a fantasy world where we would magically solve all our problems. Boy, was I wrong! They had houses and cars constantly on fire, aliens invading, locusts and meteorites coming upon us, pollution so bad we would need masks to breathe, and—my favorite—no real music would exist. Wow, no real music! This last one came from the musician of the group. We laughed about it, talked about it, and then I thought about it. It became clear to me that whatever we adults are saying around children, coupled with the media, have a great affect on how Detroit's youth envision the future of their home. I couldn't leave such a dystopian vision hanging in the air. My meticulous curriculum went out the window.

Over the following days, we read Derrick Bell's *The Space Traders* and focused on various mythologies, beginning with the Dogon myth of the alien Nommo imparting knowledge. Then we dove into Detroit's own Afrofuturism through Drexciya, the electronic music duo who created the aquatopian myth of pregnant African women who went overboard during the Atlantic slave trade, populating an underwater world. Drexciya's music is the sounds emanating from this aquatopia. In response to this myth, the students drew their own mythology and created sound art to accompany it.

I then decided it was time to address those dystopian visions, and so a comic book was in order. The superheroes had to really think about how they became superheroes and how they learned of their powers, as well as how to use the powers correctly. They especially had to think about who their nemeses were, and how the superheroes would defeat them, resolving the issues the villains created in that dystopian world. I was hoping this exercise would help my students create a bond with their superhero characters in preparation for the movie that was to be made the next week.

The group chose a team name, ATEN, an aspect of the ancient Egyptian sun god Ra (as in Sun Ra). I love how they unconsciously, without any direction from me, brought it back to the Godfather of Afrofuturism. For their movie, *Team ATEN Saves Detroit*, the students made costumes, props, and their own G-rated weapons based on the comic book stories. To see their creativity expressed through a variety of media was exciting. We shot the movie in one day. Cole-Mind edited it, and the movie was exhibited during the Detroit Design Festival. At the end of it all, the class seemed to have a good grasp of the central message: They control their destiny and shape the future.

I'm so proud of my students, my heart bursts when I think of them. It became clear to me that within my students is AFROTOPIA, and the Young Futurist Academy allowed it to shine through.

So tell me, what is your superhero name?

Blowing Bubbles at Hart Plaza, African World Festival, 2010 / Patricia Lay-Dorsey

Concert of Colors, 2010 / Patricia Lay-Dorsey

Aerobics Class at Hannan Center for Senior Learning, 2008 / Patricia Lay-Dorsey

Streetcar Tracks

Michael Eugene Burdick
and Francis Grunow

A more poignant city thing you'll likely never see. Yes, the cream-and-red-striped streetcars are gone, long gone. But their track lives on, and in plain sight, grotesquely hacked up as fence posts to guard unsuspecting parking lots—oh, the iron—emerging on its own accord, ancient hot-rolled steel chrysalis, desperately trying to shake off a smothering asphalt cocoon. Cass and Davenport. Vernor and Junction. Street names read as epitaph to the streetcar, the way people used to travel to their everyday, by electric motor in the Motor City; they still do, in lands far away, in cities that don't shrink.

Legally Blind in
The Motor City:
A Pedestrian's Lament

Pamela Sabaugh

WHEN I WAS FOURTEEN YEARS OLD, I was diagnosed with Juvenile Macular Degeneration: a disease that attacks the macula, in the retina, which is responsible for our central vision (where we see fine detail), it's what we use for reading or driving.

"You'll lose that straight-ahead vision," the doctor explained, but you'll retain your peripheral vision. Think of the nerve damage like rust on a car. We don't know how extensive the corrosion will be, but once the rust sets in, there's no getting rid of it."

Despite being told my retinas were "rusting," or having had my vision go from 20/20 to 20/200 in a matter of months, I was not so terribly upset with this diagnosis. That is, until two years later when it dawned on me: Holy God, I'm trapped! It was 1984, I was sixteen, and I couldn't drive!

Let me remind you where I was living—in Sterling Heights, a subdivision of Detroit: Detroit, The Motor City, home of the big three auto makers that did their best to crush any plans for a public transportation system. There are blueprints for subways and rail lines that never saw the light of day. This is where the grand Michigan Theater was gutted—not demolished, but gutted, its core ripped out and replaced with a multi-level parking garage. Above the upper deck of cars, the ornate plaster ceiling still stands nine stories high. You could look over the cement barrier on one side and see the proscenium arch, and part of the red velvet curtain still intact. And on the other side, where bits of concrete have crumbled away, you could look through the wire mesh and see the carpeted staircase ascending to the upper balcony. A city stuck in transition, never quite reaching its renaissance.

But there was a time when the old Motown's urban center thrived, when the great architecture of the high Victorian or Art Deco eras flourished. When homes and offices and stores were occupied, and people could walk, or take buses or the trolley to their destinations.

My dad talked about taking that streetcar as a kid. I have a distinct memory of one time in particular. It was a weekday morning in the middle of summer. He walked in, and out of the blue said, "You kids want to go catch the ball game?"

My kid brother and I leapt at the chance. Going to see the Tigers play ball was nothing new, but going like this, on a total whim—with my dad just waking up and deciding to take the day off work—that never happened.

So the three of us climbed into his blue Ford Fairmont and headed down I-75 to the corner of Michigan and Trumbull to watch the Tigers play the White Sox. And he told us the story of how as a kid, one of his favorite things to do was to just pick up and go see the game. He'd catch the M1 trolley at Woodward Avenue and take it all the way down to that famous corner.

"Yep, I could take it right down to the stadium, then get a ticket for the bleachers, buy one hotdog, and get back on the trolley home … all for a dollar."

But those days were long gone. The streetcar service was discontinued in 1956.

What remains to this day is a slow, slapdash, inefficient and underfunded bus system. And the legendary Tiger stadium stood in a part of town, like so many others, that had been decimated by urban blight.

I remember feeling my father grow more and more tense as we walked from the parking lot through the bombed-out rubble of the old Corktown neighborhood, over the Fischer Freeway and into the ballpark. And though he may not have given up on his home team, my dad had certainly given up on the city a long time ago. On our way home from the game, he gestured out the window to that gray fractured wilderness receding in the distance, "As far as I'm concerned, they should pour gasoline on it and torch the whole damn place."

No! Don't say that!

This is our city, our downtown. And people still live there, and try to make it work. And yes, it has crime and crushing poverty, but it also has character. Throughout the metropolitan area, majestic ballrooms and buildings, emblems of its heyday, stand there, vacant, whispering their stories of how this city was once a contender. And amidst those echoes of the past, there is a gritty sort of vitality, a thrumming pulse. You're just going to need a car to find it.

And if the Detroit transit system was sagging and largely defunct, the subdivisions never had one to begin with. Subdivision: "Tract of land which has been divided into smaller lots for the purpose of constructing residences." These are not gated communities, nor are they those quaint old towns with at least one main street and a commercial center. No, we're talking a nondescript, sprawling landscape—developed, not designed—dotted with gas stations, fast food joints, strip malls, and windswept parking lots all built to the size and scale of the automobile. Where sidewalks might end suddenly and I'd find myself in a ditch or along a narrow shoulder of road, with cars whizzing past, or where I would get stopped by the cops for walking, as it looked suspicious.

In the 1950s and '60s, the country was transformed by a powerful vision, known as Urban Renewal. A seed perhaps planted by Henry Ford, and brought to full fruition by Robert Moses, it sucked the life out of urban centers. The car became king, and the interstate highway the great deliverer. And those living in the shattered inner cities and decentralized subdivisions, who for whatever reason were unable to drive, became the lowest of the low; the indigent, the outcasts, the unfortunate souls left behind in the wake of progress.

And this was where I was at: a legally blind pedestrian, without central vision, living on the sprawling periphery of an obliterated center.

On the Automobile

Rachel Reed

In 1908, Henry Ford built the Model T, and the Model T built Detroit.

I. Detroit

It's 2:06 a.m., I'm drunk, and there's a man I'd card for cigarettes sprinting away from my 2001 Ford POS. Dully, I note a dollar-store screwdriver poking out from the ignition where a key should be. Rage slowly washes over me like a hot tide, but by now he's long gone. I try to turn the engine over, but it just whimpers at me. I don't bother to call the cops.

II. The Suburbs

My dad's favorite car was a 1968 Chevrolet Chevelle called Black Betty (a relic of its former owner). An old Super 8 reel I found shows him stepping out of its cherry red chassis, laughing as the wind whips his sandy hair. The camera ignores him as it pans admiringly over the car's body, higher in the back than the front, on its magnesium wheels that look like proto-spinners. It wasn't an endurance car, he said, but in drag races it did just fine. He sold it to pay for community college.

III. Detroit

The sun is beating today, but there's a breeze coming through the open windows. It smells exactly like baking bread, owing to the whiskey factory across the strait. We drive slowly, aimlessly across the island, stopping occasionally to walk a pier or throw sticks into the river. We eat Chinese food directly from the cartons in the overgrown grass by the Carillon, and I know I'm in love.

IV. The Suburbs

I am sweating, swallowing huge gulps of air as I steel myself against tears because they'd only make it worse. I'm so preoccupied with my own concerns that I do not notice or care about the guilt and shame that distort my father's face. The economy's in the shitter, and they don't need engineers, or him, like they used to. They use the phrase laid off instead of fired because it sounds nicer.

People aren't buying cars anymore, Rachel.

I worry only about whether I'll be able to return to college next year.

V. Detroit

We're making out in the back seat of the Ford Tempo my parents helped me buy in high school just a year or two before, and some iteration of Transformers is playing on the giant screen in front of us. We pause for air and sips of Bud Light Lime, and I feel cool and sexy for the first time in my life. I have never been to a drive-in movie, never been reckless or wild, and it is everything my imagination had promised.

VI. Detroit

It's a few days after the Doogie Howser of grand theft turned my Taurus into three thousand pounds of dead metal and plastic. My father is wearing his favorite Carhartt coat, hood drawn up against the December cold. As has become our ritual, I stand helplessly next to him as he checks the engine, the ignition, the parts whose names mean nothing to me but might as well be of his own body for how well he knows them.

It's a bit different this time, though. The look on his face tells me he can't fix it. Shit's messed up good.

Snow begins to fall lazily, blanketing the ground around our feet.

Everything is going to be alright. Nothing will be alright.

Carlessness

John G. Rodwan Jr.

"OH, I DIDN'T EXPECT ANYONE TO BE HOME since there wasn't a car in the driveway," the stranger standing on our front porch said when, in response to knocking, I opened the door to the house my wife and I had just rented.

Rather than telling her that we didn't own a car, I simply learned her name, told her ours, and appreciatively accepted her homemade welcome-to-the-neighborhood cookies. I already knew that many of my fellow citizens viewed possessing automobiles as intrinsically American—even in Portland, Oregon, where despite all the determined bicyclists zipping around town, oversized four-wheel drive pickup trucks appeared to rival electricity/gasoline-powered hybrids as the preferred vehicle. Many residents exhort each other to "Keep Portland Weird," usually via bumper stickers on perfectly normal automobiles. On the strangeness scale, being able to afford a car but deciding not to have one matches declining to watch television (or bake cookies for new neighbors). If drivers didn't express bafflement at our voluntary carlessness, then they assumed we were making an environmentalist statement. When our landlady learned of it, she said she "respected our lifestyle choice." Yet we didn't define our identities by our non-driving status. We weren't tacitly judging car owners and their "lifestyle choice," and we didn't want apparent eccentricity to serve as a self-righteous political gesture.

For many years, well before we moved west, we found it easy to live without a car. We thought it was a viable, sensible option, and, for quite a while, it was. In the mid-1990s, we lived in Geneva, Switzerland, where we used the reliable, affordable light rail and bus system to get around the city. We could also easily move about the country, and indeed much of Europe, without having a car. We traveled frequently but rarely resorted to taking taxis.

Nothing beats walking as a way to get to know a place, to see things close up and get a feel for one's surroundings, but taking public transportation provides real insights into national, regional, and local priorities and conditions. In striking contrast to the United States, many Western European nations made it easy to get from airports to major and even not-so-major cities' downtown areas by train, and they also had developed comprehensive national rail networks. A friend we made during our Geneva days called Switzerland a life-size train set, which she could have said about many of the countries surrounding it. We can count a number of the reasons for this difference—in addition to transportation polices, there is geographical size (with the United States dwarfing Western European countries), population density (in heavy pockets dotting the U.S. map), and historical and technological factors (such as the United States' relatively young age when cars started rolling off assembly lines. It cannot be reduced to a more collectivist outlook, as represented by publicly financed transport systems, on one side of the Atlantic, and pernicious individualism, as symbolized by private cars, on the other. After all, those roads folks drive on sure aren't free, and they aren't privately paid for either. No simple explanation can fully account for the dissimilar attitudes toward and approaches to getting around, but it's fair to say that Europeans displayed a commitment to public transportation that Americans never mustered.

Of course there are exceptions to this generalization in the form of US cities with highly developed, not-primarily-automotive transportation systems, and when we left Geneva, we moved to one of them. In New York City, owning a car would have been an expensive nuisance. Some people we knew in Brooklyn spent as much monthly for a space in a parking garage as we had paid, a few years earlier, for a two-bedroom apartment in another city. More typical were those who, apart from the occasional call to a car service for a trip to the airport, lived mostly automobile-free. For us and most people we knew, car ownership would have been superfluous, since it was simpler to get around without than with one. (Unlike the Brooklynites with the paid-for parking spot, we had neither children nor a summer home outside the city, factors that propel some New Yorkers out of carlessness.) Living near several different subway stops, we could easily and cheaply get just about anywhere in the city we wanted to go. While the communal commute definitely had its downsides—brutally hot subterranean stations in summer, uncomfortably crowded cars year round, occasional maddening delays due to mechanical breakdowns and the like—the upsides compensated for them. For much less money than we would have paid for a car, or even for parking, we could circulate throughout the city. When, after more than a decade of subway ridership, we decided to move elsewhere, we knew we'd miss those trains.

Still, we wanted to do without a car even after leaving New York, and we deliberately chose a place where this seemed possible: Portland, with its seemingly handy combination of buses, light rail trains, and streetcars. The apartment we rented for our first year there was around the corner, not from a neighborly cookie baker, but, better still, from a bus stop where many routes intersected. Almost any northbound line went downtown, while several southbound buses could carry us to a big grocery store. Completing the picture of comfortable carlessness were roads with bike lanes, including one I often used to get to a cornucopian farmers' market, or simply to take in the occasional glimpses of the river from between the tall, hilltop trees.

Every now and then, however, we felt the indignity and inconvenience of bus dependency. Though habituated to mild winters, Portland experienced an especially snowy one our first year there. Many residents told us they simply didn't know how to drive in snow. Apparently bus drivers shared the same deficiency. Ending up stranded with groceries at a stop where no buses materialized as icy wind lashed our faces made me question our choice—of both city and means of navigating it. Those owners of cartoonish big-wheeled trucks suddenly appeared vindicated. As people who did their work at home, we viewed the expense of a car (or truck) an unjustifiable extravagance, but that frigid afternoon outside the Fred Meyer made it look less frivolous after all.

Carlessness became harder when we moved to the other side of town. Despite the storm that discombobulated the city for a week, we still held public transit in generally high regard. Our perspective, and our habits, changed when we found ourselves in a neighborhood with more limited service. The city could boast of a great system—for those who lived in and traveled between the right areas. As we quickly discovered, we no longer did. After enjoying the luxury of many bus line options, we had to adjust to the constraints of just one. We could still get where we wanted to go—if we planned carefully, checked schedules diligently, made sure to head home early, and never went anywhere on Sundays. Such limitations soon started to grate, since nothing feels more like wasting time than waiting for a bus. Never once in our years in New York did I consider buying a car, but after a few years in Portland I began entertaining the notion, if only when feeling stranded at a bus stop.

§

I was not an obvious candidate for carlessness. It might be common for native New Yorkers, but it was not a normal condition in Detroit, where I was raised. During the decade or so I spent in Brooklyn, I met many people who entered adulthood without obtaining a driver's license, an unquestioned rite of passage in Motown. Well before I got my license at sixteen, I found cars fascinating. I don't know if my father subscribed to Road & Track magazine because of his interest in them or mine, but I pored over every issue and could name almost any make and model I saw on the streets. I even became something of a car snob, disdainful of the local product. German and Italian sports cars rarely seen in my hometown appealed to me in a way that the all-to-common Chevy, Chrysler, and Ford never did. For many years, my carpool ride to school took me past a billboard that electronically displayed the number of vehicles extruded annually by local assembly lines. The figure changed so quickly and grew so big that it seemed unreal, unconnected with the hulks in freeway lanes beside me.

Even better than imported exotica were customized cars—the modified machines displayed at the Autorama. While the annual cavalcade of vehicular oddities always included automotive stars from TV shows like *Batman* and *Dukes of Hazzard*, as well as pristinely preserved or restored classics from bygone eras, what kept me coming back to the convention center downtown year after year were the four-wheeled freaks: the radically reworked cars with fat rear tires and engine parts sticking out through holes cut in their hoods and the trucks transformed into rolling rooms with colorful murals airbrushed on their outer walls. The more improbable and impractical the better. Lots of chrome and flames painted on the side—that's what cars ought to have.

My enthusiasm for such things ended before adolescence did (except, that is, for a suppressed, Autorama-inspired longing for a tricked out early 1970s Ford Econoline van that I've not been able to shake). Even though I never became the sort of person who'd spend time tinkering with motors, cars still mattered to me in other ways once I became old enough to operate them. In *Half a Life*, a memoir concerning a deadly car crash, Darin Strauss says, "when you drive in new post-adolescence, you drive with friends." I did spend much time in cars with others around my age when I was a teenager, but I also drove alone a lot, usually late at night after dropping off others. At times like those I could really listen to music, which ceased to be background noise behind conversation. Taking the slow way home via surface streets rather than expressways—just driving by myself in the dark—stands out in my mind as typical of that time as much as any non-solitary excursions.

A couple of bucks to put in the tank and a glove compartment full of cassette tapes contributed mightily to a teenager's sense of self-sufficiency. Like many male Americans before and since, I smilingly recall the first car I ever could call my own—a double-hand-me-down that my father first passed along to my older sister. By the time I ended up with it, the 1977 Datsun 280-Z was rusted and crumpled, but I didn't mind. It was still low-slung, powerful and grumbly. One winter, routine weather-wise (which meant more snow than Portland ever saw), the old thing proved especially prone to flat tires, and a friend and I became an adept mobile pit crew. I kept the space-saver flat tire inflated behind the cramped back seat along with a plank of wood (found roadside and needed to raise the car without the jack pushing through its rotted underside). After the first couple times, we could change wheels in mere minutes. When I dispensed with the oil-thirsty silver sports car and started driving a fusty Ford Escort inherited from a grandmother, I no longer cared much about cars as technological or stylistic achievements, as I had as a child. If as a new driver I saw cars as representing independence with a dash of residual romance, after a few years in traffic (and several flats), I regarded them as simply a means to move from here to there and back again. Having to buy a car, as I eventually did, and pay for insurance (notoriously, scandalously expensive in Detroit) hardly added to automobiles' fading allure.

Nonetheless, I had yet to imagine life without a car. If growing up in Detroit didn't instill more than fleeting affection for its most famous product, it did persuade me of the inevitability of car ownership. Even if during my youth, Japanese vehicles like my Datsun and other imports became common on the Motor City's pot-holed roads, cars of some sort or another seemed intrinsic to existence there and, I presumed, everywhere. Detroit is physically large, close to 140 square miles, and the shrinkage of its population (a phenomenon that began before I was born in the late 1960s and accelerated forcefully thereafter) left it feeling expansive and partially empty. A city of contrasts, Detroit consists of non-contiguous areas of relative vibrancy separated by tracts of almost abandoned wasteland. Not surprisingly, Detroit never earned a reputation for excellence in mass transit, and for good reason. Conducting oneself through such a conurbation called for a car.

Although Detroit didn't make cars like it once did, with factories racking up the kinds of numbers proudly announced during my youth, Detroit was made for cars. So, when we decided to return, we knew our carlessness had come to an end. We continued to work at home, and even moved into a house within walking distance of a grocery store, a luxury not many Detroiters enjoy. However, unless we wanted to sacrifice even more time waiting uncertainly for buses—a soul-crusher too many Detroiters suffer—then we would have to do the all-American thing. If in New York a car would have been a hassle and in Portland an extravagance, in Detroit one felt like a necessity. While it might theoretically have been possible to lengthen our experiment in automobile-free living, it would have taken a fiercer commitment to the idea, a stronger devotion to the "lifestyle," than we ever possessed. After a fifteen-year absence from the city, one of the first things I did when I got back was head to a car dealership. After an even longer post-childhood indifference to the aesthetic of automobiles and the relative merits of makes and models, I went with one manufactured by the sole Big Three company actually headquartered within the city limits, which is to say a Chevrolet. After so much time without doing it, driving regularly again made the homecoming complete.

Nonetheless, the appearance of carlessness persisted. Whether it's because their garages are too full with the accoutrements of lawn care, because their vehicles are too large to fit, or because of some other reasons, Detroiters often prefer to park their cars in their driveways. If nothing else, in a city with a sad surplus of vacant structures, the practice lends houses the appearance of occupancy—at least when the cars are actually there. As a single-car household with a two-car garage, we were able to store the lawnmower, rakes, shovels, and the inevitable miscellaneous items and still put the vehicle shelter to its intended use, which resulted in an episode of déjà vu. Soon after we moved back to Detroit, I opened the front door to a friend who said, "Oh, I didn't know if you were home; I didn't see your car in the driveway."

Kevin Robishaw

East Side Bus Stop, 2008 / Patricia Lay-Dorsey

The Line

Maisha Hyman Sumbry

I SEE STARS ON THE GRAY PAVEMENT AHEAD OF ME—glistening sunbursts of fresh spittle—the light of the sun reflected in the slick viscosity of mucus. I don't have much else to do in the cold of the Detroit morning. I push my chin deeper into the protective warmth of my coat and will the line to move.

I don't dare ask how much longer we have to wait. I shift my eight-year-old weight from one frozen foot to the other, thinking of better ways to spend my Christmas vacation. I jam my mittened hands deeper into the pockets of my light blue Weathertamer coat.

The line snakes around the building—only once today. There are times when it has wrapped twice, a double-belt of unemployed auto workers.

They are mostly men, around my dad's age or maybe older. All of them are imposing with their worn winter coats and dusty work boots. Their sizes differ—they are short and tall, some of sinewy build and others are large. A few women garnish the line; they talk tougher than the men about working in the plants, mostly the Lynch Road and Dodge Main factories that had recently been closed. Their speech is punctuated by the gray and white ash that falls from the cigarettes hanging from their lips. Every last one of them, men and women alike, carries the same expression: an undeniable willingness to work, and a confusion as to why they have to fight for the right to support their families.

My dad gives easy, three-part handshakes to the other men. I don't understand most of the conversation, and I tune it out. Mainly because I don't want to have questions later about why things are the way they are. I don't want to hear my dad give a non-explanation for Dodge closing a plant and notifying thousands of workers via a radio announcement. I don't want him to get annoyed at me for asking how much longer we'll be out in the cold.

There are other children here, too, boys and girls around my age, but it is too cold to make friends. And an unemployment line is not exactly a play date. We are all wide eyed and cold—comrades and victims.

As we approach the entrance to the squat, one-story, sandy brown brick building with tinted glass doors, the forced air brushes pleasantly over my face. It will be nice to come in from the frigid winter, but there will be no seats inside. The orange molded plastic chairs, stuck to steel pipes bolted to the floor, will be occupied, and chivalry does not apply here. No man gives up seats for women and children. They curse loudly and with abandon; they don't offer a bite of Egg McMuffin or a sip of coffee. Sometimes, a "say bro" will get a match or the use of a lighter for a cigarette. No one here is giving up cigarettes either. In this place, it's every unemployed soul for itself.

I am happy that I ate a substantial breakfast. I know that we will be here for hours, and there is no leaving the line. This is not the grocery store or the school lunch queue where people will hold your spot or give you cuts.

Our number is eventually called, which is good this time. There are times when the numbers never seem to move and people get upset because the unemployment office closes before they're ever able to get to the glass window with the surly lady behind it. I'm sure that the lady is different, but in this place, they are all the same with their brown skin and their hard straightened hair that sits like plastic helmets above their foreheads and their pea-green sweaters and their burgundy polyester pants and their hopeless voices that call the numbers and say "comeonback."

It's the behind-the-glass ritual that confounds me most. Rows of metal desks sit atop dirty, stained carpet. There's often just one chair next to the desk—no place for a child accompanying her father in search of benefits and work. There are typewriters and papers and wastebaskets. And there are mostly files, on the desks and falling from drawers and stacked on the floor. I wonder how much hope is in a file on the floor, if less hope is contained there than in the file in the drawer or the file on the desk. I wish for my father's file to be on the desk, because maybe that will mean that he will be smiling as he drives the green van home. Maybe it will mean we can stop at Burger Chef and I can get a Fun Meal and a prize. Maybe it will mean that we won't have to come back here the following week and start all over again.

January in Detroit,

or Search for Tomorrow
Starring Ken and Ann

Ken Mikolowski

I think it is interesting
though not exactly amusing
how we go from day to day
with no money. How do we
do it, friends ask, suspecting
we really have some stash
stacked away somewhere.
But we certainly do not
and we also do not know
how we do it either.
You sure are lucky,
some of our friends say. I am
none to sure of that though,
as I wait for the winning
lottery numbers to be announced
on CKLW. Thursday in Detroit
is the day of dreams. We have
been dreaming of a place
in the country lately and I'm
none to sure that is very healthy,
and speaking of health that's
also been a problem that probably
has something to do with no money,
since we've all been sick lately,
taking turns politely of course.
Could you bring me some more
tea one of us will ask,
and the other will.
In between the coughing and

worrying our thoughts
have often turned to crime.
We seriously wonder how we can
get away with a bundle with
as little risk as possible.
Last week we took our last
$12 out of the bank
and noticed how much more
they had there though
we had none. Of course
we wouldn't rob that bank,
they know us there
as the ones who bring
the rolls of pennies in.
And just yesterday they
fish-eyed us for trying
to cash our son's xmas bond
from his grandparents
after only one month.
So we wouldn't try to rob that bank,
but I do know of one up north
that may be possible. . .
I know this just seems like
romantic dreaming
but I practically make a career
of reading detective stories,
and God knows, I have no other.
Anyway if the right opportunity
comes along, we are more
than ready to meet it.
But this is a time of waiting,
the I Ching says, though it does
not say how we are to eat
while waiting. And soon
we will have another mouth to feed --
Ann now in her seventh month,
and that is often in our thoughts.
Besides all that we are both
over thirty, artist and poet,
still waiting to cross the great water.
Meanwhile, day after day,
there is still Detroit
to be dealt with—a small pond
says our friend Snee.
Big fish we used to answer him,
but that was a while back.

Now we think maybe Lake Erie
is the great water referred to
in the I Ching, and if we wait
long enough we can
walk across—to Buffalo
or Cleveland. In a healthy person,
says the philosopher, self-pity
can be a forerunner to action:
once the problem is seen clearly,
a solution may be found at hand.
And as I said, I think it is interesting
though not exactly amusing.

Trembling in the Temple of Tears at the Feet of Buddha

M.L. Liebler

Ron Allen Detroit Poet 1947–2010

After Allen Ginsberg

Who stood in the concrete fields and alleys of the Cass Corridor
With hope as wild as weeds in the every day sidewalk cracks
Of Detroit. Deep pockets filled with poetry and Black Arts
Theater that could tell the truth of the future beyond our hidden dreams.

Who understood and shared the phraseology of Donald Goines
A holy language—spun it into surrealistic parables
And laid them upon the dead bones of America's sunken chest.
A blood fever of poetry and ideas to bring new life to our city.

Hipster, futurist, teacher of the theater and poetry of backroom cafes
Who knew the way to the heart was through song and word and not
Through the lackluster academy and institutions that built themselves
Upon their own self pride while quickly diminishing and condemning
The outside world of the streets into the skull cages of formalism.

Who knew the plight of the Bantu before America understood,
And who held twenty-four-hour peace vigils sitting Shiva for freedom
And equality in South Africa before the television and newspapers would
Report the daily murders and violence in the broken houses of Soweto.

Who held, with tenderness, the grieving hands of Detroit mothers
And grandmothers whose children had been lost to murder—killed
By other children in the mean streets of Detroit under vanishing skies
Of gray smoke, blue metal revolvers in the night.

Who put prayer in motion through Zen workshops and

Provoking koans that kept folks thinking of and dreaming for
New answers in the universe of ourselves beyond the here and now
And beneath the heart and skin of God.
Who was aware of the brewing hatred in America's "post-racial"
21st century between city & suburb, black & white, rich & poor.
The invisible barriers that continue to kill the spirit and destroy
Who we are and what we should become.

Beautiful Buddha angel spirit who left Detroit to live
In warm sunshine of Los Angeles and to build
Another community of art and life in a distant city
Where pain was as real as the broken hearts
Of our Detroit. Where theater was not respected nor welcomed.

Where you took Zen meditation to the Nth degree,
And beyond the long road that led you
Through Vietnam, Cass Corridor, LA and back
To your Detroit—of community and grace.

You now, sweet Brother man, have returned to us
To live forever in the shade tress of our memories.
East side forever—reminding us always of who we all can
Be if we trust each other and heal and nurture
Each other back to life once again in the spirit of love and art.

For the Long Haul

Desiree Cooper

ABOUT TEN YEARS AGO, Curtis Lipscomb attended an HIV/AIDS program in Detroit. As the founder of KICK—a nonprofit that serves Detroit's African American, HIV-positive community—Lipscomb had attended many such gatherings before. But this meeting in 2005 was different.

"Most African American gay men—especially those with HIV—are isolated and live in fear," said Lipscomb. "But I distinctly remember seeing Tony Johnson in that room. He wasn't like the others. He was very confident and full of faith."

The two became immediate friends, joining forces in KICK's mission to create a stigma-free, safe space for LGBT African Americans who are HIV-positive. Johnson was so taken by the mission, he started catching the bus three days a week to manage KICK's calls and to become an intake specialist.

Johnson is disabled and lives on a fixed income. In 1993, he discovered that he was HIV-positive, but the virus has been undetectable in his blood since 2004. "I've come to terms with it, but I can't believe that there are still new cases being diagnosed," he said. "If I can save one person from getting it, it's worth it."

Lipscomb quickly discovered that he had not only gained a friend, but a valuable ally in the fight against AIDS.

"When you are in crisis and you call KICK, you get Tony—a real, warm, caring person to help guide you," said Lipscomb, whose organization receives no public funding. "He's the frontline person for our organization, and the key to our development."

A decade later, Johnson is still riding the bus to work at KICK three days a week. What makes it remarkable is that Johnson has never been paid a dime.

§

Don't bother talking to Johnson about his leadership in Detroit's African American, LGBT community—it would only embarrass him. He's more interested in talking about service.

"I decided that I can't stay at home and do nothing," said Johnson. "I have to get out and help others."

He not only volunteers with KICK, but he also serves at the United Sisters of Charity soup kitchen in Highland Park twice a week. He is also one of the founding members of a support group for HIV-positive veterans.

"I was despondent three years ago when a social worker referred me to the support group," said Sidney Skipper, a veteran and retired medical technician who is both HIV-positive and bipolar. "I had given up on everything. But Tony helped me realize that when you help others, you find your voice and realize you have something to say. When you help others, it lifts you up as well."

The difference between Tony and most people, Skipper added, is that he isn't in it for personal gratification. "If you're volunteering to seek reward, you'll quit after awhile, and move on to something else," said Skipper. "Tony doesn't seek reward. He's in it for the long haul."

Lipscomb agreed. "You can't have a movement without people willing to give their time and talent to the cause," he said. "Tony doesn't need his shoulders brushed off or his collar popped up. He comes from that spirit."

§

The drive to serve others seems to be natural for Johnson, but it's derived from a lifetime of struggle.

The oldest of three children, Johnson was raised on Detroit's west side by his mother and grandmother.

"I never had a coming out," Johnson, who announced his sexual orientation to his family at age 23. "They said that they already knew. I wondered why I hadn't gotten the memo!"

But that doesn't mean that he didn't suffer the same kind of backlash that LGBT people often experience in the black community.

"I knew I was different from the age of nine," said Johnson. "I remember one of my grandmother's friends talking in another room. I heard him say, 'He's going to be gay.' The way he said it, it was as if I was nasty or dirty. My grandmother said, 'That's my baby. If he is, he is.' But I was hurt. People don't realize the ramifications of what they say to children."

As he grew up, Johnson pretended to be straight to make life easier. In high school, he dated a girl from another part of town.

"Her father said, 'My daughter isn't having sex until she's married,'" said Johnson. "Well, that was fine with me."

In 1984, Johnson enlisted in the Army in order to save money for college, but mostly to get away from his family. "I wanted to explore who I was," he said, "but I went out of the frying pan into the fire."

He wasn't prepared for the physical rigors of military basic training. And the taste of independence made it harder for him to live an inauthentic life. By the time he left the service three years later, he was ready to live independently as an openly gay man. But the pull of family was too much.

In 1987, his grandfather got ill, and it was assumed that Johnson would be the one to take care of him. "Sometimes family members assume that because you're gay and you don't have kids, that you are always available to babysit, or give them money," said Johnson, the oldest grandchild. "They think you don't have a life."

Then, in 1993, Johnson faced his first major health crisis. "I found out that I was HIV-positive," said Johnson, whose partner at the time stood by him. "I was devastated. I thought people would be able to read it on my face."

As the person who was used to giving to others, Johnson found it difficult to lean on others. But he found that he had many friends and supporters. His boss noticed his medication in his cubicle at work. "Her friend had died from HIV and she knew what was happening to me," he said. "She became my ally."

In 1999 at age 35, he suffered a stroke. His boss paid his insurance co-pay for several months as he recovered. He was never able to go back to work. Seven years later, he had a second stroke that left him in a coma for two months.

As he battled back to health, he tried to make sense of all of his life. "I believe that God left me here for a reason," he said.

That reason, he believes, is to make life better for others. That's what drives Johnson to volunteer as dependably as if he were earning a paycheck. That's what pushes him to share little gifts with his fellow bus riders, or a joke with the people in the soup line.

"At the soup kitchen they say that I'm always so happy," said Tony. "But you have to laugh to keep from crying. If they had to walk one day in my shoes, I don't think they could handle it."

still of it

adrienne maree brown

i am still of it
this world
full of sorrows
i trace the lines back
from my fingertips
to my heart
the feelings all start with distinction
such unique purpose
only to pool and to pulse together
and i want to un-utter
certain passions
in my cellular structure
i taste on my tongue
her absent kiss,
the three dead names i always called him,
the wet hitch of goodbye
as that failed father enters his prison,
the acidic bite in detroit
gasping as hands tighten at her neck
and they bruise her soil,
and the sharp raging bitter
of gaza
my god, some god, somebody. . .
can i blame it on the moon
she thinks we are hers
because we are water
with her ink on our spines
can i blame it on mercury
patterning fuckery
is this envy or legacy,
all this human catastrophe
can i recall the prophet
who spoke of joy and sorrow
carving out spaces

from each other's bodies
why don't we find out
there is no place outside ourselves
to put this daunting sorrow
while we breathe we are still of it
what is the science
for this bent over grief
crying us to sleep
in this solitary cosmos
can i still wonder
feel wonder
when i am still of it
...
when my breath stops
flood me with joy
i feel room for oceans
here in my veins

Work Hard Play Harder: Brush-Adelaide Park / Megan Snow

Brown and Proud / Gabriela Santiago-Romero

In the House Where Poetry Lives

Peter Markus

Look in the mirror of the burned down house, the faces of God we see. See the man who cuts the grass, who sweeps the street, who picks up the brush to name what was once lost or tossed to the curb or left in a vacant lot. Here where a house once stood. Here where a child once played in and ate the dirt. A man pushes a shopping cart down the street even though its front wheel no longer spins. A mother cracks an egg. The skillet blackened by bacon grease. To be fat is to be holding, to be held. Fire eats the wood and the wood does not say a word. A Bible with pages missing, pages ripped out, words we all know, or don't. A sky is a bird and the roof of this cathedral. A church where cars are made. Rust is what, in the end, our ashes have become. Where the dead now live there is grass seed at our feet. The laces of our sneakers. The white sheets of a single mattress. They take. When I get out and walk, when I say my name. These are the stories we tell. These are the songs that don't get sung. The records I used to play spin on the rooftops. A chair might be a chimney. A stone that floats is a poem that cannot be spoken. Give me an imperfect circle, a shape that I can become. If the taxi does not stop then walk. When the stars burn out who will fix them? The penny on the sidewalk is showing heads. Leave it there for the next guy who comes along who will find it shining in the dark. When I shake your hand I always look for dirt beneath the nails. Your knuckles are rivers. *Don't eat the fish* but still we fish for what can't be seen. Where do the birds go when they fly away? The watch says wake up, the house keep out. Under the porch a baby doll without a child to coo it to sleep. Her hand is raised. I touch it once before turning. Before I make my leave. For it might not be here when we get back.

When we get back the house is gone. *Our words become the house we live in.* And if there are no words, what then? What is the name, the sound, of sorrow, of solace, or sacrifice? There is a hole in the ground. There is no door for you to knock on. No windows to look in through. On the other side of this city, in Delray, when a house was turned to splintered wood, a slag heap of words never said, the old man who was my grandfather knelt in the dirt and the broken glass and bricks and made a garden.

Hair white and haloed like a dandelion gone to seed. If there were weeds he would pull them. When the tomatoes fell red and ripe from the vine we would eat. For the child puts the word in his mouth. When I said just now *word* what I meant was *world*, though if there's one thing I've learned is to always trust our mis-sayings, our typos, our mistakes.

If there's anything to learn then memorize this: that behind every story is a scar. A boy writes, *My face is a book of invisible scars. Each scar tells a story. Each story begins, Back when I was small.* But what about the house where poetry lives? With a chair nailed to the roof. In the attic where the walls breathe and sweat. In the back yard with a tire swinging from a rope. And the tree that offers no leaves. And the tree that is ours to climb. In a nest at the top two eggs waiting to hatch. But what if they are stones? What if when they break open there is no song? The sky is blue. There are days when to look is an act of witness. *Perhaps we are here if only to say, or to not say*, to say how can we, or how can we not. When my daughter was small she gave me the words of a poem. *My mouth/ is wet/ like rain.* A poem, I know, is never finished, only abandoned. Detroit is a poem written in couplets, a poem that resists rhyme, a poem that is at times too easy to abandon, a poem that is rooted in the nouns—*house, sky, fire, river, mud, automobile, brick*. And for each of these words there is only one verb: to sing. Yes, to sing, sing—this is why we are here—even if no one hears it.

Belle Isle Song

Nandi Comer

for JM

When winter weaves a wind
song that slits through a city

I watch. A mother and her children
scatter across the lake's shoreline

like beads to a broken necklace.
I listen to the river slosh under

their shoes. Canada geese wobble
between weeping willows. Your long

fingers point and name a note
between cloud and river.

I plant dull sound in dirt and motor oil,
mark the mound with a leaf, watch

note-like sprouts overtake grass,
how concrete buckles

under its wiggle and stem.
I skip beat on trails alongside

a heap of brush, while sheets of ice strike
the bank, crash into rocks. This is no song

for dead ears. You scoop up a mad
pike from that river, dump it, slapping in my lap.

I listen for its breathing. I listen to it starve.

The Imam I Knew

Omar Syed Mahmood

THIS IS THE STORY of how I remember a man whom Detroit knew as Imam Luqman, who once led a neighborhood mosque in the city.

I had been there as part of the annual food drive that my own mosque sponsored during Ramadan. We waited expectantly in the fading daylight, standing by our U-Haul truck in the middle of that road, surrounded by burned-down houses with boarded-up windows, cars with their twenty-year-old paint now all but rusted. This had been prime property, once upon a time when this was still the Motor City and when it was said of Detroit that its perfect neighborhoods were lined with houses like teeth. But now the unkempt, tangled grass that used to be the well-groomed background to blooming flower patches had taken over the cracks between the decaying bricks and the splintered cement of the ruins of this now Muslim neighborhood. We stood by the house that had become its mosque, Masjid an Noor, the Mosque of Light.

I paced the wild-looking lawn adjacent to the mosque as we waited for our team to assemble. I looked around at my friends. These were the guys I'd grown up with; we'd been doing this together for six years, and yet we looked, as ever, out of place. Smartly dressed, jeans right up to our navels, and sporting schoolboy haircuts. We looked around shiftily, as if tensed for a gunshot. This wasn't our territory.

We were on our third-to-last stop. There was a rusting basketball hoop with the net half on, groaning under years of getting dunked on by Bad Boys fans. A few youngsters, most not older than ten, played around with a worn black and red basketball, doing their best to avoid the cracks out of which sprang weeds bent on taking over the asphalt. Another child rode around on his RipStick, wearing glasses, an overlarge shirt for his skinny four-foot frame, and a pair of black Shaqs with the laces missing. I had had the more refined Wave board for a couple years, so I hastened to take my chance to befriend the youth. "I got a trick for you," I promised the child. I made the most of my celebrity, playing basketball on the RipStick while the kids chased me. I would like to think that it's still a fad there.

My passion for Detroit is born of a propensity to romanticize the past. I care about tradition. I yearn for the days when Detroit really was the automotive capital of the world. But who am I to yearn? Who am I to romanticize a city whose hardships I never lived, a city I know only as a skyline? Were these even *my* people to help? Did I have a right to feel sorry for them? No, I really had no right to be a privileged suburban kid doling out packaged boxes of ketchup, rice, and cereal. Guilt was the only righteous emotion that day, the only emotion that I did not feel guilty about.

The neighborhood was, as most Detroit neighborhoods are, almost entirely black. On the corner, though, there was an East Asian Muslim family, probably Indonesian. A little girl skirted the sidewalk outside the house with a white headscarf of a style peculiar to that part of the world. A boy in a flowing *jubba* and a prayer cap, her brother, came rushing out to go play *Call of Duty* with another boy who had just gotten the game. Soon after the people assembled outside and greeted us, we began to unload the boxes of foodstuffs that we had packed earlier that day at Sam's Club. It was then that I saw a young man about my age in a do-rag climbing into the U-Haul to help us unload the boxes. He was, as I studied him, distinctly South Asian. He had rounder features and a mud-brown complexion, tanned and sweating from a day out in the sun. I figured he was Bengali, there being a large Bengali community in Hamtramck, not far from Masjid an Noor. But I do not think that his friends or my friends saw him as anything other than black. He spoke like them, he was part of them, and he had even come to look enough like them, with his large plain blue T-shirt and basketball shorts, that a casual observer would have noticed nothing unusual.

That there lived in this neighborhood an Indonesian family and a Bengali family gave me some solace. I'd had always felt that I could never be a proper Detroiter because I was not black. But here was living proof that my worry was misplaced. These could be my people. My own father was born in Bangladesh. I turned around slowly, taking in the Detroit air. It was not much different from the air that I'd grown up breathing twenty minutes away on Maple Creek Boulevard. Life here was serene. The families all knew each other, the kids grew up joyous and kicking . . . Their laughter on the street could be heard clear as the call of birds against the reddening sky, in the cool glow of the coming evening. There was a beauty in this simplicity.

All of a sudden, a thundering noise rent the air down the street. A rusting, beat-up old Ford pickup turned the corner down in the distance. It was a wreck of an old beauty, with peeling red paint and a gas pipe spurting painfully. The pickup drove down the street with reckless impunity. We tripped over ourselves back to the grass as it came by us, and without so much as slowing down the car burst onto the pavement of a driveway and stopped all at once. Here was Imam Luqman. He was a rough-looking man with a black turban, a blue jean jacket, circular spectacles, and black boots into which he tucked the cuffs of his jeans. He was tall and skinny, and he looked worn through by age, by hunger, by misfortune. His beard was a barbed mess, his clothes ragged and loose. I had certainly been scared a second ago when his car had nearly mauled us, but at the same time I felt an instant pity for the man. He walked up to us, all huddled together waiting to leave, and gave each one of us a big, tired hug. He was smiling widely, infectiously, but it looked painful, like it required unknowable effort.

He took out a list of people in his flock who had signed up for food. As he looked over the paper with the organizer, his face fell. We were short a few boxes. There were a few moments of awkward silence. We had already given extra to the places we'd been before, and if we emptied even more here what would be left for our coming stops? But then the imam looked up and nodded slowly, mumbling in a voice so humble that it haunts me more than anything about his story, that his family could go without that winter.

Suddenly I felt enormously guilty for being a self-righteous suburban kid, a self-entitled worthless child who was feeling good about himself for doing all this to help the less fortunate while braving the hunger of his fast. Who was I in that moment? All that mattered then in the world was that Imam Luqman should be given the keys to our mosque, to our cars, to our houses, to Sam's Club. I trusted him in that moment with all I owned. Only an hour ago I had believed the notion that I could be a true part of this neighborhood. But I knew with those words of Imam Luqman that hunger here was real. I had no right calling these my people. I had not lived their lives, their hunger. I had no right to be a hero. What had I done to deserve the hearty meal that was waiting for us volunteers at Dearborn's Cedarland restaurant? What had Imam Luqman done to deserve a winter of hunger? The only human thing for me to feel in that moment, again, was guilt.

On an October afternoon two months later, my sister called up from downstairs as I sat in my room: "Imam Luqman's on Yahoo!" I typed in the address on Firefox, and the page, I will always say, took an eternity to load. Not because it took an eternity, but because the next feeling that hit me was so sudden, so quick to stop my heart, that it was as if I had been living in slow motion just before.

The previous night, the FBI had cornered a gang of Muslims in a warehouse in Dearborn. They had been caught selling contraband. Actually, the FBI had been tracking them for months, and it seemed that at times the officers themselves had planted the contraband. Surrounded, the men had come out from behind the cardboard boxes that hid them, one by one and with their hands on their heads, out of a U-Haul truck. The same kind of truck we had used to deliver food. One man did not come out, and a K-9 officer was let loose on them. The man shot and killed the dog as it attacked him, and in the next second, his last second, he must have known only a searing pain as the firing squad shook him with twenty-nine bullets.

When I left for school the next morning, it was only after being coached by my father in the most severe of terms to keep myself in check and not talk loosely about what had happened. If anyone asked, I was to say simply that I had no idea. That day in drawing class, my teacher had the *Free Press* propped up on her desk. She was a blonde, carefree middle-aged woman, going deaf, who loved to gossip and who was hard to read. Her gaze tarried on me a bit much as she talked about the headline. She was the last person in the school to be prejudiced, and yet I imagined that her lips were pursed in a way that suggested she expected something of me, something more than a glazed, trained stare.

I found it hard to stay silent. I wanted to prove that I was part of a story that made national headlines. I was a big deal. I had met Imam Luqman. No, I had met the terrorist in the news. I knew the terrorist who was caught smuggling contraband in a Dearborn warehouse, where he was killed in a shootout with the FBI. The one who killed that police dog. Actually, it would be far more impressive if the terrorist had nearly killed me. And hadn't he, with his big old truck?

And so I decided to tell part of the story. Even today I cannot forgive myself for taking advantage of that situation. If I had been honest that day, I would have yelled about how the imam had been set up, how it was all a farce, how he was a hero and would always be. But I convinced myself that I was ignorant, that those were raw emotions that I could never be sure about. So I told the class about how I nearly got killed by a violent, bearded, turban-wielding man in a rusting red pickup in Detroit. My art teacher shook her head, bewildered. "Well that's not a good sign," she said in her usual way, though now it seemed to be dripping with disdain.

The next day I sat again in drawing class, and the same scene met my eyes. My teacher had the *Free Press* next to her coffee, but this time the news bore a rather different headline: "**Terrorists, Thugs, or Innocent?**" I smiled sadly. The headline proved that there must have been some truth to the Imam Luqman I had known. But I had betrayed the man's memory.

From then on I was quiet about Imam Luqman, though I shuddered in anger as I read articles about him, how those who loved him had always known him as a hero, a man who 'fed the kids.' I shuddered in anger when I read hateful comments on those articles, asking *Where's that niga muzzie's grave? I need a toilet.* I shuddered in anger when I found that no one really cared who he had been. But I had been just as willing to paint him that way for my own end, so I could feel important.

I have to believe that the real Imam Luqman was the one who gave me a hug on that day during Ramadan, a fellow faster and a leader humble to his people. That was the imam I knew. But the truth of the matter probably lies deeper than any hug. My overwhelming impression of Imam Luqman was only one of pity. It was not complex. As soon as he got out of that red pickup, I was hit with a wave of stifling sorrow at his lean figure. I felt sorry for him, and guilty that I should be the entitled suburban kid handing out food to him, as if he were less than me.

To be honest, I know nothing about that neighborhood or Imam Luqman. Other than that Ramadan encounter, I only know newspaper articles and rumors. I knew him only as a hungry man. And until I have lived his hunger, I have no right to be his judge. I will always see him standing in front of me with open arms in ragged clothes, sweating of toil, hungry. That man could never shoot anyone.

I have no right to be a hero. I have no right to be a judge. I have no right to act cool in art class at my prep school, to speak impressively about how I once knew a terrorist. I would never suffer myself to pass judgment on anyone. I would hate to be in the place of those *12 Angry Men* shouting at each other over the fate of a boy whose life they have never lived. I suppose that someone must shoulder that burden, but it could never be me.

Who, then? I would say that the best people to judge a man are those who share his story. The red pickup comes to mind, the one Imam Luqman drove. I don't know what the make of the car was. To me, it was a wreck of peeling red paint. I felt sorry for the car, in a way. But maybe if you ask the kids of that neighborhood, they would tell you stories of that car. They would know where it had been and what it had done and what it had survived. They might even be impressed that it was still running. They might be impressed that it had *any* paint still left on it. And if one day it crashed and killed a stray dog, those kids would not blame the driver. They would blame the engine, or the brakes, or the steering. They would know where the car had been broken.

Every morning on the way to Country Day that week, I would see the Detroit skyline looming out of the shadows from the vantage of Northwestern Highway, and I would think of Imam Luqman, far removed from the deciduous canopies of Beverly Hills and West Bloomfield. Somewhere out there, another art teacher would be reading the news, and she would shake her head in scorn. A hard-line Detroit Muslim cleric with a history in the Black Panthers had been smuggling contraband in a Dearborn warehouse when he was killed in a shootout with FBI agents. The terrorist had taken with him a K-9 officer. But the art teacher could never have heard his broken voice on that Ramadan day, saying so softly that his family could go without that winter. She could never have known that he had been hungry. She could never have known where he had been broken.

The Fixer

John Carlisle

T HEY'RE SWARMING AROUND HIM TODAY—like they always do. And though he's waiting for customers, he's getting visits from everyone else.

It's a hot summer afternoon, and Gus Mills is seated on an overturned milk crate in a deserted parking lot. A hand-painted wood sign propped on the sidewalk announces his business: What it Dew Lawnmower Repair and Sales.

For two years now, every day but Sunday, the 47-year-old has spread out his tools next to an abandoned dry cleaner on Gratiot near McNichols. He sits in the deep shade of a wild tree sprouting from the side of a neighboring building.

He'll fix your broken lawnmower on the spot, usually within the hour. Repairs are a flat forty-five dollar fee.

"It might be a couple of things wrong, but for forty-five dollars you're going home with it running, as opposed to when you take it to the other side of Eight Mile—they want thirty-five dollars just for you to walk into the building." He gets about a dozen customers a day.

He works from April to August, saving most of what he earns so he can attend community college the rest of the year. He's polite, hard-working, determined to project a professional image despite his rough surroundings.

But this makes him a target for hangers-on and hustlers. In this neighborhood, where a whole lot of people don't have jobs or much schooling or much of a future, a place where scrapping or selling drugs are common careers, a guy like Mills stands out for trying to do an honest day's work. He becomes a center of gravity, like a sun with lifeless planets orbiting him.

Mothers come up and demand that he teach their son a job skill. Transients come looking for a couple hours' work. Men clutching bottles in bags pull up seats, flanking him in the shade, wasting his time and theirs, hoping for some scraps.

"I get the impression that everybody's watching me," Mills says wearily. "Everybody comes up, they're like seagulls. And I'm tired of it. Go away—oh, man."

§

On some days, business gets so good that Mills could use some helpers. But few around this neighborhood are qualified. And the handful who do have skills don't have much of a work ethic. "I can't keep them. I give them a couple dollars and they're gone. Let a cat get twenty bucks, man, he's outta here. Then he'll come back, he's drunk, high, and everything else."

A pickup truck roars into the lot. "Speaking of the mechanics," Mills says, "here they come now."

The driver is young, maybe early 20s, and he's got the sly smile of a schemer. His passenger is older, dumber, possibly drunk, and he is missing all his top front teeth. He gets out of the truck and roams among the lawnmowers and the tools spread around Mills, while the driver distracts him with questions about a guy in the neighborhood, about the weather, about that old lawnmower sitting there. It's as though they can't decide whether to hustle him or work for him.

"You still got my number, right?" the driver asks. Mills shakes his head no. "I ain't seen you," he says. These two don't show up enough to be taken seriously as potential employees. "If I don't use a number within thirty days, it deletes." The driver's face becomes quizzical. A phone that deletes numbers on its own?

"But that's your new phone!" he protests. Mills just carries the ruse further. "I shouldn't even have said thirty days. If I don't see you within ten days it deletes it," he says with a straight face.

They drive off, and Mills shakes his head.

"I call them Heckle and Jeckle," he says. "They're annoying. I mean, you see how they talk?"

§

He gets other kinds of attention too. A beat-up pickup truck pulls up, driven by a middle-aged woman. She's a neighborhood junk collector, and she's got a thing for the lawnmower repair guy.

"Hey, you got a cell phone on you?" she asks, without saying hi. "My sister wants to ask you about something." He tells her no, he has no phone. Meanwhile, his phone pokes slightly out of his pocket.

The woman visits often, usually on some pretext to talk to him. Today's it's supposedly a relative who has a question for Mills. The woman dials on her cell phone and hands it to him. "Tell her you the lawnmower man," she says. There's nobody on the other end, though. He gives her the phone back. She frowns, suddenly promises to return and drives off, as stacks of appliances and metal sheets rattle in the back of her junk truck.

"She wanted to go out," Mills explains, "and it was crazy. She would come and post up. I'd tell her I might close at four o'clock or five; man, she'd be here at three-thirty and sit right over there. I'm waitin' on customers and I'd have to go tell her, 'Well, I'm gonna be here for another hour.'

She'd leave, and I'd take off," he says, laughing.

In this neighborhood, a guy like Mills is a catch. He has a job, he has goals, and he's respectful. For someone like the junk lady, he's gold. "But she's probably backed off a little," he says with relief.

§

Mills spends his days in this lot because he wants the building that sits here. As soon as the dry cleaner went out of business, he had his eye on it. It's got a big parking lot to the side and plenty of room for a waiting area and a workspace. Wait until it goes into foreclosure or tax lien, he figures, then snap it up and open his own small engine repair shop. None of that has happened yet, though.

He's not the only one eyeing that building. Scrappers noticed it too.

"Scavengers, man, they just demolished it," he says. "I've called the police on some guys going in there. And I have had some altercations. They wanted to be belligerent to me—'Mind your own business' and blah blah. I have to tell them, 'You guys don't scare me.'" But the electrical system is already gone. So's the plumbing. The building becomes more worthless by the day.

A thin, sweaty little man rides up on a bicycle and begins tinkering with his bike, using Mills' tools without asking. Mills knows him; the man volunteers to do cleanup for him sometimes. It's either ironic or nervy. "He's the same joker—I wanted this building, and he stripped it," Mills says. In this rough area, a dead building is up for grabs. So is everything else.

"Oh, my goodness," he says. "You name it, brother; you'll see it through here. This is the most action that any one man should be able to see unless he's going to Vietnam or somewhere."

Last year, he watched a man running past on Gratiot get shot in the back and collapse in the middle of the road in front of him. Just the other day, he saw a band of kids chasing someone, shooting wildly. "The newer dudes, the younger kids nowadays, man, they can be bananas coming through here, running through here. Just as long as they stay away from me."

Compared to that, a scrapper is benign. And this one sits right next to the man whose dream he's dismantling, pipe by pipe.

§

A few days pass, and Mills sits in his spot under the high sunshine, but no customers pull into the lot. The pests are intimidating to people, and today the pests are swarming.

There's little Mills can do about them. This abandoned lot isn't his. It's everyone's by default. He could move to another spot, but this is the neighborhood where he grew up, and this is where he wants to be. And he wants to keep watch on that building.

"It's crazy. The little peace that I want I just can't get to," he says, defeat in his voice. "I'm just tired."

As the hot day wears on, four raggedy guys amble up and sit behind him, talking among themselves, while Mills just sits silently with his head in his hands and his eyes looking down.

Joseph Smedo

Aaron Waterman

The Next Move

Ryan Healy

A TALL, MIDDLEAGED MAN crouches down to pick up his opponent's pawn, palming the large black plastic piece off the nearly lifesize chessboard before snapping down his own. His opponent, hovering over the board, barely waits for the move to be finished before making his own capture.

§

On the northern side of Michigan Avenue near Woodward in downtown are two outdoor plastic chess sets installed by Quicken Loans CEO and local real estate mogul Dan Gilbert. The sets were installed in August this year and receive heavy use throughout the day, with most matches falling in the late afternoon.

It's no secret that Dan Gilbert and his partners have gone on a veritable spree, snapping up vacant and underused properties in downtown Detroit. Among the latest purchases are highrises at 1505 Woodward and 1265 Griswold, which does nothing to dispel the belief that Gilbert is betting and betting *big* on a Detroit rebound.

Gilbert has bona fides as a giant in the mortgage industry and a venture capitalist. His move into Detroit's real estate don't seem to stem from the greater fool theory of real estate, where prices are driven up solely by the belief that prices will keep rising. Rather, the developments are pragmatic while marketed as championing a spirit of rejuvenation. But Detroit's recovery appears to be a fragile one, so only time will tell if Gilbert's moves are savvy or overly optimistic.

Detroit's future is uncertain, and these gamblers are betting on a longterm recovery, not a five or even tenyear turnaround. The homicide rate is disgraceful, public school performance is dismal, and the $18 billion in debt is still an unsettled behemoth, at the time of this writing, as it awaits judgment in bankruptcy court.

§

I've watched a few of these games on Gilbert's boards and handily lost one of my own. The pieces get put away after dark and on Sundays, but otherwise players have carte blanche to do controlled battle on the oversized 8x8 blackandwhite grids. There's usually banter, bawdy but amicable, and plenty of backandforth play. One Monday afternoon, I watched a trio of games between two men.

The first game was a slow and gradually unwinding showcase of tension. Midgame, it can be impossible to get a sense of who's probably going to win. The game remained obscure until a strong move by white produced inroads against black's king, safely blockaded. Endgame revolved around a tactical mistake on white's afile rook, giving black freedom on the back rank. Checkmate was close at hand, and white conceded.

"That's what this game is all about. Whoever makes the first mistake."

§

Gilbert's investment in the city totals $1.1 billion in addition to his philanthropic projects, which are separate. Gilbert's philanthropy may be understood best through Opportunity Detroit, a civic improvement arm working to make quality of life upgrades in order to draw more residents to the heart of downtown.

The moves, if successful, will benefit Gilbert's real estate holdings in the area, but even if the strategy is astute and pays dividends for downtown, localized redevelopment and the myth of one man aren't enough to save an entire city.

Behind Gilbert's Quicken Loan headquarters, the two men play for a small audience. One is wearing clothes better suited for the weather and with fewer creases on his face; the other, the teetotaler of the two, a sweatshirt hoodie.

Rodney, a 47yearold former felon and a prison chess veteran, tells me that back when Capitol Park used to be the bus terminal, along with the drinking and drugs that come with a public transit center, there were table chess games. Excons who had honed their skills in the most claustrophobic of conditions typically made hay of armchair grandmasters from the civilized world. Drinking, small bets, and cursing can still be found over the chessboards outside 1001 Woodward.

The two men begin playing again. They're just playing friendlies; not even a dollar changes hands from loser to victor, so the game is loose, not pensive. They play faster than I can annotate. In the second game, white loses significant material early and never recovers. Black gradually leverages the advantage to relieve white of his territory, and white concedes again, this time in latemidgame.

The hollow plastic pieces thud into one another as the men reset the board.

§

Capitol Park is where Rock Venture's recent purchase 1265 Griswold is located—it's where former governor Stevens T. Mason is interred, and it's in the shadow of the gorgeous Stott Building. It's also a target for an entertainment and pedestrian thoroughfare by Opportunity Detroit, planned to include amenities such as solarpowered Wi-Fi recharge points, a stage, and seating where Shelby Street runs along the park currently. It's one of the six downtown districts outlined for renovation and rejuvenation and, as of today, easily the most desolate.

Rodney reminisces about playing chess in Capitol Park "before you were even born," and though he acknowledges his knowledge of chess is connected to his criminal past, he tells me how he's learned to think differently with age. After spending five years in prison, he enrolled at WCCCD and passed his first classes. He's now taking psychology and sociology. He still plays, but that Monday he's just interested in talking chess.

The two men switch sides and begin the third game. At first my notes can keep up, but pawn exchanges begin while Rodney and I chat and the moves become a quick scabbarding for territory. The game evolves into a tense hydra of positional midgame, a doubled pawn on white's d-file the only notable weakness. I continue talking to Rodney, listening to his perspectives about the downtown rejuvenation versus the city's outward erosion, and pieces come flying off the board. I mention Dan Gilbert, and Rodney is visibly impressed.

"In ten years, all this will be worth billions of dollars," he says, motioning at the skyline. "And that's gonna be great for *them*, but I wonder what they're gonna give back to the city."

That might be the consensus about downtown developers right now. They're making savvy, buylow moves that may strengthen the nucleus of the city and leverage its keystone assets, but the rest of the city is seeing piecemeal investment. The city's core may become invigorated while significant pieces are left to grassroots investment, if any at all.

White and black are trimmed to pawns and checking each other with their queens. The game ultimately ends in the cold five o'clock sunset when Rodney reminds his friend, playing white, that they're running late. The last move, for that afternoon, simply stays on the board.

Ghost Shops

Michael Eugene Burdick and Francis Grunow

In the space of a dozen paces, folks want for a subtle change of scene. The character of retail shifts from butcher to baker to candlestick maker, giving the city its verve and its bite. In Detroit they did it too. The stores of Hamilton, Livernois, and Michigan on the west vied for attention with the Hastings, Chenes, and Gratiots of the east. All the world beckoned, come over from Poland and Germany, China, Hungary, Alabama, and Kentucky, just around the corner, thirty feet away. On Woodward, awnings kept the rain and sun at bay, storefronts articulated with deep inset plate glass glistening, hand-painted blade sign projecting over terrazz, and finely tiled entryway, only to give way as a game day spot for your Ford F-150.

The Fauxtopias of Detroit's Suburbs

James D. Griffioen

Detroit rose to its greatest height (and fell as far as it did) in part because Henry Ford didn't want to work too hard. As a child, he hated farm tasks that required physical labor; a neighbor once recalled young Henry as "the laziest little bugger on the face of the earth." Ford's lifelong love of mechanical processes was born out of frustration with manual labor: "I have followed many a weary mile behind a plough and I know all the drudgery of it," he said. "When very young I suspected that much might somehow be done in a better way." Science Fiction writer Robert A. Heinlen might have had men like Ford in mind when he said, "Progress isn't made by early risers. It's made by lazy men trying to find easier ways to do something." Ford worked very hard to change our very understanding of work. His fanaticism for efficiency led to the Highland Park assembly line; the five dollars his line workers took home each day eventually led them to the middle class; the cars they bought with that money eventually took them to the suburbs.

When he was sixteen, Henry Ford moved in the opposite direction, from his family's farm to downtown Detroit, where he worked as a machinist and later as an engineer for the Edison Illuminating Company. Ford worked so close to his home at 58 Bagley Avenue that he would often sneak off to his own workshop (while still on the clock) to tinker away at the one-cylinder internal combustion engine that would power his quadricycle. When the time came to take it out for a test drive, he discovered that the door to his workshop was too narrow, so he famously knocked down a wall to drive the vehicle out into the streets of the sleepy, horse-drawn metropolis. They say Henry didn't invent the automobile, but that night he might have invented the garage door with his sledgehammer.

A few years later, Detroit was in the midst of its gilded age and was the fourth-largest city in the United States. If you couldn't find work in the auto factories there were jobs building skyscrapers meant to rival those in Chicago and Manhattan, or plenty of other jobs serving the growing population. Historic old Detroit needed to make way for the new. During this time countless historic structures were demolished to make way for new construction. By 1926, Henry Ford's former home and workshop stood in the way of a new theater to be built on the site and was reportedly demolished before construction began. Completed in August, the 4,050-seat Michigan Theater was designed in the French Renaissance style, with a four-story lobby decorated with European oil paintings and sculptures, faux-marble columns, and giant chandeliers. At its unveiling, the Michigan Theater seemed to embody Detroit's decadent optimism for the century ahead, fueled by the surging sales of the automobiles the city and its citizens built. A plaque on the outside of the theater identified it as sitting on the spot where sparks met the tinder of the burgeoning industry.

Meanwhile, in suburban Dearborn, Henry Ford was nearing the end of his decade-long effort overseeing the construction of the sprawling new factory down the Rouge River from his Fairlane estate. The Rouge was Ford's opus, the largest vertically-integrated factory in the world, and embodied nearly all of the innovations and ideas Ford spent his lifetime developing. Upon its completion in 1928, he walked away from it, retreating to a plot of land just upriver from the factory, where he'd built a painstaking replica of the childhood farm where he'd learned so many early lessons about hard work. The man who'd helped usher in a new twentieth-century way of living abandoned it to focus his energy on recreating the nineteenth-century past he'd left behind. He spent much of his time and wealth collecting the artifacts and buildings that would become a different part of his legacy, the major regional tourist-attraction known as Greenfield Village and the Henry Ford Museum.

Reenactors near Greenfield Village entrance (2009)

Today 1.5 million people annually visit nearly 100 historical buildings "preserved" in the walled 240-acre compound, many of them chosen and situated to represent a typical American village between 1870 and 1910. Many of the buildings represent people or places significant to Ford's vision of industrial progress (the Wright

Brothers' bicycle shop, Thomas Edison's Menlo Park laboratories), but the heart and soul of Greenfield Village are the buildings associated with Ford's own life and the growth of his automobile company.

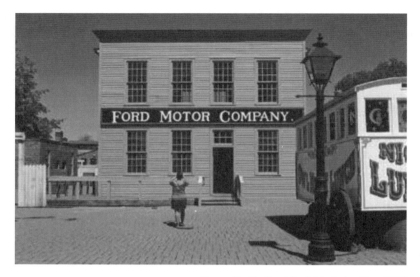

Quarter Size Replica of Ford's Mack Ave. Plant (2009)

Ford deeply regretted not saving his former home and workshop that stood in the way of the Michigan Theater, and he was forced to settle for a full-scale replica of the workshop.

56 and 58 Bagley Street (Ford Historical Archives)

But then in 1929, Ford's friend Charles B. King discovered that the original home had not actually been destroyed, but jacked up on rollers, moved, and turned ninety degrees so that it now faced Grand River Avenue. 56-58 Bagley had been given a modern facade at 514 Grand River and was open to the public as the "Lola Bett Tea Room." The house where Henry Ford lived when he built his first car was now where the before-theater crowd went for pots of Earl Grey and cucumber sandwiches.

*Lola Bett Tea Room in 1930s (*Detroit News *archive photo)*

Ford rushed downtown and confirmed it. After negotiating with the owner to buy, remove and replace a large number of bricks, he ordered his workers to incorporate them into the replica workshop he'd already built at Greenfield Village. According to Ford biographer Sidney Olson, the workers accidentally took bricks from what would have been Number 56 Bagley—the wrong half of the duplex—and to this day at Greenfield Village you can visit the bricks from Henry Ford's neighbor's home that were used to recreate a replica of the workshop where he built his first automobile.

The Lola Bett Tea Room was later demolished to no fanfare. The site, like so much of historic downtown Detroit, is now a surface parking lot. The lavish theater that originally displaced Henry Ford's workshop met a better-documented fate. By the 1960s, the decadent optimism of its unveiling had faded with its carpets as Detroit faced recompense for its Jazz Age giddiness. The badly neglected Michigan Theater barely survived to show grindhouse double features and host rock concerts. In 1976, it closed for good. When it was discovered that demolition would compromise the structural integrity of the adjoining office building, the interior of the theater was gutted to create a 160-space parking garage. Today, commuters park in a three-story garage with gilded seraphim of the old proscenium arch looking down at them from above the shredded remnant of a maroon velvet curtain.

Photo taken March 1, 1933 of the newly-built replica of Henry Ford's garage at Greenfield Village incorporating bricks from the original structure at 56 Bagley (original photo from my collection).

The Bagley Workshop Replica, Greenfield Village (2009)

Michigan Building Parking Garage, 2008

It is arguably Detroit's most breathtaking ruin, beloved by photographers, journalists, and academics for the easy irony of Ford automobiles parking in a ruined theater on the site of the garage where Henry Ford built his first automobile. What's more interesting, I think, is how this building represents a sort of unintentional preservation. At least this is not just another surface lot. And with so much of the rest of the historical city lost to development, demolition, and abandonment, there is the deeper irony that fifteen miles away Henry Ford moved so many historical buildings brick-by-brick from elsewhere around the country and "preserved" them as decontextualized structures in a counterfeit community.

§

The nostalgic fantasy of small-town life on display at Greenfield Village is what most of the beneficiaries of Ford's $5-a-day plan thought they would get when they left Detroit for the small towns surrounding it: They sought a pastoral atmosphere, far from the clanging of streetcars, the factories, and the crime. "We shall solve the city problem by leaving the city," Ford said. With his cheap automobiles, anyone with the salaries he provided could escape the dirty city's ethnic neighborhoods, and (like Philip Roth's Swede Levov) cast away their immigrant shadows. With the fresh air and personal fiefdoms found on every new block of the suburbs, anyone could be baptized as an American in that most American of places: the small town. Frozen in time, Greenfield Village serves as the perfect template for this utopia. Aside from the occasional sputtering of ubiquitous Model Ts (the only cars permitted inside Greenfield Village's walls), the roads are safe for foot traffic. There is no graffiti or crime of any kind. There are plenty of options to buy old-fashioned crafts or dine on historical comfort food. Everything is wholesome and good. And none of it is real.

The Noah Webster house, behind Greenfield Village's walls (2012)

Like some medieval village, Greenfield Village is surrounded by a ten-foot wall. You must drive there and leave your car in a vast surface parking lot before paying twenty-four dollars to get inside (parking is an additional five dollars).

Greenfield Village parking lot during the off-season (2012)

Every night the streets are emptied and the gates locked and guarded. Even the costumed interpreters abandon the village for four months every winter. Henry Ford, the man who famously said, "history is bunk," spent the last part of his life building an unoccupied historic village without any actual history. It has now existed there for eighty years. New buildings and attractions have been added, but since it was created in the 1930s it remains perpetually and intentionally frozen in the 1890s. This village Henry Ford built has, for eighty years, existed solely as a simulacrum of the world Henry Ford destroyed.

*Greenfield Village construction, 1930s (*Detroit News *archive)*

If Greenfield Village represents the sort of wholesome, idyllic (and sanitized) environment that most Detroiters sought in the suburbs, then the city of Detroit has for several decades come to represent its opposite: seedy, gritty, blighted, ruined, overgrown, dangerous, poor, and Black. Yet in the era of exurban sprawl some parts of Detroit have lost so much housing stock they are starting to resemble the pastoral environment Cadillac found there two centuries before the city became a symbol of American industrial might (three hundred years before it came to symbolize its failure). Today these parts of Detroit look more like the actual world Greenfield Village has always tried to represent than many of its once-bucolic suburbs.

That's because for the last fifty years, Detroit's suburbs have been where the action is. One of the reasons metro Detroiters get so upset when journalists and photographers represent Detroit as a city of ruins is the reality that there are millions of people living in safe, well-kept neighborhoods in dozens of prosperous suburban communities. Many Detroit suburbs have walkable, thriving business districts that resemble gentrified neighborhoods in other cities. Southfield has more workers and office space than downtown Detroit. But with big-city amenities come big-city issues of traffic, parking, and overcrowding. And of course, most suburban open spaces long ago gave way to subdivisions, strip malls, and parking lots for shopping malls and big-box stores.

East Side neighborhood, Detroit

Meijer Supercenter Parking Lot, Livonia (2012)

With all the recent development and growth, it is easy to forget that these suburbs of Detroit have their own histories. There was a time before sprawl when these small, historic communities and their citizens provided the lumber for Detroit's homes and the food for its tables. Last year, I started taking an interest in the histories of these communities and visiting all the historical museums and sites that I could find. There are dozens of historical societies in these suburban Detroit communities, many of them quite active. I quickly learned that in more than eighteen suburban communities, an effort had been made since the 1970s to preserve historical structures that were "in the way of development" through the creation of a series of historic "towns" (basically mini-Greenfield Villages) that surround Detroit in every direction the highways go.

Over the past few months, I've visited each of these historic parks to observe and document what so many communities surrounding Detroit did when their history was threatened by sprawl—after all, the drastic and sudden change that sprawl brings to a small town is as devastating to its history and overall character as upper- and middle-class flight was to the city of Detroit. By the 1970s, the suburban pioneers who first moved to these communities were getting older, and it was clear that the small town atmosphere they sought there was doomed. The newer residents of the new subdivisions were just another kind of immigrant seeking refuge and hope in a new place. And there were millions of them. I was interested in the idea of history each suburban community has preserved and presented in villages where no one would actually work or live and where none of the buildings had been preserved in their original context. What did they want their history to look like? Where would they fit that history now that land had grown so scarce? I photographed each village in the state in which they spent most of their time: vacant, empty, and silent (some even behind locked gates).

Livonia (note: this park does have a caretaker who lives in the 1924 Methodist parsonage moved to the site in 1977; also, a few of the many buildings at Greenmead are original to the site, including the 1841 Greek Revival Simmons farm house)

Troy

Goodells

Westland

Northville

    These communities all preserved and presented a nearly-identical set of nineteenth-century buildings to create eerily-similar, lifeless fauxtopias. Each boasts at least one pioneer log cabin, a rescued one-room schoolhouse, a small church and a general store.

Goodells

Clinton Township

South Lyon

Livonia

Flat Rock

These are the structures that form the bedrock of community: the rustic hearth, with separate spaces for education, religion, and commerce. These historic parks are perfect symbols of the romantic small-town fantasy most people first thought they would get when they moved out of the city. That today they are besieged on all sides by freeways clogged with rush hour traffic, thriving businesses and office parks, and neighborhoods full of homes show that no one escaped the city: They brought the city with them.

§

I keep thinking about those bricks Henry Ford knocked out of a perfectly functional building and hauled back to his walled town to incorporate into a replica of a modest turn-of-the-century workshop. What did he think those bricks meant? What strange power did he believe they held? Does it even matter, in the end, that the bricks came from the wrong house, when the underlying idea of moving any bricks from one place to another to represent some physical space of historical significance is so ludicrous? What story does a building tell when it has been removed from its original context: the mill from its stream, the general store from the community it served, the log cabin from the path of civilization in which it stood? What does Robert Frost's home in Greenfield Village mean if we can't walk down the same sidewalks he did when we leave it, or past the same hills where he gazed while dreaming up verse? And what about historical buildings rebuilt entirely after they were razed in war or some other disaster? Or historic buildings gutted to shells and filled with Chinese drywall and modern ornament? In the end, is any building really anything more than just mud and carbon?

It seems we are capable of interacting with history only through limited means. The first way is through the tangible. When we hold an antique or view something in a museum, we understand that we are interacting with the same object in the same way as others throughout history. Henry Ford believed very strongly in this tangible history. He created a legacy where future Americans would understand *living* history through interaction with ordinary objects—that's why he collected so many thousands of ordinary tools and handicrafts and machines. But the second (and perhaps more important) way we interact with history is through the intangible; through our imaginations and the inspiration of others' memories, their spoken or written words or artistic and photographic records. "History is about places of the mind," writes historian David Starkey. Appreciating history through architecture requires some of this imagination. When we visit the Roman forum, we like to tell ourselves that we are "walking in the footsteps of Caesar," but those bricks and columns have been toppled and rebuilt and broken again before being screwed together by dozens of archaeologists thousands of years after the Republic fell. Still. We believe architecture brings us closer to history the way medieval pilgrims believed relics brought them closer to Christ. They must have known that chunk of wood probably didn't come from the true cross, but still, they bought it. We know a building is really just wood and bricks, but still we tell ourselves it's something more, and open our imaginations to the wonder of those who came before us.

§

I have never lived anywhere so burdened by nostalgia, which is a sort of enemy to history. How many older suburbanites cluck on and on about the state of Detroit today and then wax nostalgic for how good it was in the good old days? If it was so good, why did any of them leave? Most of the folks who live in the communities I've discussed above do not trace their origins to whitewashed steeples or quaint one-room schoolhouses that have been saved as a nostalgic reminder of a past most never really experienced. They trace their stories through Detroit, and the old world beyond it. While Detroit rots, the nostalgic, fauxtopian villages that surround that city are a vision of history some would rather embrace. This is what happens when we try too hard to preserve the past. We create towns without memories. We abandon buildings by saving them. We create history without any history. A history of nowhere. A history that is, I suppose, easier to contend with.

My Detroit

Joseph Lichterman

THE HOUSE WHERE MY GRANDFATHER, Ben Friedman, was born no longer exists. There's just an empty lot on Clairmount Street now. Around the corner is Brady Elementary School, which he attended and where Annie, my grandmother, would later teach. The low-slung brick school sits empty, its doors chained and windows boarded shut. The building that used to be a bowling alley is covered in graffiti. There are empty fields, with grass blowing in the wind, where apartment buildings used to stand.

"My God," he mutters. "Nothing is here." He repeats it again and again. "This was a great neighborhood."

Detroit is his city. My zayde, which is Yiddish for grandpa, grew up here. He met my bubbe (Yiddish for grandma) here. They began their family, my family, here.

He lived in a house on 29th Street near Michigan Avenue until his family moved to Clairmount Street when he was in first grade. That house is also now an empty lot. The shul (Yiddish for synagogue) where my zayde had his bar mitzvah was around the block on the corner of 29th and Michigan. It's also been destroyed. The Greater Mount Huron Missionary Baptist Church, which occupied the building, moved into a new home. The candy shop that my zayde would go to as a boy is also gone.

On Tuxedo Street, the squat brick house at 4229, where he lived from junior high until he and my bubbe married, still stands. But the neighborhood has changed since his family moved there in 1945, shortly after his father, my great-grandfather, died. After all, it was already changing when my grandparents, with three young kids in tow, moved out of Detroit and into the suburbs in 1965.

The vastness of the place is what I noticed first as my zayde and I drove around northwest Detroit recently—the area that Detroit's Jewish community used to call home, though most have since moved to the northwest suburbs. In 1940, the Jewish population of Detroit was 85,000, and there were nearly fifty synagogues throughout the city. Today, the Jewish population in the city proper is marginal, and there's only one freestanding synagogue left.

But as we drive through the city, there are vestiges of Jewish life everywhere. The Clinton Street Greater Bethlehem Temple, a vast red brick Apostolic church, used to house Shaarey Zedek, one of the oldest synagogues in Detroit. A Star of David is engraved on its façade, high above a row of decorative columns and three arched doorways.

The former Adat Shalom Synagogue, where my dad had his bar mitzvah, is on Curtis, just west of Livernois. The congregation's name, in block Hebrew letters, is engraved above the main entrance. But the building, which has a copper dome that's since turned green, is now the Bailey Cathedral. Four large stained-glass crosses look out over the street.

Every few blocks, we pass a church that used to be a synagogue. When my bubbe was a girl, she'd tell me later, groups would walk from synagogue to synagogue on holidays to visit friends. It's heartening to see that new communities have come together around these old buildings. But I can't help but feel a pang of sadness for what was lost.

My zayde and I spend about two hours driving a 41.6-mile loop through the city, starting and leaving from his brick ranch in Huntington Woods, the suburb where I grew up. After he and my grandmother were married, my zayde drove a taxi at night to support his young family while he went to law school during the day. It's remarkable how well he navigates the city as we maneuver deftly down side streets he hasn't visited in half a century.

"I know the city. The streets are the same," he says. But a handful of times we drive past streets where we need to turn. The landmarks he once used to navigate aren't there anymore. The street names may be the same, but the city isn't.

As the city's black population grew, the Jews moved farther and farther out of the city. "The blacks would come in and the Jews would move farther out," my zayde tells me. That was true of all white Detroiters, who left for suburbs such as Dearborn, Warren, or the Grosse Pointes. But the Jews moved en masse. It was a trend they've followed every thirty or forty years, ever since the Jewish community first established here in the 1840s.

In the nineteenth century, Jews congregated in the Lower Hastings neighborhood on the city's east side. By the 1940s, the Jewish community moved to the Dexter area, where my zayde's home on Tuxedo is located. The last migration within the city was to the far northwestern reaches of Detroit. That's where my grandparents bought their first home after they were married; it's the house where my mom was born.

Their 1,000-square-foot home on Leewin Street was brand-new when they bought it. "We thought we'd died and gone to heaven," my zayde says now. But in 1965, with three kids, they uprooted and moved to Oak Park. After places like Oak Park and Southfield, the Jewish community mostly moved even farther out, to suburbs like West Bloomfield or Farmington Hills, where my dad's family moved in 1967, a month before the riots. My dad, who was eight at the time, says he remembers sitting in the back seat of his parents' car that July and seeing smoke from Detroit, which was burning, rise in the distance.

§

Every seat in the small second-floor sanctuary of the Isaac Agree Downtown Synagogue was filled for Friday night services. I sat on the hard wooden pew and looked around as the setting sun streamed in through the stained glass windows. "Let's go, my beloved, to meet the bride, and let us welcome the presence of Shabbat," the congregation sang, but in Hebrew. The Jewish Sabbath, which lasts from sundown Friday to sundown Saturday, is often referred to as a bride, and that week I welcomed her surrounded by the congregants at the only synagogue in Detroit. I had sung the prayer thousands of times—I didn't even need to look at the prayer book because I'd memorized the words in elementary school—but that Friday night I wasn't so interested in singing. I just kept staring at these people, this diverse group of people young and old, who were part of a small, but remarkably vibrant Jewish community in Detroit. I'd grown up in various synagogues my whole life, but I had never seen a congregation quite like this before.

After services, everyone gathered in the brightly painted social hall to eat a vegetarian meal prepared by members of the congregation. Sipping on PBRs, people discussed an upcoming film series, the synagogue's attempts to promote urban farming, and an ultimately successful online effort to raise $60,000 to pay for renovations to the synagogue, which is housed in a former industrial building on Griswold Street.

Though their numbers may be few, and though their building is a little rough around the edges, they are here as an active Jewish community in Detroit proper. The only one left.

§

Detroit was founded as a French fort and trading outpost in 1701. Sixty-one years later, in 1762, the city's first Jew, a German-born trader named Chapman Abraham, arrived. He remained in Detroit for about twenty years, but the city's Jewish population remained small until the 1840s, when Germans began immigrating to the United States in large numbers. By 1850, Detroit had a population of about 20,000, and of those 20,000, there were 51 Jews: 29 men and 22 women. Though they were nearly all immigrants, Detroit wasn't their first stop. The city was a growing hub of trade, and they had all come from elsewhere for economic opportunity—a theme that would continue for people moving into Detroit over the decades.

Twelve German-Jewish families founded the first synagogue in Detroit, Beth El, in 1850, in the home of some of its congregants. In 1861, the congregation voted to join the more liberal reform denomination. Seventeen members decided to leave the congregation and form Shaarey Zedek, a more conservative Orthodox congregation. And though they've since moved to the suburbs, both congregations still exist today—in fact, my grandmother was the principal at Temple Beth El's Hebrew school for many years. As the nineteenth century turned into the twentieth, more Jews kept coming to Detroit, mostly from Eastern Europe. By 1920, there were 35,000 Jews living in Detroit—a 247 percent increase over a decade prior. Detroit's overall population, then nearly 995,000, grew by about 114 percent over the same time period. By 1940, there were 85,000 Jews in the city, and there was a well-established community, replete with Hebrew schools, a hospital, Jewish delis, and more.

This was the community my grandparents grew up in. My great-grandfather was caught delivering illegal whiskey in Poland, and he fled the country, coming to Detroit, where his brother lived, in 1923. Quotas put in place by the United States government prevented my great-grandmother and her children from meeting him in the U.S. Finally, in 1926, the family was reunited, and in 1931 my zayde was born, the youngest of four kids and the only one of his family born in the United States.

"I was their American dream," he says.

My bubbe, then three years old, arrived in Detroit with her parents in 1938. They emigrated from Palestine, which was then under British control, because her father, a carpenter, was unable to find work. They had family in Detroit, and the three of them planned on staying for a year to make money before returning home to Ramat Gan, in what would later become Israel. But when World War II broke out in 1939, they were unable to leave. Detroit was home now.

Their stories are typical of people of their generation. People came to Detroit because there were jobs. They came for economic opportunity, and stayed for the communities.

They made Detroit their city.

§

Early in our day together, as we drove by abandoned house after abandoned house, I asked my zayde what he thought of Detroit's miniature renaissance: Downtown and Midtown are doing well, of course, and despite the city's bankruptcy, people outside the city view it as full of opportunity.

"It's not a destination," he says. "The schools are bad. It's no place to raise a family."

He's right. Nobody really vacations in Detroit, and the Detroit Public School system is broke and failing. But if you're thinking of moving to Detroit, you're not looking for a destination, you're not looking for good schools for the kids you may have one day. Rather, you're looking to be part of a change that's been a long time coming; you're looking to reclaim your heritage.

And as my zayde and I drive back toward the suburbs after our day in the city, back toward our actual home, my zayde told me that this was the first time he's been back in his old neighborhood in nearly 40 years. And as we crossed over 8 Mile Road out of the city, he cited an old Yiddish song written by a Holocaust survivor upon returning to his hometown for the first time after the war was over.

"Where is the street where I grew up? Where is the house where I lived? Where is the girl I used to love?" he roughly translates for me.

This Detroit is no longer the city my grandparents knew, but maybe one day it will be mine.

By The Time This Reaches You

Deonte Osayande

I love you but by the time this reaches your ears
it will be too late
I will be headed back
within the mouth of the beast.

In my hometown
2 men aged 16-25 are murdered
each week, which means men my age
have asphalt graves dug by trucks
made in the ghost factories of our homes.

We are cracked futures,
buried in abundance
as if something is supposed to grow there.
Our lovers forget our names like subtotaled receipts.
After we fill up the garbage cans
we are heaped on top of one another,
like tables overflowing with the dishes of deaths breakfast.

By the time this reaches your ears
I will be cursed in betrayal.
I'm ripping down the wallpaper of my heart as we speak,
dragging an ax along carpets where I once laid in love.

I've replaced all the doors with windows.
I've become more open but I'm letting less people in.
My ventricles are wrecking balls.
My arteries are arson art exhibits.

Little children watch in awe
but in my hometown
Little boys and girls have pistols for mouths.
They all have similar targets and I've slowly begun

to grow a large red dot on my chest.
There is an orange circle around that,
and a yellow halo around that.
Every time I try to talk to them I see their tongues twitching.

I tell rooms full of strangers
things I don't tell my best friends.
Those who I see an oasis in desert me.
There are vultures and hyenas that have long circled my failures,
and I fear I will disappear searching for you.

Your attention is worth more to me
than the attention of millions.
I don't know the depth of your damaged heart
but mine has been broken
into small enough pieces across Detroit
that it will fit in and fix it.
I've tried to repair my soul with a hammer
for so long that I know how impossible it is.
I face myself in the mirror knowing that I
have loved bricks that think they are wrenches.
They will have wrecked more than they repair.

If you told me to swallow gasoline
to get that kiss from your flamethrower of a mouth
I would engulf every motor in my city.

I am just a man with a woman's heart.
There is a landmine between my neck
and my navel and all I want you to do is fall for me.

But by the time this reaches your ears,
I will be back in the mouth of a beast
that wants nothing to do with me. Its teeth will be stars.
Its gums will drip comets.
I will suspended the sky above my head
waiting for you to notice me and
the crazy thing about stars
is what you see is really an image of something that died a long time ago.
like an egg broken before being boiled for breakfast,
like a dying animal watching the scavengers
wait for a meal, or a victim of its surroundings
waiting for someone, anyone to show them love.

Detroit I-75 Overpass at Sunset, 2013 / Melanie Schmitt

Aaron Waterman

Aaron Waterman

David Blair and the Hannan House Choir, African World Festival, Hart Plaza, 2008 / Patricia Lay-Dorsey

Music as the Missing Link

Keith A. Owens

DETROIT IS NOT AN EASY TOWN FOR MUSICIANS, but then Detroit is not an easy town for anyone. If you want the Big Easy, head south. Here in the Motor City, we take an almost perverse pride in doing things the hard way, or whatever way that means we can be left alone to do our thing however we want.

In Detroit, we don't always play well with others. Sometimes we pay a steep price for that. But when it comes to the music, the results would indicate that this sort of middle-finger independence has worked to our advantage. From Motown to techno, from jazz to blues, from rap to rock, from hip hop to R&B, Detroit has proven to be the international gold standard when it comes to musical creativity. If you don't believe me, try and name any other city anywhere with such a deep bench of musical heavy hitters across so many genres who either were born here or began their careers here. Don't wanna brag but . . . well . . . I kinda do. It's not overselling when it's the truth.

And yet, despite the apparent fact that our cast-iron cup runneth over with talent, even as the city's fortunes as a whole continue to decline at an exponentially accelerated rate, Detroit's musical community hasn't really been taken seriously at the local level—or at least not as seriously as it should be—since the days of Motown. Or, if you want to reach back even further, to the days of Paradise Valley, when Detroit actually had a musical district that provided gigs for some of the world's best musicians seven days a week virtually around the clock. If live music was what you craved—and Detroit has always been a city in love with notes—then Paradise Valley was where you went to satisfy that craving.

As for Motown, it wasn't just the quality of the music that made Hitsville USA stand out so prominently, it was the jobs that the music provided. Granted, there were some grumbles about how much—or little—the salaries that came with some of those jobs actually were, but the fact remains that Motown was a local business that put people to work while providing high-quality entertainment on a regular basis for Detroiters who were only too happy to spend a portion of their (very) hard-earned money to see a show.

Today, the music is still here, but the venues available to perform that music to an appreciative audience have shrunken dramatically. There is no music district anymore comparable to Paradise Valley where music lovers can stroll in and out of clubs checking out the scene, like they still do today in Memphis on Beale Street, or up and down Bourbon Street in New Orleans. If you want to check out the music in Detroit, you need to know where to go and whom to ask. But no matter who you ask, the fact remains that finding live music performed by local musicians in Detroit is a much harder task than it used to be, which means it is much harder for Detroit musicians to nail down gigs that pay more than enough to buy a hamburger on the way home.

For a city that has given, and continues to give, so much music to the world, you would think there might be a little more appreciation and a little more recognition that since this is something that we Detroiters tend to do better than just about anybody else, perhaps we should harness that ability and convert it into fuel to help run the sputtering engine of the city's recovery. Granted, there are organizations such as the Detroit Sound Conservancy that have taken it upon themselves to be a particularly active and aggressive cheerleader for the city's music scene. By working to preserve and promote the city's musical history for research and study as well as for simple enjoyment, the DSC is helping to reignite a pride of ownership for a city that has cast perhaps the longest musical shadow of any city in the world.

But despite all of our accomplishments, it still seems like we're so accustomed to being surrounded by all this musical talent (because it's been here for so long) that Detroiters just take it for granted, assuming that it will always be here and therefore is not in any need of special attention or consideration.

This could prove to be a serious mistake. Today it's hard to even count the number of top-flight musicians who have been forced to leave the city over the years to make a name for themselves—and some money—but let's just agree that it's a lot. If just a fraction of those who have left for greener pastures were still actively employed here in the city sharing their talents and having those talents utilized as teachers, performers, producers, and composers, among other things, just imagine what a difference this could make as we all struggle to define where Detroit goes from here.

Because wherever Detroit goes from here, if Detroit music isn't helping to steer the wheel then we're bound to wind up lost.

Movement 2012 Electronic Music Festival, Hart Plaza / Patricia Lay-Dorsey

Awakening

Maisha Hyman Symbry

O N THE EDGE OF THE DIRTY CONCRETE RISER, I stand with Lynara Carter, crunching on contraband Better Maid Hot chips and drinking a verboten Pepsi. Mommy would kill me—like dead—if she caught me consuming such garbage. I keep a five-stick pack of Doublemint in my pocket because, well, all the cool girls do it, and because it collects all the chip fragments from my teeth while it freshens my breath. Plus, Mommy doesn't mind gum.

My cheap spiral notebook covers leave streaks of damp color on my sweaty forearms and along the front of my short-sleeved shirt. My bangs had long lost their curl and had become mini-afros around 1:26 p.m.—a full hour before we got off the yellow-cheese bus to head over to the DDot bus stop to catch the Wyoming—Lynara to Fenkell, me to 8 Mile Road.

"It's hot as HELL out here." Lynara pushes her permed hair back. "Shit."

I study her side profile. Lynara is one of the cool girls – but not too cliquish to allow me, a lowly sixth grader, in her circle of friends. She used to be best friends with one of my best friends from elementary school. They fell out over a skinny boy named Paul with Skippy peanut-butter-colored skin and curly hair. He was one of a few phenoms in the school—the curly–haired boys with the maple syrup–colored eyes. He was "fiiinnne." Us Detroit girls know how to put the dirty south in mid-word-occurring vowels. "Fiiiiinnnne" (add an eye roll and a lip curl, and chase with a swig of Faygo Redpop).

I, on the other hand, am kind of pathetic. Super smart, yes, but super unpopular too. My clothes are not cool, and I'm a ten-year-old nervous wreck around boys. I have, however, perfected the art of the code-switch and wield that as my sole weapon in the Nationalist/Pan-Africanist family environment versus Detroit Public Schools battle for my soul.

I walk to the edge of the curb, looking to see if the Wyoming bus was anywhere in sight. I contemplate if I have enough time to walk across the street to the gleaming white tiled Wimpy's hamburger restaurant for an order of chili-cheese fries in soggy wax paper. I debate it with Lynara.

"You gon' miss the bus! Shit. And then you gon have to stand out here for another HOUR. Plus you might get that mean-ass lady busdriver ...."

"And I ain't got my bus card," I finish for Lynara. "Damn."

"See?"

Lynara sits down on the riser in front of the Texaco gas station. Some high school kids from MacKenzie strut across the asphalt behind us. It's late May—hot in Detroit. The girls remind me of the Rick James song "Seventeen and Sexy"; their bodies push the limits of the seams of their T-shirts and jeans. I look at my own body, blossoming in strange ways—and ask Allah if, like, he could do me a favor, and shit.

School is almost out, and no one is taking this shit seriously anymore. Well, at least that's what the high schoolers behind us are saying. I agree inside my head then remember that I have a couple of essays to do for school that evening.

"Where's the fucking BUS?" Lynara yells at the heat.

I rather don't mind the hot weather. Much prefer it to shoveling snow and sitting in a cold house where maybe there was heat or not, depending on how Mommy's bill money landed for that month. In the summer, there's no need for cooking gas or hot water for the radiators and showers. Summer is just fine.

I take a long pull on my cold Pepsi, abandoning the idea of heading across the street for greasy fries, when I feel a lurch inside my chest. Followed by another, and another in staccato repetition. My notebooks vibrate in my arms.

Lynara stands up and dusts off her colored Levi's, a smile easing the muscles on her face, pinched in response to the afternoon sun.

"That's my *JAM*!"

We both turn around and watch a shiny black Dodge Charger rumble into the gas station parking lot. The bass booms and bangs around the car and out of its hundreds of paths of least resistance. Lynara raises her right hand, her elbow bent at a right angle, and twists her wrist—the Errol Flynn. She rocks side to side.

"Who's THAT?" I ask, taking on her recently abandoned frown. "That don't even *sound* right."

"Girl, that's Run-DMC . . . 'it's like that—WHAT and that's the WAY IT IS . . . HUUH!'"

"Who??"

"Run-DMC! Girl, wait til you hear 'Sucker MC's,' that's really my jam. My cousin got the tape the other day. We wrote down *all* the words."

"What kind of NAME is that? Is it just one person?"

"No . . . it's a GROUP—Run and DMC!"

"Oh . . . so Run and DMC?"

"NO! Run-DMC. It's their names, but they don't put no 'and' in between it. It's just Run-DMC."

"That don't make no sense."

I stood in stark opposition to things that made no sense. Like why my parents split up in the first place then acted like friends and confused me. Or how my dad always had the nice new stuff at his house and Mommy didn't. Or how you could get discounts on food at Farmer Jack if you paid using the coupons you clipped out of the newspaper, but you could actually *pay* for food with the colorful food coupons that you tore out of the book that came in the official-looking envelopes in the mail. Just didn't make sense.

My spine tightens against the name. Run-DMC. What kind of group is that?

It feels awkward to say the name, with its missing conjunction.

I watch Lynara, head bobbing in time with her Errol Flynning arm. She mouths the words about record unemployment, people dying, wars, famine, escalating bills, and I'm taken in. The cowbell contrasts against the pavement-crashing beat. I feel my neck become convinced.

"It's the jam, right?" Lynara looks over at me.

"Yeah. It's the jam."

Game Not Over

Veronica Grandison

O N A HOT SUMMER SATURDAY NIGHT, a crowd of hip-hop aficionados gathered inside Foot Klan Skate Park, an indoor skateboarding facility on Grand River, to hear beats and rhymes by some emerging hip-hop artists from the D. The room where the hip-hop showcase took place was dimly lit, except for bright, multicolored lighting that pointed towards the stage. Urban graffiti images adorned the walls of the venue, and amateur skateboarders performed tricks toward the back of the room.

The crowd gathered around a large wooden stage as Detroit rappers Faded Agenda, Fame the Ripper, and Ams Fresh took turns getting busy on the mic. The Klan became the house of Detroit hip-hop that night. This showcase, known as "The Air Up There" has become a gem in the hip-hop community. It's been going on since 2009, and it is one of the main spots for up-and-coming hip-hop artists to showcase their talent.

Tashif Sheefy McFly Turner, the founder of The Air Up There, is a hardcore advocate for Detroit music and his showcase is part of the second wave of hip hop hot spots that have embraced the genre and given artists an outlet to be creative.

§

In the early- to mid-1990s, venues such as the Shelter were a staple within the local hip-hop scene. Located inside the basement of St. Andrews Hall, the Shelter was one of the main spots where many Detroit hip-hop artists got their start. Rappers like Eminem, Royce da 5'9, D12, and Slum Village (with the late J Dilla) performed there before their careers took off.

There was also the Hip Hop Shop, a clothing store on 7 Mile that doubled as an open mic venue. Fashion designer Maurice Malone opened the shop in 1993, and it became one of the main destinations for rap competitions. Its famous rap battles inspired scenes from the film *8 Mile*. Unfortunately, the Hip Hop Shop closed its doors in 1997 when Malone relocated to New York to focus on his clothing line.

These venues housed a different generation of artists, many of whom are now in their 30s and 40s. Now, there is a new crop of hip-hop artists coming up, and more outlets are being created to nurse this homegrown talent.

"Because of *8 Mile* and Eminem, it was like a rite of passage if you played the Shelter. But it's not like that anymore," says Brent Smith (aka Blaksmith) a local hip-hop artist.

"It's almost like the Shelter (and St. Andrews) is going through a transition period because they see that the newer venues are more environmentally friendly for artists," Smith says. "St. Andrews knows they can't just rely on their reputation from years ago."

Smith is one half of the rap duo Passalacqua and a founding member of the rap group Cold Men Young. When Smith started out, he says venues like the 5E Gallery embraced his music.

This new class of hip-hop spots includes showcases such as The Air Up There and venues such as the Untitled Bottega, and the 5E Gallery.

The Air Up There was originally held at the Detroit clothing store Bob's Classic Kicks. Turner interned there in high school, so the owner let him use the spot to hold a hip-hop show. The showcase received a lot of buzz and eventually became a monthly event.

In addition to being a party promoter and artist, Turner is also a hip-hop artist. He started this series so he and his music peers could be heard.

Turner says he was surprised at the positive response the show received.

"I wasn't all hip-hop oriented when I first started. But, once it got big, I felt like I had a position to play and I had to step up to the plate and make it a staple for the Detroit music scene," says Turner.

The Air Up There was a monthly showcase for two years, and it even garnered sponsorships. The showcase went on hiatus for about seven months, but Turner started it back up recently.

Like Turner, artist and Detroit native Flaco Shalom wanted a space to express his artistry. Shalom studied fashion design at Alabama A&M and the International Academy of Design and Technology in Chicago, but no art galleries in the city would showcase his work. So, in 2011 he started the Untitled Bottega, an uncurated art gallery that welcomes all up-and-coming-artists (not just painters).

"When no one would accept any of my work, I said it's just four walls with white paint on the inside that puts art up, and I said I can do that myself," Shalom says. "After doing that I said I wanted to do that for other people, and that's pretty much who comes in my doors."

The Bottega hosts many events, including fashion shows, fine art shows, poetry sessions, and hip-hop showcases. Two well-known underground hip-hop showcases, Mixtapes and Pancakes and The Carter, are held at the Untitled Bottega.

In addition to being a performance and art venue, the Bottega doubles as a store where artists can sell their music, art and pretty much whatever they want. As a bonus for artists, they get to keep 80 percent of their sales.

The Bottega was originally located on Iron Street in Detroit, but it moved to a new location in a 4,000-square-feet building on East Baltimore.

The 5E Gallery is another venue that has become a local mecca for all things hip-hop. The nonprofit visual art and culture gallery was founded in 2008 by DJ Sicari Ware. Ware has worked with stars such as Eminem, D12, and J Dilla, and is also a youth program coordinator for the Detroit Hispanic Development Center.

The gallery's mission is to further bridge the connection between art and hip-hop culture. The 5E offers educational programs and performance opportunities for DJs, graffiti artists, photographers, bands, and poets.

Its most well-known event, The Foundation, is an open mic session specifically geared toward female hip-hop artists and was founded by Detroit hip-hop artists Invincible, Miz Korona, and 5E Galley co-owner Piper Carter.

Earlier this year, the gallery faced some economical challenges and had to relocate from its building on Michigan Avenue to the Cass Corridor Commons.

This summer, with start-up funding from Cognizant through the Kresge Foundation, they started Sonic Maker Space, which offers classes in music production, video, photography, electronics, robotics, and painting.

They are currently seeking funding for the purchase of a building and for programming.

Turner says that the 5E is one of the biggest supporters of the hip-hop game, and they, along with the Untitled Bottega and The Air Up There, are continuing to make an impact on young artists. But, regardless of where the music is played, Turner says rappers just want to be able to break out their mics and show off their skills.

"At the end of the day, hip-hop is wherever people set the speakers up," he says.

Misguided Faith

Karen Minard

I T'S A SUMMER DAY, and I'm sitting in my living room when I get a call from a woman in New York. She identifies herself as part of a research team that is compiling a database of Johnny Mercer's work, an electronic songbook as it were, to coincide with the hundredth anniversary of the songwriter's birth.

She says, I understand he collaborated with your husband.

"Ex-husband," I correct her, but she ignores my rebuff.

Was it just on one song, she asks, or were there more?

"It was so long ago," I answer, "and quite honestly, I just don't know."

Perhaps you can remember the year, she presses on, until I feel compelled to stop her in her tracks.

"You know, we divorced a long time ago," I say, "and he's been deceased for many years."

The song we're looking at, she continues, was called "Sanctifying Grace." Then it looks like it was changed to "Misguided Faith."

I don't hear a question in what she is saying so I decide to offer one of my own. "Would you like my son's phone number?" I ask. "He can probably give you the kind of information that you want. He's a songwriter too, and he spent a lot of time with his dad before he died."

Yes, she says, and thank you. But she still won't let me off the phone. She wants the correct spelling of my ex's name, his place and date of birth. But the only thing I can say with any certainty is that he was born in Liverpool, just like my son.

England? She wants to know.

"Yes," I reassure her, "just like The Beatles. His last name used to have an s on the end that sometimes he used and other times he didn't. It's there on our marriage license but not on the divorce decree. As for his date of birth, I'm not sure. He had more than one birth certificate, each with different dates on them."

There's a pause on her end of the line. It's a long pause, and it's hard for me to tell if it's because she's surprised by what I've just said, simply processing it all, or taking notes. And so I add, "He was a bit of a character, you know."

When she speaks again, she asks, Would you remember the year they worked together, and how and when they met?

I think back. A flood of memories come pouring in. "It was the seventies. My ex was a bartender at the Plaza Hotel. Johnny Mercer must have been staying there; that would have been how they met. I remember he called me on the phone, one night, all excited to meet a song writer of Mr. Mercer's caliber; next thing I knew, he had handed him the phone. Here I am, lying in bed in the middle of the night in our apartment in Astoria, and giddy as a schoolgirl to have Johnny Mercer on the line. And he was so sweet, acting like I was doing him a favor by talking to him and apologizing for the intrusion." The Mercer period wasn't all bad.

The woman wants more information, dates, details, and timelines. But I'm too busy beating down the bird to even hear what she is asking. What I really want to do is scream at her: Why the hell are you calling me? Call his sister! Call his family! Don't you know that man caused me more grief than you have the right to make resurface? Don't you know he kidnapped my children, dragged them across country, then out of the country, and, when I got them back, followed us here to Detroit where he dragged us through judicial hell? And he lied, schemed, plotted, and plagued us for ten years when he couldn't get his way. But, of course, I don't say any of that. She doesn't know the story, and why should she? Just because it made the front page of the *Los Angeles Times*—then again, that's not the research she doing.

I stand up and take a deep breath, my albatross hanging low. I clasp one arm around the other to keep my beating extremities calm. "I really have to go now," I say. "Call my son." I hang up the phone.

It had been a long time since I had thought about all the connivances of those custody battle days: the trials, lawyers, officers of the court, clinicians, press, and various preachers. All were institutions in which I had once put my faith. In the end, many tried to boil things down in black-and-white terms: my ex was white, and I am black and that's all there was to that. Although I disagreed, I never really found a suitable simplistic answer with which to retort.

I should be over it by now, I guess, but PTSD by any other name is still PTSD, and I still struggle to make sense of it all. A few things I can say, however: I am proud I stood by my convictions at that time, and I am even more proud to have raised two healthy and wonderful kids. I am grateful that I have lived this long to write and tell about it. And today is a sunny day.

Learning to Roll Our Tongues, Detroit 1986

Nandi Comer

Ms. Alvarez flips up a flashcard and shows us a faded
red sphere. Two leaves cling to its stem. *Manzana*, apple.
All together, we say it. She nods, smiles. We sit
cross-legged, her rug with a map of the world, frayed
under us. Our upturned eyes set on her pictures,
we wrap our brown lips over her florid sounds,
flicking the fruit off our tongues.

Oso, bear. No breakfast before school, our mothers
have sent us to repeat Spanish words. We suck
the sugary heads of animal crackers for midday snack.
The small cookie bodies softening in our mouths.
Some of us sneak an extra cookie bag. I've stuffed mine
in my pocket for later. One time Lawrence
choked from trying to swallow a lion whole.

The word *platano*, banana, is easy on our teeth.
Two blocks away, a man knocks a woman to the ground.
Libro, book. The man is one of our fathers. *Cerdo*, pig.
His dry hands tighten around her throat. *Mariposa*, butterfly.
We mimic our teacher's pitch, curl the *P* out like a pout.

Gato, cat. We are anchored
to the rug's blue-red-green. *Azul. Rojo. Verde.*
He hits her again. Her knees scrape pavement.
España Angola, Japón. I trace my fingers
over each country's translated names, imagine
the sounds at each border. She tries to escape.
No one stops his hitting. *Pajaro*, bird.
A robin stares sideways from our teacher's card.
It does not sing. It does not know trees,
nor nesting, nor migration.

Up in the Morning & Off to School in Detroit

Tracey Morris

O N MY FIRST DAY OF SOPHOMORE YEAR IN 1982, I transferred from St. Martin De-Porres High, a very small, very focused, very caring Catholic high school, to Northern Senior High School, a very large, very chaotic, very cold public school. A steep tuition increase at DePorres (along with one at St. Cecilia, the Catholic elementary school I'd attended and my baby sister was attending) meant, as my mother had tearfully explained to me weeks before, a sacrifice had to be made.

Walking through the doors of Northern High with my mother for enrollment on that late August day, I was that sacrificial lamb.

I had few friends there—most of the kids in my neighborhood dismissed me as the "stuck-up girl who went to private school." They didn't want to have anything to do with me, nor I with them.

The other kids I encountered were standoffish, bored, and eager to be anyplace else. The staff working that day cycled back and forth between being sullen, overworked, and overwhelmed. Finally, after being shuttled from table to table, room to room, desk to desk, to standing in one line after another, my mom and I found ourselves standing in front of a chipped folding table in a hallway that smelled like gym shoes, speaking to a woman (I think she was a guidance counselor; I can't remember exactly) who didn't try to hide her hostility as she asked for my paperwork. I handed her my ninth-grade report card and my school transcript, proud of the fact that I was an honor student and carried a 3.8 GPA. The woman behind that folding table? Not so much. She looked at my papers, rolled her eyes, and handed them back to me with a sigh.

"Girl," she said, sucking her teeth, "you sure don't belong here." And with that, school was in session.

Remember your first day of school? How your outfit had to be just right? Or how the crusts had to be cut off your sandwich and carefully placed in the lunchbox with your favorite cartoon character on it? Was your backpack brand new or the beat-up one handed down from an older sibling? Were you excited about your new teacher, or were you planning ways to skip class?

That first day set the tone for the rest of the year, defining who you were and setting your place in your classroom universe for the next 180 days. Every experience you lived, every person you met, helped form your persona, and continues to frame your existence to this day.

For me, that existence is one of persona non grata. You see, every school I attended—from Head Start to twelfth grade—has closed. Every. Single. School.

St. Agnes Head Start.

Brady Elementary.

Sanders Elementary.

St. Cecilia School.

St. Martin DePorres High School.

Northern High School.

Each one gone forever.

Only Northern still has students in its classrooms. It's now the Detroit International Academy for Young Women, which, according to the Detroit Public Schools website, is the only public all-girls K-12 school in the state. St. Cecilia's academic program is no more, but its regionally renowned gymnasium still functions as a training ground for promising young basketball players. St. Martin DePorres moved locations three times during its decades-long academic history before finally being claimed by declining enrollment and increasing operational costs. Sanders Elementary, which once stood in the shadow of the Herman Kiefer Health Complex, was razed a few years ago—even the playground equipment that the neighborhood kids used long after the school closed its doors was torn down, leaving behind only a weed-choked vacant lot. The buildings that housed Brady Elementary survived the threat of fire from a nearby commercial laundry, but it's currently up for sale by Detroit Public Schools. St. Agnes Church and School—once a majestic complex of buildings that survived the brunt of the 1967 riots—is now a decaying hulk of buildings, long picked clean by scrappers and scavengers.

Try to imagine what it's like to wake up one morning, like I did recently, to realize your childhood has been boarded up, abandoned, padlocked. It's a very disorienting feeling.

Sadly, that disorientation is something many children in Detroit are experiencing every morning as they grab their backpack, put their lunch money in their pocket, and walk past the neighborhood school that was taken from them for reasons beyond their control. They find themselves in a classroom that may not be willing or able to provide them the nurturing learning environment they deserve.

Today, watching the kids in my neighborhood walk or ride to their first day of school, I realize they are walking toward an uncertain future. The plummeting enrollment, population drain, and economic woes that claimed each of my alma maters now stalks a new crop of students. Some are headed to Thirkell Elementary, the last public grade school in my neighborhood. Its classroom windows and playground sit in direct view of what remains of St. Agnes, a crumbling preview of what the future could look like. In recent years, parents, local activists, and the school's students and staff have banded together to fight off the threat of closure—a threat that still looms over the school, despite having some of the best test scores and parent ratings in the

DPS system.

A handful of neighborhood kids are headed a few miles south to the Detroit School of Arts, a nationally recognized academic and performing arts high school. It's a public school run by an experimental self-governing board that nonetheless faces the threat of budget cuts that diminish the very music and art programs that make the school great. Other kids are headed to Durfee Elementary-Middle School and Central Collegiate Academy a couple of miles to the north—schools whose ongoing academic and financial problems led to them being absorbed into the state's Education Achievement Authority for Detroit's lowest performing schools.

Continuing financial and management problems plaguing DPS, along with Detroit's bankruptcy crisis—the largest municipal filing in US history—means that the city we know and love, the only home many of the kids walking into Detroit's classrooms each morning have ever known, will face more unanticipated changes. The changes that come to Detroit impact the region, the state, and the nation. I'm honored to share my experience of the Detroit I've come to know, love, and sometimes dread over the past forty-six years.

Hello, Detroit. School is now in session.

The Corner: Reid Building / Megan Snow

Apartments v. Houses

Michael Eugene Burdick
and Francis Grunow

Just a lifetime ago, Detroit was home to the most single-family houses on earth. Hundreds of thousands, each filling a neat lot, with a separate yard, planted in blue grass, divided by a drive, connecting to a garage, light penetrated four sides, with a certain disdain for the party wall. We took great pride in the idea of everyone owning the *American Dream*. Wherefore art thou apartment house? Many in the world never have to cut the grass, walking to the park instead, with neighbors down the hall, often having pretty great views, and still get to own their ideas, too.

Stand

Steve Hughes

OF COURSE THE FISH ARE DEAD. They dried up and curled at the tail. Fish need water. I've tried to explain this to her. I don't know why I bother. I'm talking to the wall here. And she looks at me like I just kicked her in the shin, but I didn't touch her. I maybe bumped her ankle earlier with my wheelchair, and that probably left a bruise, but that was an accident. She takes an armful of my laundry and crams it in the dresser. There's no good reason to be mad at me just because I'm trying to make a point.

She forgets stuff. First she forgets how Martinez turned her out and how I let her come back, and then she forgets how I saved her. Sometimes I think I shouldn't have. I sure as shit wouldn't be so messed up now. That was the night she poured that floor polish into a cup and drank it right in front of me. Out of spite. She would have swallowed more if I hadn't slapped it from her hand. It made her shake and flip around the floor. Her arms bent up like a praying mantis. I tried dragging her to the car, but it was impossible with her jerking around like she did. Finally I called the ambulance, which was smart because I was loaded too.

Two days later she blinked awake out of the coma. Two more days and she came home to fill the house with the sharp smell of her stomach. She is sick still, brainsick. But for some reason God wanted to make her better. I guess he wouldn't let her die—not until she finished the hard work of ruining my life.

I'm in this wheelchair now because I let her drive. We were coming home from Martinez's. My old friend Martinez is up on 7 Mile. He's the guy with the good stuff. So, she had the wheel and she was killing my buzz, arguing about something and going too fast through nowhere Detroit, just not looking at anything and pointing her finger at me. Truth is I wasn't paying attention either, until she hopped the curb then slammed into the telephone pole. That's when my femur snapped like a carrot. Metal hammered into my leg and my ankle ground up like blender ice. Bones popped out of my skin. "Bloody Mary. Dirty Harry," I said, and then I think I passed out.

I got a room at the hospital. They set me up with a foxy nurse. She had a tattoo of a lady's face on her neck. She was the bearer of some very good pills too, not as good as Martinez but better when you double them up. After a four-week stay, they sent me home with a goodie bag full of them, and ten pages of instructions in print too small to read.

I'm getting better still, but it's been some months since I worked, doing my job at the transfer station, and then I had to have surgery and then the infection happened because who-knows-why, and then more surgery. At least they didn't take off my leg and toss it in the scrap pile. One day, they say, I might be able to walk again, only I don't know. Below my knee, the thing is all swollen up like a watermelon. It doesn't look like a leg at all.

It's snowing out tonight, and I wonder how long this winter can last. It's been forever already, living in gloom. It's all cold and bad and tumbling out of the sky and sticking on the cars and streetlights, putting its sick freeze on the world.

She wheels me to the kitchen in time to grab the phone. I'm just sitting there listening to the radio, waiting for her to hang up. She puts it to my ear, so I can hear. It's the electric company's computer again, calling to say they are going to shut us off. "Bastards!" She says. "What the hell are we going to do without power?"

"Light candles. I guess."

She opens the fridge and pulls us some beers. We sit at the table and look at each other. The radio is playing a good Led Zeppelin song. When it's over the announcer starts yammering about Kwame.

"Oh shit, did you hear about this," she says, "the fucking mayor is in jail. That one on Conant. Hah! I hope they leave him there forever. Lying bastard."

"What do you have against him? He's not the one turning off our power. You don't even know him."

"I know he's a fucking liar." She's rubbing her hands together. Making a sound like sandpaper. "Where's my hand lotion," she says.

I point to the TV.

"How did it get behind the TV?"

"I don't know," I say. "Why does anything get behind the TV?"

That's around the time somebody starts pounding on our front door. We're not expecting anyone. I guess it shouldn't be a surprise. None of it should be. But bad news always is.

She looks at me and scowls. After we hear the feet tromp back down the steps and the car roar away, she goes to check the porch, returning with an official paper surrounded with wide swaths of blue tape. It's a bad joke signed by a judge. It declares eviction. She throws it in my lap.

"I guess we don't have to worry about our power getting shut off anymore."

"What am I supposed to do with this?" I wad it up and throw it at her as she walks from the room.

Mostly, I'm ready for another beer. I can almost get one on my own, but I can't because she keeps them way in back where I can't reach from my chair.

I wheel into the bedroom and ask her to get me another can. She's in the closet emptying her clothes from the rod and dropping them on the floor. I work myself into the bed using the railing and my one good leg. I can do it, just barely.

"What are you doing?" I ask

"Packing."

"Why?"

"Didn't you hear? The bastard bank is taking the house, baby. We have to go."

But leaving seems ridiculous. The whole building is filled with our stuff. It's huge. Two stories tall with a basement and an attic. We can't afford to move. It's impossible. "Call the fucking DHS. It's inhumane. They can't throw us out. It's snowing."

"The DHS isn't going to do shit."

It's funny then because she's found the big bottle of whiskey that I stashed in the back of the closet, just before the accident. I had forgotten about it. Holy shit. Happy day! She undoes the screw top and upends it.

"Hey, let me have some," I say. She guzzles a good amount. "You share with me — I share with you."

"Shut up," she says. "You don't share."

There is some truth to that. I know. It's getting late. She sits on the bed with me, and we take turns with the bottle. Already my stomach is hurting, so I chase with antacid.

After a while, she pulls off her clothes until she's wearing nothing but her bruises. "Where's my fucking underwear?"

"How could you lose them? Check the floor," I say. "Check behind the TV. How about the fishbowl? Oh, that's right. That's where the dead fish live." I close my eyes and listen to her flat feet banging around the room.

But then she is pouring more booze into my throat. "Thank you," I say, and I mean it. I am grateful. She settles back into bed and we drink more. I look over at her. She is turning orange. What are we eating to make that happen? Her lips are as chapped as her face.

"What are we going to do, sweetie?" she says.

"I don't know. Go to your aunt's place. Go to Martinez's. Find a shelter."

"I'm not staying in one of those places. There's no way."

After a while she says, "I want to fuck one last time in this crappy old house." That sounds alright I guess as long as she's careful about my leg. But first we need these special fuck pills. I have a couple more that I got from Martinez. I take one and wait for something to happen. "I don't think it's going to work," I say. "My dick is too drunk."

We lay next to one another. Me with my hand in the kink of hair between her legs. I don't want to look at her. I just want to lie there. I want to remember how she used to be. I try, but all I can think of is that nurse with the tattoo on her neck. Something about her reminded me of the circus. I used to try and dream about her. I'd sleep with my hand between my legs, and I'd think of her mouth and all the great things it might say if she let it.

Now my woman's got me in her rough fingers and is flipping me all around, but it's not working. After a while she swears and gives up. My dick is just such a useless flap of skin.

"Remember that time with the gasoline?" she says. She's smiling and glowing with whiskey.

"Yeah, that was funny as shit."

"You didn't have any sense then either," she says.

It's only that we were out of lighter fluid, so we used gasoline and dumped it all over the charcoal. The fire exploded. It flashed a bright pop and shocked the air, and an orange fireball rolled up the backside of the house. It was like a little bomb went off. The air shuddered, and we stood there with our salt shaker and our meat on a plastic plate and our beers and watched the siding curl and twist, stunned that something so stupid was happening right in front of us. Instead of trying to fix it, I kept thinking how I needed to start over, and try that again, and this time not fuck it up, and probably just move the grill a little farther from the building. Who cares about the mulberry tree anyway? Not me. The blackest, most foul smoke rose into the sky and got pushed back down between the houses and spun all around us.

"Get the hose!" she yelled, then smacked me in the head. I started running, only I couldn't get the thing to thread on the bib. I turned the water on, and it blew off the pipe. She was standing in the grass next to the gas can and yelling to hurry. My skin was pink and burned some. The hair on my arms had shriveled down to kinks. I was trying to get the threads to line up and make the hose work when she said, "Oh, fuck it. Forget it."

When I finally looked back up, I saw the siding had melted to stringy plastic, and the fire had burned itself out. She was laughing her ass off. We were okay. We didn't burn up our house or the neighbor's. I didn't start laughing until I realized the fire had singed her eyebrows to dark little stubs. Oh, shit. That was a good day. We grilled our meat and drank ourselves to perfection, and my dick still worked that night when she got hold of it. It worked fine. That was one of the last times.

She touches me now, still trying to get the thing to stand. I never meant to end up like this, unshowered and bad smelling with a watermelon foot, my woman unable to make my dick work.

"Relax," she says.

"How can I? We have two days before the bailiff comes with the cops or whoever. Before they throw us in the street. Or before I shoot them all in the head."

"We should just torch the place," she says. "We should."

"Damn right."

"I'm not kidding."

"I'm not either. I'd burn it right to the ground before I'd give it to those assholes."

She kisses me, which is a surprise because when was the last time she did that? It's been forever. And I know I'm on to something. My heart beats with the idea. It's pounding hard, with steady even thumps. It feels right, and somehow this talk of burning our life to the ground has got me feeling young again.

I know just where that gas can is too. It hasn't moved in months from its spot next to the garage door. We're only two blocks from the service station. Who cares what it looks like—my old lady, filling up her container so late at night with snow falling everywhere. Carrying it home in a laundry bag. It's not illegal to buy gasoline.

"Fuck those bastards," she says.

I can see a happiness, swirling in her eyes. She is kissing me. There is a wild heat in her mouth. Her tongue is a flame. She touches it to mine, and for the first time in months, she sets me alive. She sets me burning, and I'm filling with heat and blood, and standing up. God damn it—I'm standing up. I'm ready for her.

"Come on, baby," I say. "Come on."

SOBs and Dummies

Karen Minard

Remember the *Seinfeld* episode in which Kramer gets a gig playing a patient with gonorrhea? Well, there is a lot of that going on right here in metro Detroit (play-acting, I mean, not the clap).

Wayne State University's School of Medicine has one of the most comprehensive Standardized Patient (SP) programs in the nation. People, primarily actors, are hired on a part-time basis to portray sufferers of a wide range of complaints: headaches, shortness of breath (SOB), gallbladder attacks. The list goes on.

The whole idea was the brainchild of the late physician and educator Howard Barrows. Back in the 1960s, he was working at the University of Southern California, where he naturally had access to a lot of underemployed thespians. So he hired them, trained them, and set them to work. And nowadays, since 1991, there is even a nationwide professional association that regulates their ongoing work.

Behold the boon. For many first- and second-year medical students, interviewing and diagnosing these faux-patients represents their first face-to-face encounter with a live, human specimen, and gives them an opportunity to practice bedside manner. These neophytes are nervous. They flush. Some of their hands shake as they enter the room. Racing through their brains can be a long list of dos and don'ts: Do confirm the patient's name, practice active listening skills, make eye contact but don't stare the patient down. Don't stereotype or appear judgmental.

The pressure is on. They may only get seven to twelve minutes, tops. They know they're being recorded, videotaped; and, at any given moment, their professors may be watching.

And it doesn't get any easier as they advance in years through the program. By the time they become residents, more sophisticated training tools are in play. Pretend ER patients may fall out and have to be hooked up to a heart monitor, in which case they are swapped out with a mannequin or dummy that a student doctor would have to resuscitate.

Bag and mask! Chest compressions. Is there a pulse? No pulse. Let's shock 'em. Clear! Clear. No change. Let's do it again; this time, three hundred joules. Clear!

The SPs are an interesting group (actors usually are), who readily respond when the call goes out for SOBs and Dummies. The money isn't great, but at the end of the day, all they're really hoping for is a clap (applauses, that is, not gonorrhea).

Aaron Waterman

Down in Detroit

Terry Blackhawk

"Help me! I live in Detroit."
Sign taped to a tip cup on the popcorn counter
of the Maple Art Theater in Bloomfield Hills, Michigan—2003

Remember when the flight attendant had us prepare
for landing in "Honolu...oops, Detroit"
and the whole plane laughed?
And did I tell you the one about the ex-
Michigander who turned her back on me
& pointedly bestowed her life story (Border Collies
and Harry Potter included) on another woman
waiting for the Napa Shuttle after I winced
& replied yes, yes, **in** Detroit, I live
IN Detroit. Or the librarian from Auburn Hills:
his "You live down in Detroit?" still echoes
down, down, down.
                        Tough enough to love
this town without the shocked looks, dropped
jaws of fellow citizens who assume whiteness
unites as they eye you, reassessing instantly. Still,
"The D"—dear "D"—must have some magic in it.
How else to explain the doubled take, the suddenly shed
disguise? In less than an eye-blink, I've had men
switch from flirt to default mode, their mental
U-turns screeching with chagrin. Such power
in a word: to make a person give himself away.
        Dee-troit, *day–twah*, strait in French, place where waters
move swiftly.

Aaron Waterman

Playing Ball

J. M. Leija

Baseball is in my blood. Not in the traditional way, not in any way you're think-ing—I have lousy hand-eye coordination, and I've never been able to sight the ball well enough to hit it. I could probably field grounders, but I'm useless on pop-ups. The extent of my baseball career was a season of middle school softball that I quit midway through because I was afraid of learning how to slide.

It's the men in my family who are talented players. My pops, Grandpa Felix, was a five-foot-five Mexican powerhouse behind the plate: compact, quick, with a filthy mouth—before World War II and the Jefferson Assembly Plant and twelve chil-dren. My dad was a sandlot pitcher with a nasty curve before he went to Vietnam and, later, in the industrial leagues out of the Chrysler plants in Detroit.

My brothers (Baseball Gods bless them) are gay and indifferent. Jim's hands are made to play the piano, and Jeff's body is made to play football—for that matter, so is mine—and they quit baseball long before their high school years.

I can't say why I was pulled in and they weren't. Both of them, according to our father, had at least a bit of talent for the sport. I have none. But I love the long minutes of lazy play and the tense stillness right before a pitch. I love the bursts of too-fast movement, the baseball that only looks right when it's in motion. Maybe because there's peace in the three-hour contests, easy silence in the living room that doesn't need to be broken—though Pops talked more during baseball games than any other time, and a particularly good pitcher will almost always set off my dad's stories about old teams and old men and old times.

For my brothers, there's nothing beautiful about the behemoth baseball sea-son, the 168-game marathon. They couldn't seem to catch the rhythm of it, but I never heard anything else.

§

The rhythm of the season goes something like this: Sometimes I watch with a book in my hand. Sometimes I don't even look up for the hits. Sometimes, if I'm not in the park, I'm watching just to remember what it feels like to lose. Baseball is just as much wanting to win as learning how to take a loss gracefully. See: The Tigers' last three bids for the World Series.

With our latest failed attempt, this year makes twenty-six seasons of faithful waiting for me. For Dad it's twenty-nine. GrandPops had grown old during his twenty-nine-year wait, but he saw the Series in '68 and listened to it in '45. He told us both to be patient. The bald, cantankerous, hunched, ninety-year-old Mexican who could barely manage to wait ten minutes for my dad to cook his breakfast told us to be patient.

This is what Detroit baseball teaches you: patience, loyalty, fighting well for something worth fighting for—no matter how many times the other team knocks you ass backwards.

And what can I tell you about Detroit? My city is ripped down the middle. It's a place that is two parts post-apocalypse and three parts stubborn as hell. A city that keeps running on idealism mixed up with cynicism, covered over by pragmatism and sprinkled with the long-lasting poison of racism. But we still build your cars. We still make your music. We still bottle the best ginger ale in the world and have championship hockey and basketball teams and the only international marathon course in the world and my Tigers. My Tigers who bring together almost 42,000 people every time they play—black, white, yellow, red, green. My dad, the old Mexican, teases the young white girls who come for social Friday nights and icy daiquiris and have no idea how batting average is computed. There was the Arabic man in front of us who put a cap back on his young daughter's head, and my dad leaned forward to ask what her name was, and when the man looked back, Dad said, yes, this one's mine, the son I always wanted. My daughter Jennifer knows more about baseball than the Skipper.

Which is not expressly true, but you get the idea.

I looked at his daughter, and I wondered if I'd be teaching her in a few years. I don't get many Middle Eastern kids. I work on the north side of the city where my students have trouble getting home safely in broad daylight, let alone getting three square meals a day. But when they come into my classroom they ask me about the game the night before, they tease me if we lose, and on the day we lost the World Series in 2012 twenty-five fifteen-year-olds held a moment of silence at the beginning of each class period to mourn with me.

Detroit's like that. It takes you in if you let it, and it's impossible for me to explain because I'm of it. Because if you asked me to move away, the first thing I would say is, "But, my Tigers . . .," and when I said it, I would mean, but my students, but my parents, but my family, but my city.

And baseball is like that too. You spend so long at the games that the people in the seats around you start to become familiar. You high-five strangers when the big hits come. There's communal shaking of heads at each fielding error. I'd comment to my dad that the Ace's fastball is looking sharp and be answered by the seat in front of me—that his mechanics look just right, the arm coming over, the leg moving behind. Or the seat behind me might say that the Skipper threatened a stint in Toledo, a month in the minors if the pitcher didn't shape up. Just to show the men I know what I'm talking about, I'd mention the pitcher's record offhandedly, his last three or four starts were excellent, the WHIP was fairly low considering the line-ups he was facing, and what followed would be a conversation of a few minutes or half-an-hour with my father looking on bemused at the old black man and the middle-aged Italian usher arguing the viability of WHIP as a pitching statistic with his twenty-five-year-old half-white daughter.

It's an unforgivable cliché to say that the bleachers make us better. It's too much to believe that the sun in our eyes and the slap of the curve ball get us closer to who we wish we were. After all, there's still a club on the wheel of my car in the parking lot on Madison, and walking down Brush Street to the gates, there's a panhandler on each corner. There are still more white people in the luxury boxes, and at the end of the game, a traffic jam of spectators flees up I-75 and I-94, northward toward 8 Mile and the imaginary white line.

But inside the park, that fades. Look up and the view is marvelous, the deep centerfield built facing the river and the skyline instead of the desolation of Woodward heading north, out of the city. The orange Guardian Building, the blocky, pointed First National Building, the Penobscot with its radio tower and flashing red ball atop, all still standing proud, struggling to be maintained. Just the tip of the marquee of the Fox Theatre. Dad remembers when it was practically a flophouse, but it was restored to jeweled brilliance and plush velvet the year I was born, so I've never known it as anything but beautiful.

Lower your gaze to the walls of Comerica Park, and the simplicity of the playing field calls 42,000 fans together: the long white chalk lines, the quilted velvet green grass, the hard pillowed bases, dirt brushed smooth around them before the players take the field. And the D, my D, our D, the only embellishment, stamped proud and clear into the grass behind home plate.

The people, the city, it's all just a little bit easier when we're playing ball.

Detroit Tigers Playoff Game, Comerica Park, 2011 / Patricia Lay-Dorsey

Night, Briggs Stadium, 1960

Gail Griffin

I AM TEN THIS JULY, and I might be dreaming.

This is my birthday present. Strange, to be leaving for the city after dinner, driving into the hot night. Someone is taking me, down Woodward past the Zoo and the big cemetery where you hold your breath forever. Someone takes me straight into the city's heart, corner of Michigan and Trumbull.

Berberet behind the plate, Bunning on the mound.

We converge on it with all the other people. It looms, a big gray fortress. Who shepherds me through the crowd toward the numbered gate? Everything slows as I lean forward up the ramp, through a tunnel that is like a portal.

Cash, Bolling, Yost at 1st, 2nd, 3rd, Chico Fernandez at short.

A rectangle of night sky opens ahead. Brilliant banks of lights against the black. The low crowd hum, rising, like a sea sound. Then acres of green seats and then, below it all, the blazing diamond, emerald they should call it, nothing has ever been so green.

Left field, Maxwell. Right, Colavito, the outrageous Cleveland trade, who points his bat at pitchers like a gun.

Humidity haloes the lights. Men yelp HOTdogs, HOTdogs, PROgram. I am transfixed, dizzied by the vastness. My stomach lurches like on the Ferris wheel at the State Fair when it surges up and I can almost see Canada. How can an entire world fit inside a building? It's a gleaming secret, a hidden kingdom, an alternate planet shining at the core. Secret garden, emerald city, wonderland. The night breeze licks my skin. I might be dreaming.

In center, who else, the Center. The press calls him Mr. Tiger; the bench calls him 6.

Next year they will change the name of this place, call it after the team. In forty years, when I am older than my parents are tonight, they will tear it apart, seat by green seat, nail by bolt. But at the corner of Michigan and Trumbull there will be a ball diamond. As the city surrounding it festers and starves, some locals will keep it clean and mowed and watered. Some of them are here tonight, with me, dreaming.

Lost in Hockeytown

Matthew Lewis and Aaron Mondry

JOE LOUIS ARENA (JLA, or simply "The Joe") is hallowed ground in Hockeytown. Since relocating from Olympia Stadium in 1979 to this downtown riverfront arena, the Detroit Red Wings emerged from the lamented "Dead Wings" era, reaching the postseason each of the last twenty-two seasons (the longest such streak for any franchise in major American sports) and winning four Stanley Cups.

The arena itself, home to one of the most robust and energetic fan bases in all of hockey, deserves some credit for the Red Wings' success. The widely acknowledged elasticity of Joe's wood-backed boards—a unique feature among all other NHL venues— gives the Wings a distinct home ice advantage. It's not surprising that the Wings hold the NHL record (set during the 2011–2012 season) for the longest home winning streak (twenty-three games).

For the last thirty-five years, the Joe has been a great venue to watch a hockey game, but its days are numbered.

On February 4, 2014, the Detroit City Council approved a deal that would transfer roughly forty-five blocks of land in the Lower Cass Corridor neighborhood to the Detroit Development Authority. This entity will lease the land to Olympia Entertainment (at no cost), enabling the construction of a $450 million arena with assurances of $200 million in additional funds towards spin-off real estate developments in the district. Over half of construction costs are expected to come from public sources.

At the time of writing, Olympia Entertainment's plans for the new arena district are vague. But the project has captured the attention of local media, sparking public discussions about local hiring requirements and the potential gentrification of the Lower Cass Corridor.

But surprisingly little attention has been paid to Joe Louis Arena and its fate.

According to some reports, the state will foot the bill to demolish the Joe shortly after the new arena opens, but no firm guarantees exist. (It took the city eight years to demolish Olympia after the Wings relocated to the Joe).

A proper evaluation of JLA's successes and failures is necessary to inform the design and construction of a new facility and determine the fate of the riverfront site that the Joe currently occupies.

§

From prehistoric times when Native Americans settled in Southeast Michigan to the present day, one of Detroit's defining features and most valuable assets has been its riverfront.

During Detroit's industrial heyday, the western portion of the riverfront currently occupied by JLA and Cobo Center was heavily utilized as a transshipment point where raw materials were conveyed from lake freighters to railroad cars.

By midcentury, the west riverfront was seen by city planners as an area with great potential for redevelopment. The zeitgeist in major American cities was to restructure downtowns into regional entertainment destinations in order to combat the exodus of residents and tax base to rapidly developing suburbs. Detroit was no different.

In 1947, the Detroit Chapter of the American Institute of Architects contracted the firm Saarinen & Associates to develop a plan for a new civic center in downtown's west riverfront district. Most elements of this plan were largely incorporated into the city's 1951 Master Plan, which called for a widened Jefferson Avenue, a county-city municipal building (the Coleman A. Young Municipal Building), a "large landscaped plaza" on the riverfront (Hart Plaza), "a convention hall and a civic auditorium" (Cobo Hall and Cobo Arena), and a "downtown expressway loop" (the John C. Lodge Expressway) that passes underneath the convention center and connects with Jefferson Avenue. The near west riverfront of today looks remarkably like the conceptual drawings of the 1951 plan.

This period of massive scale downtown redevelopment coincided with the early stages of Detroit's long-term population decline. By 1960, when Cobo Center was completed, the city had 180,000 fewer residents than in 1950, experiencing its first loss of population since its founding. Many of these residents, however, had not left the metro area and still used downtown as an occasional playground.

The 1973 Master Plan continued the course set by the 1951 plan, prescribing further redevelopment of downtown into an entertainment destination. Special attention was given to the riverfront:

> The plan is designed to assist the city in making maximum use of its riverfront resource and to capture more fully the potential of the Detroit River as Detroit's most outstanding natural resource. A major objective of the city is to encourage and facilitate the development of the riverfront by *uses which derive a particular benefit from a riverfront location*. [emphasis added]

The plan is also the first document to suggest the development of a sports stadium near the civic center:

> Special commercial-residential areas are indicated just east of and west of the Civic Center . . . These areas should be developed with a major office headquarters complex, an international gateway, or *a major spectator sport facility of regional significance and supporting uses such as hotels, restaurants, major institutions, medium-rise offices, and apartments*. [emphasis added]

It is clear from these excerpts that planners expected the arena to have a harmonious relationship with its riverfront location and generate economic spillover for the rest of downtown.

By 1977, Mayor Coleman A. Young's administration was set on developing a new downtown arena for the Red Wings to retain them in the city. The Wings were playing in an aging Olympia Stadium, located on Grand River Avenue at McGraw, about three miles outside of downtown, and, according to Young, were threatening to move to the suburbs if the city did not built the team a new facility.

Young's administration identified a site along the west riverfront adjacent to Cobo Center that was occupied by underutilized warehouses, railroad yards, and docks. These impediments were demolished to make way for JLA, the final piece required to realize the vision for Detroit's downtown civic center set forth in its past two master plans.

Joe Louis Arena opened in 1979, and the Red Wings signed a thirty-year lease to make the Joe their home. Olympia Stadium was abandoned and eventually razed. Named for legendary Detroit boxer Joe Louis, the "Brown Bomber," JLA is one of only three current NHL venues not named for a corporate sponsor.

Joe Louis Arena is emblematic of the type of urban redevelopment project favored by the administration of Coleman A. Young: massive, modern, and expensive (see also: Renaissance Center, Millender Center, Riverfront Towers, Detroit-Hamtramck Assembly Plant, People Mover). It also was a major investment in downtown development, perhaps at the expense of neighborhood stabilization and core service provision.

As a way to showcase Detroit's downtown transformation on a national stage, Mayor Coleman A. Young, a lifelong Democrat, succeeded in attracting the 1980 Republican National Convention, where Ronald Reagan, a man Young once referred to as "Pruneface," accepted the GOP's nomination inside of Joe Louis Arena.

In his autobiography *Hard Stuff*, Young writes:

> Although Detroit was and is an overwhelmingly Democratic city, and although I have traditionally been at cross-purposes with the prevailing ideology of the Republicans, as a champion of the United States Constitution and the spirit of bipartisan cooperation, I fully supported their right to assemble and spend lots of money in our hotels, shops, and restaurants. I also appreciated what the national exposure could do for the city's image, which was still characterized by the '67 riot and out-of-date murder charts. And I was thrilled to see Joe Louis Arena enjoy such a conspicuous and honorable christening. At the same time, the convention was an event that I find difficult to index historically. To this day, it sticks in my craw that Ronald Reagan was nominated in the damn building that I put myself on the line for.

The choice of JLA as the site of Reagan's nomination acceptance speech was oddly fitting. Though Detroit was the largest majority African American city in the United States and had not elected a Republican mayor in decades, the Wings' fan base was and is dominated by suburban whites. Many of the people who packed the Joe on game days would come to be known as "Reagan Democrats" for their role in helping the Gipper win the White House. The 1980 GOP convention was appropriate symbolism, for it soon became evident that the Joe was designed for Detroit's visitors, not its residents.

Some have argued that Detroit has lacked effective planning over the last half century—that the city has failed to get things done. The large-scale redevelopment of downtown and the near-west riverfront, however, has been immense in scale and anything but ineffective. The planners succeeded in setting out a vision that would take shape in glass, concrete, and steel. Whether the effects of this thorough implementation have been good, whether, the '73 Master Plan made "maximum use of its riverfront resource," is another question entirely.

After the 1980 GOP convention, Joe Louis Arena would be used primarily as a venue for hockey and other large-scale entertainment spectacles like concerts and wrestling matches. The Red Wings play forty-one home games in a given season and a handful more in the event of a playoff run. Approximately twenty-five other sporting and entertainment events are held at the Joe throughout the year. Despite these uses, there are hundreds of days each year during which the arena sits idle.

Many variables determine an arena's true worth. The Joe's interior adequately provides everything necessary to enjoy a game or show, though it lacks many of the amenities and design features found in newer stadiums (e.g. LED screens and "gourmet" restaurants).

A sports venue's value to society, however, goes beyond a slick interior, ticket sales, and a winning franchise. We must also consider an arena's potential to enhance the liveliness of the city beyond its walls. Sadly, JLA's exterior is an unqualified disaster. It has glaring aesthetic shortcomings and lacks synergy with the rest of Detroit's central business district.

A basic concern of every fan attending a sporting event is arriving at his or her seat easily and on time. In the Joe's case, this process is needlessly troublesome.

The authors have experienced this difficulty firsthand. At one point, living about a mile from the Joe, it seemed silly for us to drive to games. Unfortunately for us, walking and cycling clearly were not primary concerns for JLA's designers. There is no obvious pedestrian route from anywhere in Detroit. Way-finding signage is all but nonexistent. The only hope for a first-time attendee is following the throngs of more seasoned fans who have learned the idiosyncrasies of approaching the Joe on foot. Coming from downtown, fans can make their way circuitously around Cobo or head away from the Joe several blocks south to the Riverfront or north to Howard Street and cross the Lodge freeway. A rarely used alternative is through the Jefferson/Lodge tunnel, which has a narrow sidewalk that stinks of exhaust and feels hazardous as traffic zooms by.

Pedestrian helplessness is the result of an infrastructure that itself seems to be confused; the modes of transit surrounding the Joe are poorly integrated. A skein of vertical silos and horizontal concrete tubes litter the landscape. The Jefferson/Lodge freeway creates a moat-like impasse directly in front of the Joe's entrance. The path is made less certain by the constant intrusion of walls, fences, bollards, and gratings.

Traversing any route by foot involves navigating a dystopian, gray-washed hardscape where the actual earth is entombed below several feet of concrete. Peeling paint and cracked concrete add to the sense of chaos. On days when the Joe doesn't host an event, a sense of disquiet and abandonment pervades the district not dissimilar to the depopulated "Zone" in Tarkovsky's *Stalker*.

Veteran fans and clever businesses have developed their own methods to cope with the Joe's lack of pedestrian access. Of course, a fan can pay fifteen dollars on top of his ticket and park in the nearby structure owned by the city and operated by Olympia Entertainment. One of the rare occasions the People Mover reaches capacity is before and after a Wings game, when patrons park in paid lots along Broadway or some other street with easy access to a stop.

Some choose an ad hoc transportation service provided by a bar or restaurant. Nemo's, a classic Detroit sports bar, offers free parking and round-trip shuttle service to the arena for a small fee. Nemo's is indeed within "walking distance" from the Joe, but no simple route exists—it's simpler and safer to board a bus.

In addition to being the hub of an impractical infrastructure, the Joe is also the locus of an uninspiring west riverfront district. Unlike the handsome barn-style brick structure of JLA's predecessor Olympia Stadium, the Joe is nothing more than a big white box in a sea of concrete. It resembles an industrial warehouse more than a sports venue, making for pitiful aerial footage during TV broadcasts. The monotony is striking.

The building's designers' indifference to aesthetics extends to its riverfront location. The Joe's bland presence cuts off views of Detroit's defining natural feature. Newer arenas such as Consol Energy Center in Pittsburgh incorporate glass atriums in their designs to make the most of their surroundings. JLA's architects, the Smith Group, did not heed the clear advice of the drafters of Detroit's '73 Master Plan to "[make] maximum use of the riverfront resource."

Despite its aesthetic and infrastructural shortcomings, JLA makes the city money. 10 percent of all spending at the Joe goes into city coffers. According to an article in *Crain's Detroit Business* published in August 2011, Detroit "collected $2.1 million from its share of concessions, suite leases and ticket surcharges, the rental fee and another $1.4 million from parking fees." This is not an insignificant sum for an insolvent city; however, a major sports arena should provide other indirect benefits.

Unfortunately, the economic benefit of the Joe is limited by its design, particularly its flaws in pedestrian access. In his book *Major League Losers* (the title implies his conclusion), Mark Rosentraub critiques conventional wisdom on the value of sports venues. He measures their economic worth as "people from outside the city or county attend[ing] a game and spend[ing] money they would not have spent in the city or county for some other type of entertainment." Rosentraub assumes that individuals will budget a set amount for entertainment that remains constant regardless of what they spend it on.

Since a good percentage of the fan base is suburban, each Wings game presents an opportunity to capture outside spending. Unfortunately, local businesses receive little to no boost from the Red Wings apart from the clever few that offer shuttle services. JLA's spillover effects are inadequate given the Wings consistent success and loyal fan base.

The Joe's disconnect from the city incentivizes fans to purchase the fifteen dollar parking voucher rather than navigate the unfriendly terrain. When patrons park at the Joe Louis structure, they watch the game from opening face-off to finish. Then they leave. There is no incentive to arrive early or linger afterward. There are no storefronts, restaurants, or bars (i.e. opportunities to spend money) within eyesight of the Joe. This is the greatest of the Joe's many failings.

The Joe is so disconnected from the rest of the life of downtown that one can rightly ask why it was even built there.

§

In the article "Cities and the Financing of Sports Facilities," Adam Zarestsky writes, "When studying this issue, almost all economists and development specialists . . . conclude that the rate of return a city or metropolitan area receives for its investment is generally below that of other projects."

Despite economic indicators, America has an infatuation with building the most advanced sports venues. Construction costs regularly run into the hundreds of millions and can only be afforded by the agglomeration of many rich investors or through significant municipal subsidies. The Joe was paid for entirely by the city of Detroit at a cost of $30 million, significantly less than what it costs to build stadiums today, even when adjusted for inflation.

Sports franchises perpetually demand newer venues and subsidies to build them, threatening to move if their demands are not met—and they often are. Medium to small markets are the victims in this "sports war," as Rosentraub calls it. Cities build expensive new stadiums and often abandon the old ones. Stadium subsidy critic Charles Mahtesian describes America as suffering from "throwaway stadium syndrome."

The Pontiac Silverdome, former home of the Detroit Lions, is one such example. Since the Lions moved to Detroit's Ford Field in 2002, the Silverdome has hosted some one-off events such as a monster truck rally, an international soccer exhibition match, and a welterweight boxing bout. According to a Metro Times article, as of 2009 the Silverdome cost the city of Pontiac $1.5 million in upkeep annually. Since Pontiac was over $100 million in debt at the time—and has since gone into receivership of the state—the city decided to sell the stadium at auction with no minimum bid. The Silverdome, once the largest NFL stadium and built at a cost of $55.7 million (unadjusted for inflation) in 1975, sold for an embarrassing $583,000. In the absence of a buyer, the fate of a vacant stadium is demolition, as was the case for Olympia and Tiger Stadiums in Detroit. Neither of these sites has been redeveloped.

What will become of the Joe once the Wings vacate? In the near term, Detroit will be saddled with a facility that has poor ties to commercial zones and would prove exceptionally difficult to adapt for purposes other than professional sports and major entertainment events. The State of Michigan has reportedly pledged funds to demolish the Joe once the new arena opens, but there are no guarantees when this will happen.

It's difficult to propose a worthier plan than demolition. Current plans for renovating neighboring Cobo Center do not include the potential of utilizing an abandoned Joe Louis Arena or the land on which it sits.

Already a cause of considerable pedestrian confusion, the problems created by aging, unsightly, and intrusive infrastructure around the Joe will also need to be addressed upon the Wings' departure. These walkways and parking structures are open only during the evening of events at JLA. This infrastructure, essentially a part of JLA itself, will be rendered immediately obsolete and need to be torn down along with the Joe, adding to the already considerable expense.

We can only hope that the designers of the new arena are cognizant of the many reasons why Joe Louis Arena fails.

Aaron Waterman

Wayne County Building / Aaron Waterman

Streetlights

Michael Eugene Burdick
and Francis Grunow

Have streetlights lost their way in the dark? In the day, beautiful, finial-topped bishop hats and crooks, dripping pineapple globes that once diffused the intense light of the carbon arc, held aloft by ancient wood, rusted fluted steel, and now, even fiberglass. At night, moon towers weep from afar and the past, their curb-bound brothers and sisters cannot illuminate Detroit for Detroiters to take center stage. So much of the best of a city's life happens after the sun goes down.

Lily-Livered New Yorker Seeks Lion-Hearted Detroiters

Jaclyn Trop

WHEN I FIRST CAME HERE, in June 2008, it was supposed to be for a summer. Twelve weeks, and home by Labor Day. My friends back in Manhattan and Brooklyn thought it was funny that I, for some divine reason, was the one plucked to spend the summer after graduate school interning at a newspaper in Detroit, of all places. My only research was a night spent at home watching *8 Mile*, my hand jammed in a bowl of popcorn as I imagined finding this mythical street and meeting Eminem.

But instead of danger on the streets of Detroit, I found desolation. After I arrived at the airport and wrangled my two oversized suitcases into the trunk of my rental car, the GPS mounted on my windshield directed me through a downtown where everything seemed closed and nary a person passed through my peripheral vision. Driving down Woodward, I imagined a trio of tumbleweeds pulling up alongside my Ford Focus, as if to underscore how far from New York I'd really come.

The device guided me to a place on the edge of the city that I suspected was a housing project. The summer sublet I rented sight unseen had a lobby encased in bulletproof glass, but none of the furnishings, utilities, or riverfront views promised in exchange for the lofty sum paid. After a trip to the grocery store across the street— harrowing for reasons I cannot enumerate here—I spent my first Detroit evening in the dark, cross-legged on the living room floor, eating Cheerios out of the box one by one.

Though I didn't stay in that particular apartment long, disbelief in the dys-functionality suddenly surrounding me eventually gave way to self-defeat, which the bankrupt city seemed to be indulging in also. But the end of my summer internship coincided with the start of a national economic recession, and I accepted the paper's offer of a full-time job. That's how twelve weeks somehow turned into six years. For several of those years, lion-hearted Detroiters took to the task of convincing me that my first week here was not a normal one. Now I've been in Detroit so long, I don't even know what passes for normal. And that is my proudest achievement.

It took me many years to discover that life here is what's tucked within Detroit's crevices. But to access the spaces in between, it's necessary to learn to accept the kindness of strangers, the ones who brought me to my first school bus demolition derby and to my first visit with a renowned astrologist, who took one look at my star chart and said, "Everything in your life makes sense except for Detroit. Why the hell are you in Detroit? This says you're supposed to be in Southern California, by the beach."

This is not an easy city. But it's the city where I grew up, albeit in my late twenties, long after most people may admit to growing up. I had a lot of growing up to do.

Mine is a story of taking a bad situation and making it worse before making the choice, eventually, to make it better. It's a story of healing the gaps between lofty aspirations and lesser realities. And that's the story of this city too. Weird, wild Detroit, the Midwestern frontier with a pockmarked panorama and a passionate populace. After the better part of a decade, we have grown ambivalent together.

Motown Atlantis

Chantay "Legacy" Leonard

This city belongs to me.
Skinned knees on concrete
tasting my child blood.
Swallowed saliva and screams
like shadows on river sunsets.
Wind steals breath.
Stirring dreams
into dancing phantoms
in this clinched fist Mecca.

Motown, soundtrack of struggle
and prayers in sanctuaries.
Mingling pain with the rainfall
Windows washed in gilded tears.
Silt of heat and madness settling
on a city thriving in three months of sun.
Nine months of cold freeze us below zero.

Detroit, birthplace of smiles.
Breaker of hearts and
bringer of adolescent rage.
Lost innocence in your streets.
Lost my mind
and found revelations

and poetry
and art
and hip-hop
and jazz
and funk
and Black Bottom and my People and

God.

Found womanhood
and loved her dearly.
Found self
and loved her dearly.

Engraved in my soul.
No price renders me amenable
to part with the real estate of my heart.
Squatters' rights are revoked.
Ownership is written in veins
& the love of Detroit.

Strange City

Chantay "Legacy" Leonard

I live in a strange city.
Here suffering is eloquent.
Joy a sudden trauma.
Curse words taste delightful.
Kisses are bitter lies.
Eyes make the best promises.

Potholes and behavior patterns
buckled under the stress of living.
How do the children find shapes
in whispering clouds and starless nights?
How do we imagine ourselves out of hell?

Heaven is music rising
from hollow throats, torn paper,
scratch cuts, ancestral beats,
sobbing strings and flaring horns.
Supplicating hands, arched backs
Sweat testaments on dance floors.

Holy days are reserved
after Saturday night exorcisms.
Sermons spit in poetry.
Redemption found in the mouth
of street corner griots
and those who just need to speak their peace of mind.
Our pain is not professional.

Rubble scattered in random neighborhoods
Flower beds and organic gardens.
East and West side.
Financial divides, color lines and imagined issues.
We are all struggling.
One hand deep in our pockets.
The other gripping smoked glass skylines
attempting not to shatter with the rising sun.

Thanksgiving Day Parade Down Woodward Avenue, 2012 / Patricia Lay-Dorsey

Dally in the Alley, 2011 / Patricia Lay-Dorsey

The Detroit Virus

Shaun S. Nethercott

I. Yes, But...

Well, once again my decision-making is suspect. I woke up the other morning and said, I am going to take a long loaded bike ride . . . just to see if I can. I had Wes drag my big yellow bag out to the garage. I attached the trailer to the bike and went zooming off. It was an absolutely beautiful morning in Detroit, one of those clear blue spring days where the humidity is low and the air almost sparkles.

I cycle down to the riverfront, where the first thing I see is a fisherman pull a twelve-inch walleye from the water. He is one of the many riverside and boating fishers partaking in the annual walleye run. The riverfront is teaming with people, even though it is pretty early in the morning. I am tickled at the range of people enjoying the sight of the glistening water.

There are people of all ages, all colors, women in hijab and men in hard hats. There are youth with pants four sizes too big walking along side hipsters with pants two sizes too small. There are grandmas with squirmy little grandbabies sitting on lawn chairs watching their menfolk throw fishing line in the water and watch the red floaters bob, bob, bob downstream. There's a white-suited sailor scrubbing the sidewalk leading up to the Detroit Princess party boat. There's even a few tourists having their picture taken with Underground Railroad monument, standing alongside bronze statues, living and metal people peering mightily toward the promised land of Canada just across the water.

I am a bit of spectacle with my full touring regalia: helmet and gloves, sunglasses, and most importantly, my low-slung bright yellow trailer. I see the occasional walker turn a full 180 degrees to watch me go by. It tickles my fancy to imagine they think me some exotic traveler making my way across the city on this beautiful morning.

I leave the waterfront on the other side of the Milliken State Park, past the swaying cattails and invasive phragmites of the restored marsh. I note my mileage (on my new bicycle computer, of course) and see that I have traveled just over four miles from my Southwest Detroit starting point. I told Wes I was going to go down to the Belle Isle bridge and back. He shook his head ruefully and said, "That far?" I stuck out my chin at him: "It's only fifteen miles!"

I curve back to the riverfront by Stroh River Place. I love this part of the RiverWalk, with its restored buildings, boutique hotels, boat slips, and Coast Guard station. I am intrigued to see a Coast Guard cutter being lowered to the water. The giant crane looks like a huge praying mantis.

I am still feeling good as leave the riverfront and cross the bumpity, bumpity cobblestone streets of old Iron Street, noting the ten or fifteen new murals depicting the strengths and beauty of Detroit on the sides of a rusting wreck of old factory. I am still feeling good as I pass by the big empty lot just before the Belle Isle bridge. Years and years ago, it was an industrial site for Goodyear, I think. It has been too toxic for redevelopment and has sat fallow as long as I have lived in Detroit. Today, it is abuzz with activities. All along the fence is banner after banner proclaiming the upcoming Belle Isle Grand Prix. The lots are being set up as service areas for the racing crews.

Well, here is where I made my big mistake. If I had "the sense god promised a billy goat," as my mother would say, I would have turned around right then and there, and started my homeward trek. This was the distance I told Wes I was going to ride. It was a good run.

But no. Blinded by the beauty and ecstasy of my ride thus far, I turn my bike onto the Belle Isle bridge. It is gorgeous to look up and down the river. There are geese, and swans, and ducks paddling with their babies. I am committed now. The Belle Isle run, if I circle the island is another 5.5 miles. But hey, I'm feeling good, so why not?

I pull my trailer up the bridge and notice for the first time, how much drag the trailer creates on a hill. I huff and puff up the bridge, then scream down the other side, pushed by the trailer, find the corner to the right quite a bit of challenge with the push of the trailer, and drive right into . . . a construction zone.

All along the river road, giant concrete barriers are being put up along the race route for the Detroit Grand Prix. The barriers block the view. I weave in and out of heavy equipment, tents for workers, and trucks moving racing gear. The workers stare at me. I am sure they are wondering what kind of fool would bring her bike and trailer into their midst.

A few miles later, I finally leave the construction zone, then pull into the party zone on the riverfront. It is a mess. Even though there are garbage cans every twenty-five yards or so, there are cans, bottles, wrappers, dirty diapers, food containers, and more everywhere. On the grass, on the road. It is disgusting. This is the place where scads of teens hang out on weekend nights. Every Monday morning, the place is a wreck. The debris used to be gone by Tuesday, but now, with budget cuts, it is still sitting there on Thursday.

I leave the garbage zone, and I notice that I am really starting to get tired now. I have gone about ten miles, and it is starting to get hot. I reach for my water bottle . . . empty. I am not halfway around the island, and I still have the whole way back to go.

By the time I get to the Detroit Yacht Club, I am only three-quarters around the island and I am pooped. I stop in some shade, move my pannier to the other side because my right leg is hurting, record a note on my phone, and call Wes. I tell him to meet me at our favorite Coney Island in half an hour. He asks me if I am all right. What can I say?

The ride back to the diner is long and hard. The river is still beautiful, but the temperature is up. When I make it back to the Underground Railroad monument, I am in "just keep going" mode. The tenth mile turns over so slowly on my bike computer. When I turn away from the river and make my way up the gradual climb up to Michigan Avenue, my legs hurt, my forearms ache, and my shoulders are starting to knot.

I stop at a red light to catch my breath, having climbed the bank of the former Cabacier's Creek. While I pant, a friendly fellow tells me, "You don't need to wait for the light, there ain't no traffic." I wait anyway, glad to be off my bike, even for a moment.

I meet Wes at the Coney. I am sweaty, sore, and beat. I have cycled eighteen miles without a break, carrying a forty-pound load. Wes laughs out loud as we listen to the recording I made of my pitiful self at the yacht club. ("Eleven miles in, I'm tired and out of water and don't know how I will keep going.")

"What did you expect?" he asks.

I say to him, "Well, I have answered my question."

"What question is that?"

"Can I do twenty miles in a shot."

The answer is "yes, but . . . " After I cycle the remaining two miles home, I have gone twenty miles, sure enough, but I will be sore tomorrow, and not worth much today.

Yes, I can ride twenty miles with a load, but I have also shown, once again, that I am poor, poor, poor at recognizing reasonable boundaries. And not just on bicycle rides, I assure you.

II. The Detroit Virus

The reason we are going to cycle across America has nothing to do with needing to get out of Detroit. On the contrary, we want more and more to stay. Our friend Craig describes Detroit as having "dysfunctional charisma." That is certainly true. Is there a place that has more imminence, in which the future is more present? Or that the past has more painfully marked?

We moved here in 1989, one of the first to catch the Detroit virus. We fell in love with it, with its potential, with its stark and beautiful contradictions. Since then, we have transmitted the virus to a number of people. They come to work at the Matrix Theatre Company, or with Detroit Summer, or with the Mercy Volunteer Corps, or some other organization working at street level. They find what we did: that is possible—nay required—to do really important work here that makes a real difference in people's lives and the shape of the city. They also discover that is possible to find a whole bunch of people doing similar transformative work.

Care a lot about food? You can be at the center of movement building a new food system tomorrow. Want to shape the way different ethnicities work together? Come and do the work tomorrow. Do you want to live in such a way that culture and cultural expression are embedded in daily life? That's the way we roll in the D. Once you get a taste for it, once it gets under your skin, you will find yourself staying or wanting to return over and over.

Want to break away from mindless consumerism, me-first-ism, and deadening conformism? Come on down. There's hardly a store where you can spend your money. You won't long survive without social capital in this environment where being connected and having relationships is the truer form of currency. To what will you conform in this wilding ecosystem? There is no monoculture—just the bumptious biodiversity of a vibrant ecosystem.

None of this freedom is free, of course. This is the city of do-it-yourself. That means policing your own neighborhoods, organizing your own recycling, creating your own recreation leagues, cleaning and mowing your own streets. You will pay taxes and wonder what you get for your investment.

You'll have daily contact with people this culture serves not at all. Most people here are just trying to make a way out of no way. Some of the choices available and taken are terrible. No doubt, Detroit will give you a daily dose of ugliness to go along with its freedom and social vibrancy.

You don't ever recover from the Detroit virus. Everywhere else seems pale and innocuous and inhospitable by comparison. We love/hate/need this place. It is a power spot whose vibrations are both thrilling and exhausting.

No, we prepare to ride, not to run away from Detroit, but to run toward ourselves and in so doing, run on a purer fuel when we return to the exasperating, endearing, delicious, delightful wreck of a city.

Detroit's Good-Food Cure

Larry Gabriel

WEEKEND MORNINGS are the busiest days of the week at D-Town Farm. That's when up to thirty volunteers from across Detroit come out to till the earth and tend the crops at the seven-acre mini-farm on the city's west side. They sow, hoe, prune, compost, trap pest animals, build paths and fences, and harvest—all the activities necessary to grow healthy organic fruits and vegetables to nurture the community. There is a 1.5-acre vegetable garden, a 150-square-foot garlic plot, a small apple orchard, numerous beds of salad greens in a couple of hoop houses, a small apiary, and a plot of medicinal herbs such as purslane, burdock, and white thistle.

"One of our goals is to present healthy eating to people," says Malik Yakini, Director of the Detroit Black Community Food Security Network (DBCFSN), which runs D-Town. "We think that healthy eating optimizes a good life generally. A diet close to nature allows the human body to function the way it is supposed to function."

D-Town is set in one of the city's greenest areas, a former tree nursery in the 1,184-acre River Rouge Park. It's a couple of miles downriver from Ford Motor Co.'s famous Rouge plant, which once employed 100,000 workers, and about a mile upriver from Brightmoor, a formerly devastated neighborhood that boasts no fewer than twenty-two community gardens. The Detroit City Council granted use of the land to DBCFSN in 2008. Deer ate up most of the first crop: Volunteers who planted 750 tomato plants harvested only about five pounds of tomatoes. Now a fence keeps deer out, and other pests such as raccoons and possums are trapped and released far from this feeding ground. There are even a few apple trees on the grounds that are tended by folks from Can-Did Revolution, a recently established family canning company.

§

Nowhere in the United States has urban agriculture taken root as prolifically as in Detroit. Earthworks Urban Farm, Feedom Freedom Growers, GenesisHOPE, Georgia Street Collective, and other community gardens have stepped up to help create a healthier and more self-empowered food system. The Catherine Ferguson Academy for Young Women runs a small farm on the school's grounds to teach students about nutrition and self-sufficiency. This gardening renaissance has been growing for over two decades, since the Gardening Angels, a group of southern-born African Americans, began growing food and passing their agricultural knowledge on to another generation.

There are more than 1,200 community gardens in Detroit—more per square mile and more per capita than in any other American city. The number of community gardens is just a fraction of the number of kitchen gardens that families grow in yards and side lots. Locals are learning more about nutrition and feeling the health effects of eating the food they grow.

"You're only as healthy as the food you eat," says Latricia Wright, a naturopath who champions natural, uncooked, unprocessed foods. "It's all about the minerals in the food."

§

Kesia Curtis began gardening with her parents, Wayne and Myrtle Curtis, at Feedom Freedom Growers community garden. The 29-year-old had suffered from debilitating allergies since she was 17, often missing work, unable to sleep, and suffering from sinus infections.

"I was pretty much living on Benadryl or other allergy medications year round," says Curtis.

About a year after she started gardening, Curtis began eating a vegan diet—no animal products at all. She reports that her allergy problems have gone away except for some mild symptoms in the spring.

"My parents started the community garden, and it felt like a natural thing to do with my family," says Curtis. "The more I became involved with it the more I started asking a lot of questions about food from the grocery store as opposed to what you can grow. Tomatoes that you grow taste and smell different from what you get at the store. I had tasted tomatoes before but a local tomato had so much more flavor. . . . I can't imagine someone being a farmer and it not changing your health and making some kind of positive impact on your life."

§

DBCFSN's goals include empowering African Americans within the food system and providing fresh, healthy foods in an area where access is not a given. Detroit was among the communities declared food deserts by researcher Mari Gallagher in 2007. Food deserts are communities where the kinds of foods necessary to maintain a healthy diet are unavailable, unaffordable, or difficult to get to.

"The types of food we live closest to—along with many other factors—are related to our health." reads Gallagher's report. "Unless access to healthy food greatly improves, we predict that, over time, those residents will have greater rates of premature illness and death from diabetes, cardiovascular diseases, cancer, obesity, hypertension, kidney failure, and other diet-related complications. Food imbalance will likely leave its mark directly on the quality, productivity, and length of life... "

Those are the effects of malnourishment. Eating healthy food is the cure. This is particularly important in Detroit, where the population is 82 percent African

American, the unemployment rate is twice the national average, and the poverty rate is high.

African American adults are twice as likely as non-Hispanic whites to be diagnosed with diabetes, almost twice as likely to be hospitalized for diabetes and more than twice as likely to die from the disease. "Type Two diabetes is epidemic," says nurse practitioner Yvett Cobb, a member of DBCFSN. "I've spent twenty-three-plus years in emergency medicine and critical care nursing. I've seen a lot of complications of diabetes. I've seen a lot of limbs being cut off."

Even though African Americans suffer from higher rates of these diet-related illnesses and are more likely to develop kidney failure or complications from high blood pressure, all American demographics are suffering increasingly from the effects of bad diets and lack of exercise. Getting Americans to eat a healthier diet is a growing concern, exemplified by First Lady Michelle Obama's championing of gardening and former New York City Mayor Michael Bloomberg's recent attempt to ban sugary sodas sixteen ounces or larger at restaurants. In cities across the nation, an urban agriculture movement focused on overcoming food scarcity and promoting healthy eating is driving a local food movement.

"It gives me so much tremendous hope that change can happen as we make gardening accessible," says Cobb, who also teaches yoga and has trained as a practitioner of the Tree of Life raw food diet. "As people get more and more into gardening and learning its benefits, it gives me hope. Planting gets you closer to nature, keeps your joints loose, and you get to eat all these nutritional things."

A host of infirmities could be avoided simply through eating well and getting some exercise. Both can be accomplished through gardening.

"Health is impacted by eating fresh produce," says Yakini. "Food loses some of its nutrient density over time as it is transported long distances. Food that is produced nearby and eaten soon after being harvested is more nutrient-dense and has a stronger health impact. Also, gardening is great exercise—bending, standing, and using muscles that you might not normally use."

§

Dinah Brundidge was already in the throes of changing her life when she discovered gardening. She had just kicked a twenty-year alcohol and crack addiction and was going to the Capuchin Soup Kitchen, near where she lives, to eat and shower. She asked one of the Capuchin brothers about a job, and he referred her to the gardening training program at Earthworks, which supplies food to the soup kitchen. Brundidge's recovery was still shaky, and she hadn't settled on how to spend her time when she wasn't getting high.

"I started the gardening work," says Brundidge. "It was like a healing process with me, a connection with the earth. The gardening motive gave me a purpose in life. I was used to the everyday drug life. I had tried many years to kick, but what really did it for me was urban gardening. The beauty of planting a seed and seeing food grow, that gave me a purpose. Having my hands in producing it really captivated me. How people really cared about growing healthy food."

Brundidge reports gaining weight and losing the skinny drug addict look.

Her skin became healthier, and a chronically bad complexion cleared up. She reports feeling better, although she suffers from arthritis. But the biggest thrill seems to come from doing for others.

"I invite people to come out to my community garden, and they can't believe I'm doing this and enjoying it," she says. "Last year in the community garden I did so well—I fed a lot of people."

There's plenty of space for gardening in Detroit; most people live in houses and have yards. And there are some twenty square miles of vacant land in the city that could easily be converted into arable land. Many gardening activists say they think of food as medicine. If that's the case, there is potential for a lot of healing in the city.

Planting Seeds of Hope

Grace Lee Boggs and Scott Kurashige

In 1988, WE IN DETROIT were at one of the great turning points in history. Detroit's deindustrialization, devastation, and depopulation had turned the city into a wasteland, but it had also created the space and place where there was not only the necessity but also the possibility of creating a city based not on expanding production but on new values of sustainability and community. Instead of investing our hopes in GM, Ford, and Chrysler and becoming increasingly alienated from each other and the Earth, we needed to invest in, work with, and rely on each other.

Through no fault of our own, we had been granted an opportunity to begin a new chapter in the evolution of the human race, a chapter that global warming and corporate globalization had made increasingly necessary. In its dying, Detroit could also be the birthplace of a new kind of city.

As Detroiters, we were very conscious of our city as a movement city. Out of the ashes of industrialization we decided to seize the opportunity to create a twenty-first-century city, a city both rural and urban, which attracts people from all over the world because it understands the fundamental need of human beings at this stage in our evolution to relate more responsibly to one another and to the Earth.

In pursuit of this vision, we organized a People's Festival of community organizations in November 1991, describing it as "a Multi-Generational, Multi-Cultural celebration of Detroiters, putting our hearts, minds, hands and imaginations together to redefine and recreate a city of Community, Compassion, Cooperation, Participation and Enterprise in harmony with the Earth." A few months later, to engage young people in the movement to create this new kind of city, we founded Detroit Summer and described it as a multicultural, intergenerational youth program/movement to rebuild, redefine, and respirit Detroit from the ground up.

Living at the margins of the postindustrial capitalist order, we in Detroit are faced with a stark choice of how to devote ourselves to struggle.

Through Detroit Summer, urban youth of a lost post-1960s generation, whom many adults had come to shun, fear, and ultimately blame for so many ills, became a part of the solution to Detroit's problems. Recalling how the Freedom Schools of Mississippi Freedom Summer had engaged children in the civil rights movement, we asked Detroiters to just imagine how much safer and livelier our neighborhoods would be almost overnight if we reorganized education along the lines of Detroit Summer; if instead of trying to keep our children isolated in classrooms for twelve years and more, we engaged them in community-building activities with the same audacity with which the civil rights movement engaged them in desegregation activities forty years ago: planting community gardens, recycling waste, organizing neighborhood arts and health festivals, rehabbing houses, and painting public murals.

By giving our children and young people a better reason to learn than just the individualistic one of getting a job or making more money, by encouraging them to make a difference in their neighborhoods, we would get their cognitive juices flowing.

Learning would come from practice, which has always been the best way to learn. In Detroit Summer we combine physical forms of work with workshops and intergenerational dialogues on how to rebuild Detroit, thus further expanding the minds and imaginations of the young, old, and in-between. Instead of coercing young people to conform to the factory model of education, the time has come, we say, to see their rebellion as a cry for another kind of education that values them as human beings and gives them opportunities to exercise their Soul Power.

Detroit Summer began in 1992 and has been an ongoing and developing program for more than twenty years. Since 2005, it has been organized by a multiracial collective of twenty-something young people, many of whom have been a part of our past summer programs. With this younger generation now at the helm of leadership of the Detroit Summer Collective, the organization continues to tap the creative energies of urban youth.

Some skeptics question whether a program such as Detroit Summer can make much of a difference, given the magnitude of the city's problems. They doubt that a program, which at its greatest capacity involved sixty youth, could have an appreciable effect in stemming the crises of school dropouts, violence, and incarceration that are stealing lives by the thousands. They ask how tending to a handful of gardens, painting one or two murals a year, and fixing up a house or vacant lot here and there can address the blight that has taken over much of the urban landscape. And they lament that small dialogues—between youth and elders, between neighbors, between people of different backgrounds, and between activists from various cultural and political traditions—cannot match the force of large demonstrations involving tens of thousands.

What they don't understand is that our goal in creating Detroit Summer was to create a new kind of organization. We never intended for it to be a traditional left-wing organization agitating masses of youth to protest and demonstrate. Nor did we intend that it become a large nonprofit corporation of the sort that raises millions of dollars from government, corporations, and foundations to provide employment and services to large populations.

Both of these forms of organizing can be readily found in Detroit and all major cities in the United States, but the system continues to function because neither carries the potential to transform society. By contrast, our hope was that Detroit Summer would bring about a new vision and model of community activism—one that was particularly responsive to the new challenges posed by the conditions of life and struggle in the postindustrial city. We did not feel this could be accomplished if control of our activities was ceded to the dictates of government or the private sector, even though this meant that we would be working on a small scale. However, by working on this scale, we could pay much closer and greater attention to the relationships we were building among ourselves and with communities in Detroit and beyond.

The result has been that we have been able to develop the type of critical connections—of both ideas and people—that are the essential ingredients of building a movement. The best metaphor Detroit Summer has come up with to characterize itself is "planting seeds of hope."

What has developed through both conscious organizing drives and the actions of many individual residents is a significant urban agricultural movement in Detroit. All over the city there are now thousands of family gardens, more than two hundred community gardens, and dozens of school gardens. All over the city there are garden cluster centers that build relationships between gardeners living in the same area by organizing garden workdays and community meetings where participants share information on resources and how to preserve and market their produce.

When I think of this incredible movement that is already in motion, I feel our connection to women in a village in India who sparked the Chipko movement by hugging the trees to keep them from being cut down by private contractors. I also feel our kinship with the Zapatistas in Chiapas, who announced to the world on January 1, 1994, that their development was going to be grounded in their own culture and not stunted by NAFTA's free market. And I think about how Detroiters can draw inspiration from these global struggles and how—just as we were in the ages of the CIO unions and the Motown sound—our city can also serve as a beacon of hope.

Living at the margins of the postindustrial capitalist order, we in Detroit are faced with a stark choice of how to devote ourselves to struggle. Should we strain to squeeze the last drops of life out of a failing, deteriorating, and unjust system? Or should we instead devote our creative and collective energies toward envisioning and building a radically different form of living?

That is what revolutions are about. They are about creating a new society in the places and spaces left vacant by the disintegration of the old; about evolving to a higher humanity, not higher buildings; about love of one another and of the earth, not hate; about hope, not despair; about saying YES to life and NO to war; about becoming the change we want to see in the world.

The Kidnapped Children of Detroit

Marsha Music

IT HAPPENED SUDDENLY.

One day, we'd be outside with our friends, black, brown, and white, on the warm summer days before the start of the next school semester, playing jacks and hopscotch, riding bikes. The next day, our white friends would be gone. One of my friends might have said, "Hey, we're moving," in the middle of a game of kickball, but there were few real goodbyes, or promises to keep in touch, at least not of the type associated with the farewells of kids who had been together all or most of their lives.

In the jumbled mishmash of childhood memories during those transitional years, I recall worshippers leaving the neighborhood church after Sunday service, descending the dark oak staircase from the sanctuary. In their hurry to get on with their day, it looked, from my kid-level gaze, like a stampede, during those late summer days when our integrated neighborhood was disassembling before my eyes. I will forever associate the Sunday-dressed hemlines and dark-suited pants legs with their rushing, running to get away—from us—the worshippers with whom they had just fellowshipped before God.

White parents were grabbing their kids and escaping from Detroit—and from its enclave Highland Park, where I grew up, a then solidly middle-class enclave within Detroit's borders, "a city within a city." Often, it appeared as if they left in the dark of the night, the moves seemed so clandestine. This sense of them leaving virtually "overnight," packing up and disappearing, was likely due to the white parents' reluctance to speak to their black neighbors—whom they often treated with pronounced neighborliness—about their impending moves, knowing that their departures were largely because of the color of the neighbor's skin.

I wonder if some worried that their daytime public neighborliness contrasted with their nighttime kitchen table planning, their plotting to get out of the neighborhood as soon as they could manage. Perhaps they forbade their children to speak to their darker friends about the frenetic packing going on inside. Certainly they didn't want to speak of the reason for the moves *with* the reason for the moves—though everyone, of course, knew why. Or they talked to their black neighbors pretending "those new people moving in" didn't include those with whom they commiserated. But one by one, the white families left their old homes, tree-lined streets—and us—behind.

I'm sure that some of my friends listened to their parents in their homes, as they spoke of us with words of racial hatred, while outside they smiled across backyard fences, making small talk about sod and azaleas. Perhaps black and white neighbors rarely communicated at all during this time, when our neighborhoods were soon to be re-segregated. For there was virulent racism and ill-disguised violence in areas throughout the city, and even in the late '60s, blacks could not shop in many stores. Detroit was replete with episodes of unrest and even terror in the competition over housing: whites demanded that blacks be stopped from moving into an east side housing project, which precipitated a race riot in 1943. A generation before that, Ossian Sweet, a black medical doctor, was met with mobs as he moved into his home in a white neighborhood on the near east side. Clarence Darrow would defend Sweet's right to defend his hearth, and establish, "A man's home is his castle."

My grandmother told me the tale of how, in the early '50's, she had saved up the money she made as a domestic to buy a home on Clairmont and Woodward Avenue. On the eve of the closing, the realtor came to her with the news that the white block club did not want her in the neighborhood. Grandmother refused to change her plans and sent him packing, but the realtor returned—the block club offered to pay her back the money for her down payment, plus some. Well, Grandmother took the money and ran, to a neighborhood on the near east side.

She moved near Conant Gardens, a community developed on land that had been owned by an abolitionist named Shubael Conant, who refused to sell his land to developers who sold homes with the restrictive covenants that were common in Detroit. That community was one of the first strongholds of black middle class home ownership. My grandmother chuckled at the end of her story, at the irony that by the time of her telling, thirty years later, Clairmont and Woodward was all black—the block club had obviously been unable to buy its way against the changing times.

Some whites, I'm sure, were not influenced by race baiting, but left the city solely to experience the new suburban living, or to be closer to the jobs that had moved across 8 Mile—though they knew that they were going to communities where blacks were not allowed. Some of my friends' parents were surely anguished about the decision to move, sometimes leaving behind equity and often their own parents who refused to go. Did my young white friends listen to their planning with conflicted feelings? Never mind; the torrent of change and fear that was driving white Detroiters could not be turned off.

§

And so, I say, my friends were kidnapped; snatched away from their homes, often under cover of night or in rushed moves that split friends apart for a lifetime. I watched Mary Martin fly as Peter Pan on TV, and it seemed my friends too had been lured to a Neverland. Did they cry when they were taken, missing their old friends? Did they think of what they'd left behind when they woke in homes with no deep porches or rich oaken banisters? On streets with no lush, ancient trees? Where it took a car—or two—to get anywhere, with lawns so new that grass had yet to grow? But my friends settled into their new neighborhoods, like children do, adapting and making friends, happy for the new. Glad to be in the modern houses on spread-out blocks, out of the brick behemoths, two-family flats, or frame houses of the old, dense Detroit streets they'd left behind.

One of my friends remembers the overwhelming fear that consumed his family's 7 Mile and Wyoming household—a relatively new community even then—as they prepared to leave for Southfield. He confirms that, in so many homes, there was a sense of *panic*, as his family prepared not just to move, but to *escape*, as if from some impending debacle. He recalls how, in the innocence of youth, he wondered about the reason for the terror; for it appeared to him that the black folks moving into his neighborhood were at the very least, in his child's eye view of social classes, the most non-scary folks in the world: doctors, teachers, professionals. To him, they seemed to be of a clearly higher social standing than most of the folks who were desperately moving out.

§

It happened rapidly. An elder of my church remembers that he started school in his west-side neighborhood as only one of two black children in his kindergarten class; the rest were white, mostly Jewish. By the time he left elementary school, only two white children remained. The Jewish exodus (so to speak) was an integral engine of the movement of blacks across the west side, for they were willing to break the "restrictive covenants" in deeds that had prohibited homeowners from selling to blacks, and often Jews too. Block by block, as whites moved out, Jewish homeowners replaced them and then blacks followed, with synagogues transformed into black churches.

After the 1967 riots (also known as The Rebellion, in which my own father's record business was destroyed), the post-conflagration trauma was so great, and the consciousness of Detroiters so altered by the eruption of turmoil and destruction, that it came to be said that "all the white people left after '67," a false narrative that persists even today. In reality, the exit from the city began after World War II. By 1952, construction of Northland Mall in suburban Southfield had begun, to accommodate the mounting loss of population from Detroit; it became the first and largest suburban mall in the country. Whites bought new houses in the newly built suburbs, when the schools in the city were still quite good; and really, there was no reason to go except for a change of scenery and a good use of the G.I. Bill. But blacks were straining against the "James Crow" segregation of the North, and out of the packed neighborhoods in which they had been confined. Millions of whites were worked into moving van frenzy by word-of-mouth from one home to the other, and in rabble-rousing community meetings. Importantly, real estate interests and developers—often individually, and surely cumulatively, stood to profit greatly in that rapid turnover of properties.

Some real estate companies grew rich from this race-based trading in hope and fear. Some actually identified neighborhoods and instigated the whole cycle in order to profit from the terror-driven turnover of properties. One of my friends remembers when her white neighborhood was inundated with flyers, exhorting Whites to get away from the coming dark hordes. Neighborhoods had brief, uneasy periods of "integration," marked by racial tension and police brutality, before the last of the whites would move out.

This practice is called "block-busting," creating a crazy, predictable cycle—whites move out, lured by real estate interests to leave for white communities; blacks move in and fear is escalated; whites become panicked and, egged on by the realtors and block associations, sell at ever lower prices in order to hurry and "get out." This also happened when blacks moved into communities paying higher rents or land-contract prices than the whites before them. The more whites that moved out, "dumping" houses onto the market, the more blacks were able to move in; many of them were on a lower economic rung than those who preceded them, creating a self-fulfilling prophecy.

The result—a neighborhood that had solidly "middle class" or even affluent blacks and whites, had, in a few short years, a preponderance of poorer families. These were families who were often less able to maintain the lifestyle in that neighborhood, and brought with them the problems that their children often had in rough projects or poorer communities. Many of my black friends from harsher backgrounds had a difficult time adjusting to the quiet, tree-lined life on their new blocks. In each neighborhood, they used the drugs that were flooding into the communities to deal with their anxieties of being planted in these short-lived "mixed" communities, where they were often not wanted by blacks *or* whites. This accelerated the neighborhood's crime and disruption—the final death-knell for many communities.

Another factor I remember that prompted moves to the suburbs was violence, whether threatened or carried out, against white kids, who were often tormented by black kids in outbursts of retaliation for wrongs real or imagined. Later, there was the bussing of children to schools as a tactic to address the re-segregation of the community, with the rise of agitators who whipped up a frenzy of racial fear and hatred, driving whites further across 8 Mile. A group of us stared down Klan sympathizers on the east side, singing "We Shall Overcome" in the streets during chilling episodes of anti-bussing turmoil.

As people left, so did businesses; the suburbs, an appealing, all-white commercial for modern living, were a vacuum sucking life and enterprise across 8 Mile. Many of the largest industrial enterprises had gone first, finding in the undeveloped suburbs the acres of land needed for the modern, stretched-out production facilities that could not be built in the property-dense city. Companies left behind the tight neighborhoods where residents could and did join organizing efforts of all kinds, and by the 1960s, there was a freeway system to move out workers and supplies. Detroit's infrastructure, dependent upon on the former booming tax base and not the new, shrinking one, was less able to maintain services. With joblessness that became epidemic, and the ruination of great sections of the social fabric via the scourge of crime and drugs, the urban community spiraled ever downward.

This circular, self-fulfilling, nasty game of musical chairs perpetuated itself in the Detroit area, as in other "changing" communities nationwide. As whites departed en masse, the problems they most feared came to pass. In many areas, blacks moved into a level of community that they were suddenly allowed to afford, yet unable, in the long run, to maintain. Or, blacks with means moved into communities with aged housing stock, making the next years of living a fait accompli of devastation. Later, the mortgage crisis sealed the deal of destruction in many neighborhoods.

Even so, after white flight, there were still many communities full of dedicated residents who were paragons of home ownership, with houses and lawns maintained in consummate displays of steadfast residential pride, despite the challenges of living in the midst of flight and escalating blight. Detroit still has exquisite blocks in affluent neighborhoods, and handsome, solid homes on working-class blocks—maintained by those who remained. My own neighborhood, Lafayette Park, was built in 1960 to staunch the flow of white Detroiters outward. It is still a model of diverse urban living, with those who live there committed to the city.

During the departures in the late '60s, my next-door neighbors were among the last whites to leave our block; we had lived next door to them all of our lives. He was president of a bank on Woodward Avenue, and on the verge of retirement, but I guess the changing times had become too much; whites were now moving at the sound of the drum beat of the Black Power era. The banker's wife, a white-haired lady who had known me since I was a babe, literally burst into tears across the backyard fence at the sight of my brand new sixties Afro, and asked me tearfully why I had to wear my hair "like that." Shortly after, it was time for them to go. Some waited *too* long and moved into white communities in which they were branded by the stigma of having come from neighborhoods that had long ago turned black, never to be viewed as really equal to the whites in their new towns.

But they were all transfigured into new souls called suburbanites, though many maintained an undying love-hate relationship with the neighborhoods they were forced by fear to leave behind, often viewing the city and its current residents with a mixture of contempt, dismay, and nostalgia. They pined for the old glory days of the city, following the stories of its streets and politics as if they lived within its boundaries; following the news of its decline like a lover both grieving and gloating over the travails of a lost love. In the late sixties, many of my black friends began to leave too, as the city declined, for segregation had finally lifted its weight from the close-lying suburbs. So they too moved across 8 Mile.

§

Over the years I've known many whites that work in downtown Detroit, and savor the scary, sexy power of being comfortable in the city—at least during work hours. They're proud of their ability to move around the urban landscape and to have at least daytime friends of other colors. Most whites in the Detroit area stay away, especially from anywhere outside of downtown, fearful of the community. But some former Detroiters are pulled back to their old neighborhoods—some intact, some bedraggled, some where the old home is completely gone: the decay and destruction an affirmation of their parents' obviously right decision to leave, so long ago.

I wonder if, sometimes, they suspect that somehow, that decision itself, multiplied across Detroit, was at least part of the cause of all the mess here now. That maybe the mass flight, the leaving of property all over town, the years of being egged on by whispers and realtors to cross 8 Mile, was all part of a nasty, self-destructive Monopoly game—with real properties and real lives. I wonder what might have happened in Detroit if there had never been this flight—if whites had held on and resisted the racial manipulation, if blacks had been able to push back the plague of unemployment, drugs and crime, if we had been able to live in Detroit, all at one time.

It is hard for many black Detroiters to comprehend the sense of belonging, or even entitlement, that many whites feel toward Detroit, even decades and states removed from living within city boundaries. There are those—black *and* white—that have never lived in Detroit proper, or even in Michigan, who gaze (through Google Maps) at old family homesteads, and vicariously traverse old family blocks from afar. They regard Detroit as *their* city. And I believe that the sense of being part of Detroit proper—despite living well outside of its borders for generations—is rooted in that mass evacuation. Like the movement of blacks across the city after the destruction of Black Bottom, this was an unprecedented transfer of community; and suburban parents did their best, as they understood it, to build better lives. But fear of a black city made my friends Detroiters in Exile.

Folks ask the question, Will Detroit come back? Well, Detroit never left—but three generations did. Today, regardless of the city's efforts at redevelopment, most know that they will never again live in the city of their affection. Most of the old neighborhoods are much too far from livability for them, and the city's core and urban lifestyle holds no appeal for those accustomed to suburban sprawl. But more and more of the children and grandchildren of the Kidnapped Children are finding their way home. But despite ghost-town metaphors, blank-slate pronouncements, and prairie-land descriptions of Detroit, they find the city already occupied, and these strangers in a strange yet familiar land must learn to share it with those who held on.

As the quality of life in the outer ring of the city declined, forcing more blacks to look outward to escape crime and to seek neighborhood stability, property values fell in the near suburbs—because of the age of those cities and their housing stock, because of the mortgage crisis, because of blockbusting that is still alive and well (though sometimes with more subtle practices than before). As many of the suburbs become less "exclusive" and downtown living grows, owners who held onto core city properties during the crash of their values watch their fortunes rise, after contributing to the city's vistas of decay and destruction. For decades, they held onto ravaged, abandoned structures as they waited for a time of profitability, contributing to much of the urban devastation for which black city dwellers have been reviled.

Younger generations of whites from the suburbs, who don't have their forebears' fear of the city, are moving in the opposite direction, proudly proclaiming their Detroit provenance and reveling in their new urban life. Some of them recreate suburban segregation in the heart of the city; they want life in Detroit—without Detroiters. But many more look to the city as the most exciting place in the world to live in diversity. They are led by the artists' community, the creative seraphim of redevelopment; they are the coal-mine canaries of our scorched and burned land. This community of artists has been waiting and creating for such a time as this, for Detroit has always been a city of artists. Our extreme maker impulse in Detroit is now unfettered, no longer consumed by the past that propelled, yet devoured, so much of the city's creative energy. They are side by side with those who've held on for decades, trying to make "a way out of no way."

As in South Africa, there is a need for atonement in Detroit and its suburbs. We need a restorative movement to heal what has happened here, as the working people of this town ,competed against themselves over the right to the good life. We have to share stories about the experiences of the past era. As we move forward in Detroit, there must be a mending of the human fabric that was rent into municipal pieces with the divisions of city and suburbs. Small, continual acts of reconciliation are called for here, as sections of the city rise again.

As the children and grandchildren of the Kidnapped Children make their way to the city, I believe that it is the responsibility of the rest of us—those who, like me, never left—to welcome them; to tell our new residents the real city narratives, to share the truths of what happened here from all sides. There are deep schisms that never should have been, that were orchestrated by self-serving interests; we must work to mend these wherever possible. Our new residents have a contagious earnestness, energy, and hopefulness, reminiscent of the movements of our past, and there's a difference between their sincere efforts for change and the machinations of those who would manipulate the urban crisis to their own benefit, casting us aside like flotsam in the name of progress.

Yet it is likewise the charge of our new Detroiters to acknowledge and respect those already here—to actually *see* longtime residents, *for we are not invisible.* Our new residents must learn from our history and experience; they must work alongside our earlier residents and their children in Detroit's renewal, for they are the bedrock of the redeveloped city and the nexus of its future. Let us figure out—this time—how to live together, so that more children and grandchildren of the Kidnapped Children can come home to live in the city, so that more of our children and grandchildren might also be part of a truly new Detroit. Young people come to be freed from their lives of suburban isolation and the crippling divisions of this region; they want to be a part of a new urban reality. It is true that some say that they have come to save Detroit, but *I* say, they come to Detroit to *BE* saved.

Aaron Waterman

Contributors

Terry Blackhawk (www.terrymblackhawk.com) is the author of six collections of poetry, including *Escape Artist*, winner of the John Ciardi Prize, and *The Light Between* (WSU Press, 2012). Her poetry has appeared in many journals and anthologies as well as online at Verse Daily, Poetry Daily, and The Collagist. She founded Detroit's acclaimed writers-in-the-schools program, InsideOut Literary Arts Project, in 1995, shortly before retiring as a Creative Writing and English teacher from Detroit Public Schools. "Down in Detroit" appears in *Poetry in Michigan / Michigan in Poetry* (New Issues Press).

Grace Lee Boggs has been an activist for more than sixty years. She is the author of the autobiography *Living for Change*. "Planting Seeds of Hope" was first adapted for *YES! Magazine*, a national, nonprofit media organization that fuses powerful ideas with practical actions, from the book *The Next American Revolution: Sustainable Activism for the Twenty-First Century* by Grace Lee Boggs with Scott Kurashige (University of California Press).

adrienne maree brown is a writer, facilitator, doula, and sci-fi scholar living in Detroit.

Michael Eugene Burdick is an illustrator and designer in Detroit. He graduated from the Illustration program at the College for Creative Studies in 2009 and quickly found work creating graphics and commissioned artwork for local businesses, organizations, and publications. There's a conveniently loose nail on the east wall in his studio to hang his coat up.

Detroit native **John Carlisle** is the author of the book *313: Life in the Motor City*, a collection of feature stories about people and places in Detroit, and is a columnist with the *Detroit Free Press*. Prior to that, he was a columnist for the *Metro Times* (where "Desolation Angel" and "The Fixer" first appeared, in slightly different form), and was named Journalist of the Year by the Detroit chapter of the Society of Professional Journalists for his coverage of the Motor City.

Nichole Christian is a writer and Detroit native who began her career as a staff member for some of the nation's top news outlets, including the *Wall Street Journal*, *Time* magazine, the *New York Times*, and the *Detroit Free Press*. She is co-author of *Canvas Detroit* (Wayne State University Press). Her work also appears in the books *Dear Dad: Reflections on Fatherhood* and *Portraits 9/11/01: The Collected "Portraits of Grief"* from the *New York Times*. She holds a BA in journalism from Wayne State University's Journalism Institute for Media Diversity and lives in suburban Detroit with her husband and daughter.

Anna Clark is an independent journalist living in Detroit. She has written for *The New Republic*, *NBC News* online, *Pacific Standard*, *The American Prospect*, and other publications. She is a former Fulbright fellow in Kenya, and in 2012 she founded Literary Detroit. She is a board member of Write A House and a writer-in-residence in Detroit high schools through the InsideOut Literary Arts Project. She graduated from the University of Michigan and from Warren Wilson College's MFA Program for Writers.

David Clements' photography has been exhibited regionally and nationally. He is the author of *Talking Shops: Detroit Commercial Folk Art* and photographer of *Art in Detroit Public Places* (Wayne State University Press). He continues to produce and direct television productions for advertising, business communication, and documentaries.
More information at davidclementsproductions.com.

Nandi Comer is currently the poetry editor of *Indiana Review*. She is pursuing a joint MFA/MA in Poetry and African American and African Diaspora Studies at Indiana University. She has received fellowships from Virginia Center for the Arts, Cave Canem, and Callaloo. She is the winner of *Crab Orchard Review*'s 2014 Richard Peterson Poetry Prize. Her poems have appeared or are forthcoming in *Callaloo*, *Spoon River Poetry Review*, *Sycamore Review*, and *Third Coast*.

Desiree Cooper has been a columnist for the *Detroit Free Press* and a frequent commentator for National Public Radio's "All Things Considered," the BBC's "Americana," and PBS. She also co-hosted and served as senior correspondent for the American Public Media's "Weekend America." Currently the communications director for Planned Parenthood Mid and South Michigan, her fiction has been published in literary journals including *Best African American Fiction 2010*, *Callaloo*, and *Tidal Basin Review*. She was a founding board member of Cave Canem, a national residency for emerging black poets, and is currently a fellow of Kimbilio, a national fiction residency for African American writers. A booster for Detroit, she founded an apparel company, Detroit Snob, in 2010. "For the Long Haul" first appeared, in slightly different form, in *Between the Lines*.

John Counts is a crime reporter for *The Ann Arbor News* and a contributing editor for the *Great Lakes Review* literary journal, where he runs the web-based "Narrative Map" project at www.greatlakesreview.org. His fiction has been published in the *Chicago Reader*, *Kneejerk*, and *Monkeybicycle*. His nonfiction has been featured in the *Wayne Literary Review* out of Wayne State University, where he earned his English degree. He also holds an MFA from Columbia College Chicago. He lives in Whitmore Lake with his wife and two daughters.

Aaron Foley is a Detroit native and writer living on the city's west side. He writes about the automotive industry and local culture for several outlets. "We Love Detroit, Even If You Don't" first appeared, in slightly different form, in *Jalopnik*.

Larry Gabriel is a Detroit-based writer and musician. He is the former editor of *Metro Times* and *UAW Solidarity* magazine, and was a writer and editor at the *Detroit Free Press*. He was named Best Columnist by the Association for Alternative Media in 2012 for his Stir It Up column in *Metro Times*. "Detroit's Good-Food Cure" first appeared, in slightly different form, in *YES! Magazine*, a national, nonprofit media organization that fuses powerful ideas with practical actions.

Veronica Grandison is a freelance music writer from Detroit and graduate of the University of Michigan-Dearborn, where she earned a bachelor's degree in Communications and a minor in Music History. She is a regular contributor to the online publication Model D, and has written for *Metro Times*, *Real Detroit Weekly*, and *Deadline Detroit*. She runs a music blog called Roots, Rhythm and Rhyme, which presents social discussions about African American music. "Game Not Over" was first published, in slightly different form, in Model D, a publication from Issue Media Group, a Detroit-based company.

Gail Griffin is a poet and nonfiction writer born in Detroit. Her latest book is *The Events of October: Murder-Suicide on a Small Campus*, an intimate study of two student deaths at Kalamazoo College, where she taught for many years. Her essays have appeared recently in the *Chattahoochie Review* and in the collection *Southern Sin: True Stories of the Sultry South and Women Behaving Badly*.

James D. Griffioen is a freelance writer and photographer, raising his family in Detroit. He blogs at Sweet Juniper (www.sweet-juniper.com), where an earlier version of this essay first appeared.

Francis Grunow is a public policy consultant at New Solutions Group, and is primarily an urbanist. He is a native Detroiter and has former lives as a city planner, preservationist, filmmaker, and law student. Grunow lives on Cass Park, catty corner to the Masonic Temple and a new building named Cass Tech, where he did not attend high school.

dream hampton is a writer, filmmaker, and organizer from Detroit.

Kofi Handon is the founder, president, and lead photographer for Loves Life Photography, a full service photography company officially established in 2004. Kofi is an organic photographer showcasing the natural beauty of all things through his lens. Having always had a passion for photography even as a child, Kofi is dedicated to capturing life's most precious moments through digital imagery. Given the weight of day-to-day struggles, he believes it is of the upmost importance to seize moments where the load of life is lightened by smiles, laughter, hidden messages and love. "There is no greater feeling than immortalizing a moment in history."—Loves Life

francine j. harris's first collection *allegiance* was a finalist for the 2013 Kate Tufts Discovery Award and the PEN Open Book Award. Her work has appeared in *Ploughshares*, *Rattle*, *Ninth Letter*, *Indiana Review*, and others. Originally from Detroit, she is a Cave Canem fellow and is the Front Street Writers Writer-in-Residence in Traverse City, Michigan for the 2013-14 school year. "what you'd find buried in the dirt under charles. f. kettering sr. high school (detroit, michigan)" appears in *allegiance* (WSU Press).

Kat Harrison is a lifelong Detroiter who embarked on a new career as a freelance writer after many years in the corporate world. She is currently working on several writing projects and editing a novel based in pre-Civil War New Orleans and Boston.

Ryan Healy studied poetry at the University of Michigan under Ken Mikolowski. He worked as an author of Detroit's first guidebook in over thirty years and has been published in Motor City Muckraker. He lives in Detroit.

Steve Hughes is the writer and publisher of the long-running zine *Stupor*. He manages the Public Pool art gallery in Hamtramck, Michigan, where he runs his award winning reader's series the Good Tyme Writer's Buffet. He is the author of the 2011 book *Stupor: A Treasury of True Stories* and his work has appeared in numerous publications, notably *Fence, Crimewave USA, MacGuffin, Publik Enema*, and *Monozine*. A previous version of "Stand" was published in 2008 as part of a collaborative project with artist Lisa Anne Auerbach called *Tract House*.

Nina Misuraca Ignaczak is a devoted, lifelong resident of the beautiful and battered Detroit area. She writes about the intersection of people and place, and she is inspired by those who work to make their communities shine. She lives in Rochester, Michigan with her husband, son, and daughter.

Tyehimba Jess is a native Detroiter who now lives in Brooklyn. He's the author of the poetry book *Leadbelly*, and he teaches at College of Staten Island. "Infernal" was first published in *Meg Tuite's Exquisite Duet*.

Scott Kurashige is the author of *The Shifting Grounds of Race: Black and Japanese Americans in the Making of Multiethnic Los Angeles*. "Planting Seeds of Hope" was first adapted for *YES! Magazine*, a national, nonprofit media organization that fuses powerful ideas with practical actions, from the book *The Next American Revolution: Sustainable Activism for the Twenty-First Century* by Grace Lee Boggs with Scott Kurashige (UC Press).

As a cultural producer, arts advocate and director of Maison LaFleur, **Ingrid LaFleur** has developed and organized art exhibitions both nationally and internationally. Ingrid began her academic studies with a B.A. in Art History from Spelman College and went on to pursue her M.A. from New York University with a concentration in Museum Studies and Sociology. In 2012, she founded Maison LaFleur, a boutique art advisory firm. Maison LaFleur specializes in emerging and established artists from Africa and the diaspora. Ingrid has worked with artists and arts organizations in New York, Atlanta, Paris, Johannesburg, Cairo, and a host of other cities. "Detroit: A City of Superheroes" first appeared, in slightly different form, online at the Urban Innovation Exchange (UIXDetroit.com).

Born in Washington, DC, in 1942, **Patricia Lay-Dorsey** brings her training as a social worker and over three decades as a visual artist to her work as a photographer. Her photographic practice focuses on seeing herself and others from an insider's point of view. Patricia's self-portrait book, *Falling Into Place*, was published by Ffotogallery in 2013 and is available worldwide. Her photo essays have been featured in *Newsweek Japan* and online by the *London Daily Mail*, CBS News, ABC News, the *New York Times*, and *Slate* magazine. She has had museum and gallery exhibits of her work and won a first prize in the 2013 Photo Annual Awards in Prague. In 2008, Patricia was the Detroit location scout for Academy Award–winning director Davis Guggenheim's documentary film, *It Might Get Loud*.

J. M. Leija has her MFA from the Bennington College writing seminar in Vermont. She currently works as a teacher and writer-in-residence for the InsideOut Literary Arts Project in her hometown. From April to October, you can find her most often in the pavilion seats at Comerica Park.

Chantay "Legacy" Leonard is a Detroit writer, author, performance poet, and activist. Her literary work has been featured in Stanford University's *Black Arts Quarterly*, and the anthologies *Estrology* and *The Bandana Republic*. Her debut book of poems, *I Have Come Forth By Day: A Woman's Evolution* (2011), is available on Moore Black Press.

Matthew Lewis is a writer who lives and works in Detroit. He has no plans to leave. His writing has appeared in Model D, *The Detroit Free Press*, *MLive*, and *Belle Isle to Eight Mile: An Insider's Guide to Detroit*.

Joseph Lichterman grew up in Huntington Woods, Michigan. Joseph reported on Detroit for Reuters, primarily covering the city's bankruptcy. He previously reported for *Automotive News* and Michigan Radio. Joseph was also the editor-in-chief of *The Michigan Daily*, the independent student newspaper at the University of Michigan. Joseph is now a staff writer for the Nieman Journalism Lab at Harvard University reporting on innovation in journalism.

M. L. Liebler is an internationally known and widely published Detroit poet, university professor, literary arts activist, and arts organizer, and he is the author of thirteen books including the award-winning *Wide Awake in Someone Else's Dream* (Wayne State University Press 2008). *Wide Awake* won both the Paterson Poetry Prize for Literary Excellence and The American Indie Book Award for 2009. He is the founding director of both The National Writer's Voice Project in Detroit and the Springfed Arts: Metro Detroit Writers Literary Arts Organization. He was recently selected as Best Detroit Poet by *The Detroit Free Press* and Detroit's *Metro Times*. In 2010, he received The Barnes & Noble Writers for Writers Award with Maxine Hong Kingston and Junot Díaz. His groundbreaking working-class literary anthology from Coffee House Press, *Working Words: Punching the Clock and Kicking Out the Jams*, received The Michigan Library Notable Book Award for 2011. His website is www.mlliebler.com.

Tracie McMillan, a freelance journalist whose work centers on food and class, is a senior fellow at the Schuster Institute for Investigative Journalism at Brandeis University. Her first book, *The American Way of Eating: Undercover at Walmart, Applebee's, Farm Fields and the Dinner Table*, was a *New York Times* bestseller. McMillan's journalism has appeared in the *New York Times* and *National Geographic*, among other publications, and has won awards from the James Beard and Sidney Hillman foundations. A Michigan native, McMillan now lives in Brooklyn.

Omar Syed Mahmood is a student at the University of Michigan in Ann Arbor and an alumnus of Detroit Country Day School. He has for as long as he can remember had a love for language and the pen. He wishes he lived two hundred years ago, although a log cabin in God's Country does have its merits.

Peter Markus is the author of a novel, *Bob, or Man on Boat*, as well as three books of short fiction, the most recent of which is *We Make Mud*. A new book, *The Fish and the Not Fish*, will be out in the Fall of 2014. He is the Senior Writer with the InsideOut Literary Arts Project of Detroit and was a 2012 Kresge Arts in Detroit fellow.

Jamaal May's first book, *Hum*, received the Beatrice Hawley Award from Alice James Books and an NAACP Image Award nomination. Other honors include the Spirit of Detroit Award, an *Indiana Review* Prize and fellowships from Cave Canem, Frost Place, Bucknell University, and Kenyon College. Recent poetry can be found in *The Believer, The New Republic, Poetry, Poetry Daily, Best American Poetry 2014*, and the anthology *Please Excuse This Poem: 100 New Poems for the Next*

Generation (Viking/Penguin, 2015). Recent prose appears online from *Poets and Writers Magazine* and *Poetry*. From Detroit. he co-directs the Organic Weapon Arts Chapbook and Video Series with Tarfia Faizullah. "There Are Birds Here" and "Per Fumum (Through Smoke)" were first published by *Poetry*.

Ken Mikolowski is the author of three books of poetry: *Thank You Call Again, little mysteries*, and *Big Enigmas* (Past Tents Press) "January in Detroit" appears in *Big Enigmas*. His new book *THAT THAT* will be published by Wayne State University Press in 2015. He teaches poetry writing at the Residential College of The University of Michigan. For more than thirty years he and his late wife, Ann Mikolowski, edited, published, and printed art, poetry, and collaborations as The Alternative Press.

Shannon Shelton Miller is a native of Detroit. She worked at the *Detroit Free Press* from 2005–2010 as the beat writer for Michigan State University sports. Now living in Dayton, Ohio, she works at the University of Dayton and contributes freelance pieces to newspapers and magazines.

Karen Minard is a Detroit poet, short story writer, and essayist. She was born and raised in this great city and has lived here most of her life. She writes to make sense of her life, create art, and delight her friends at dinner parties.

Aaron Mondry is a writer of fiction and occasional journalism. He has lived in Detroit for almost four years.

Tracey Morris is a Detroit-based poet and author. She is a columnist with Motor City Muckraker and she published a book of poetry called *You Said You Wanted to See Me Naked: An Autobiographical Poem Cycle*. Her poetry was included in the anthology *I Said It and I Meant It: The Soul of DUPAAS Poetry Anthology* and was a finalist in the 2013 Springfed Arts poetry competition. "Up in the Morning & Off to School in Detroit" first appeared, in slightly different form, in Motor City Muckracker.

Marsha Music grew up in Highland Park, Michigan, the daughter of a legendary pre-Motown record producer. Marsha is a self-described "primordial Detroiter," and for many years she has written about the city's music and its past and future. She is a noted presenter and has contributed to important anthologies, narratives, and an HBO documentary on Detroit. She was a 2012 recipient of a prestigious Kresge Literary Artists Fellowship and has received accolades for her one-woman show, *Live On Hastings Street!* She resides in Lafayette Park, Detroit, and writes a blog called *Marsha Music—A Grown Woman's Tales of Detroit* (http://www.marshamusic.wordpress.com).

Shaun S. Nethercott is artist, activist, and theatre administrator. She is the cofounder of Matrix Theatre Company, which has been using the transformative power of theatre to change lives build community and foster social justice since 1991. She and her husband Wes recently completed a bike ride from Portland, Oregon, to Portland, Maine, and are in the midst of completing a book about this amazing odyssey.

Ingrid Norton's essays, fiction, and reportage often address the history of cities, race, and religion in America. Her work has appeared in *Building Community Resilience Post-Disaster* (American Bar Association, July 2013) and in publications such as *Dissent, The Guardian, Next City, Religion & Politics*, and *The St. Ann's Review*. "Letter From Detroit" first appeared, in slightly different form, in *The Los Angeles Review of Books*.

Matthew Olzmann's poems have appeared in *Kenyon Review, New England Review, Inch, Gulf Coast, Rattle,* and elsewhere. He's received fellowships from Kundiman, the Kresge Arts Foundation, and the Bread Loaf Writers Conference, and he has served as a writer-in-residence for the InsideOut Literary Arts Project. Currently, he teaches at Warren Wilson College and is co-editor of *The Collagist.* "Gas Station on Second Street" appears in his book *Mezzanines* (Alice James Books).

Deonte Osayande is a poet, performer, and instructor from Detroit, Michigan. He has toured North America multiple times, and his poems have been published in over a dozen literary journals, including *Emerge Literary Journal, Prime Number Magazine,* and *Camroc Press Review.* When not doing poem-related stuff, he enjoys family, naps, traveling, and reading.

Keith A. Owens is an award-winning freelance writer, columnist, blogger, and journalist whose work has been featured in *The Detroit Free Press,* Detroit's alternative newsweekly the *Metro Times,* the *Michigan Chronicle,* Model D Detroit, PoliticusUSA, and other news media outlets. He was also a nationally syndicated columnist with Universal Press Syndicate for three years beginning in 1993. Currently, he is senior writer with Writing It Right For You, a writing services company founded by his wife, Pamela Hilliard Owens, in July 2008. He has also self-published two novels through Detroit Ink Publishing; *The Mayonnaise Murders* is a humorous science fiction/fantasy detective adventure, and *Who Stole the Zmulobeast?* is a fantasy/detective story for middle school–aged children. "Music as the Missing Link" first appeared, in slightly different form, in Model D, a publication from Issue Media Group, a Detroit-based company.

Steven Pomerantz was born and raised in Detroit and now lives in Boulder, Colorado. "Fort Gratiot" first appeared, in slightly different form, in *Belt Magazine.*

Rachel Reed grew up in the suburbs and adopted the schizophrenic city of Detroit as her home in 2008. She loves puppies, porch beers, and crossword puzzles. Not necessarily in that order.

Kevin Robishaw was born and raised in the Bay Area of California. He attended the University of California, Santa Barbara, where he studied History and Labor Studies. He lived in Oakland, California, for a year and a half before moving to Detroit in May 2013. He currently works for an immigration law firm, drafts grant proposals on behalf of two local organizations, and is engaged in the following projects on the side: the Society of Urban Sketchers and Psychogeographers, Detroit, an initiative to experience place through on-location sketching, and the Detroit Wildlands Conservancy, a tactical urbanism group working to promote the natural beauty of Detroit's informal and unsanctioned green spaces.

John G. Rodwan Jr. is author of the essay collections *Holidays & Other Disasters* (Humanist Press, 2013) and *Fighters & Writers* (Mongrel Empire Press, 2010) as well as the chapbook *Christmas Things* (Monkey Puzzle Press, 2011). His writing has been published by *The American Interest, The Chaffey Review, Midwestern Gothic, Concho River Review, The Oregonian, The Mailer Review, Pacific Review, Jazz Research Journal, San Pedro River Review, The Avalon Literary Review, The Nevada Review, Cream City Review, Blood and Thunder, Spot Literary Magazine, Philip Roth Studies, Palimpsest, Prime Mincer, Critical Moment, Free Inquiry,* and *The Humanist,* among others. His essay "Nice Things about Detroit" was named a Notable Essay in *The Best American Essays 2013.* He has lived in Brooklyn, New York; Geneva, Switzerland; Portland, Oregon; and Detroit, Michigan, his hometown and current home. "Carlessness" first appeared, in slightly different form, in *Midwestern Gothic.*

Amy Sacka is a Detroit-based street photographer who spent a full year posting a daily photograph and reflection on Detroit on her blog, Owen Was Here (owenwashere.com). The project was featured in both the *Detroit News* and *Huffington Post Detroit*, and select photos were part of the Women's Caucus for Art exhibition "Eye on the D: Seeing Detroit with New Eyes" at the 555 Gallery. Sacka's work has twice been selected by *National Geographic* online as Photo of the Day and countless times as National Geographic Editor's Picks, as well as "Photo of the Week" in Ron Howard's Project Imagi8tion.

Maisha Hyman Sumbry is a mother, wife, foodie, and native Detroiter now living, working, and writing in Washington, DC. Her uniquely Detroit upbringing is brought to life in her honest, creative nonfiction work. She always looks forward to coming home to Dutch Girl Donuts and corned beef sandwiches from Lou's. "Awakening" first appeared, in slightly different form in *Temenos Journal*, Central Michigan University's literary publication.

Gabriela Santiago-Romero is a current business student at the University of Detroit Mercy. She is a self-taught photographer who started documenting Detroit in 2010. She's loved Detroit ever since she moved to the city at the age of three and is striving to be the change she wants to see.

Pamela Sabaugh is a New York–based performer, playwright, and musician. She has worked extensively onstage off-Broadway and regionally, as well as in film and television. A Detroit native, Sabaugh's critically acclaimed solo rock musical, *Immaculate Degeneration*, about coming of age in the Motor City, has toured internationally and was selected for the "Best of the 2012 New York Fringe" at indietheaternow.com. "Legally Blind in the Motor City" is a slightly modified excerpt from *Immaculate Degeneration*.

Melanie Schmitt was born in Michigan but was raised in Sheboygan, Wisconsin. In 2009, she moved to the Detroit area for her ophthalmology residency. She fell in love with the unique beauty of Detroit and its people. She has been a part of many things, from the Detroit Derby Girls to marathons to electronic music. She has tried to capture the city, as she sees it, through photography.

Shaka Senghor is a writer, mentor, and motivational speaker whose story of redemption has inspired youth and young adults at high schools and universities across the nation. He is founder of The Atonement Project, a recipient of the 2012 Black Male Engagement (BMe) Leadership Award, and a 2013 MIT Media Lab Director's Fellow. He also teaches a course on The Atonement Project at The University of Michigan, Ann Arbor. He has a memoir about his life in the streets and in prison entitled *Writing My Wrongs* and an anthology of his writings for youth entitled *Live in Peace: A Youth Guide to Turning Hurt into Hope*.

Despite having lived in several other areas of the country, **Megan Snow** is proud to distinguish herself as a native Detroiter. She owns a small photography business, evol STUDIOS, where her goal is to bring awareness to, and understanding of, the rich history and culture of Detroit. Megan earned her BA in Early American History from the College of William and Mary, and currently volunteers with various Detroit preservation organizations.

Joseph Smedo is a professional artist from metro Detroit. He does metal sculptures and fine art photography that have been in numerous galleries and publications. He is currently working on a fine arts degree from Schoolcraft College.

Thomas J. Sugrue, a Detroit native, is now the David Boies Professor of History and Sociology at the University of Pennsylvania. He is author of several books, including the prize-winning *Origins of the Urban Crisis: Race and Inequality in Postwar Detroit*, just reissued with a new introduction on Detroit's bankruptcy. "Notown" first appeared, in slightly different form, in *Democracy*.

Jaclyn Trop covers the automotive industry for the *New York Times*. A Connecticut native and former *Detroit News* reporter, her secret wish is to sit on an ice cream sheet cake.

Aaron Waterman started capturing images at the age of six with a Kodak Instamatic and hasn't been too far from a camera since. He's as much at home on a rooftop as on the street, and he feels very fortunate to be able to share his view of Detroit. When not taking photos, Aaron is a family guy, marketing professional, and he rides his bike as much as possible.